Clues to Acting Shakespeare

Second Edition

WESLEY VAN TASSEL

ALLWORTH PRESS
NEW YORK

10 09 08 07 06   5 4 3 2 1

Published by Allworth Press
An imprint of Allworth Communications
10 East 23rd Street, New York, NY 10010

Interior design by Sharp Des!gns, Lansing, MI
Typography by Integra Software Services, Pvt., Ltd., Pondicherry, India

Cover design by Derek Bacchus
Cover photograph by www.PaulGodwin.com
Cover model: Deborah Houston
Period clothes supplied by Deborah Houston/Kings County Shakespeare Company

ISBN-13: 978-1-58115-464-1
ISBN-10: 1-58115-464-X

LIBRARY OF CONGRESS CATALOGING-IN-PUBLICATION DATA
Van Tassel, Wesley.
Clues to acting Shakespeare / Wesley Van Tassel. — 2nd ed.
p. cm.
Includes bibliographical references and index.
ISBN-13: 978-1-58115-464-1
ISBN-10: 1-58115-464-X
1. Shakespeare, William, 1564-1616—Dramatic production. 2. Acting. I. Title.
PR3091.V36 2006
822.3'3—dc22
2006029749

Printed in Canada

In America, the struggle for media success often reduces the art of acting to the act of marketing.

"Nothing will come of nothing...,"
Lear observes suspiciously.

Playing Shakespeare has nothing to do with marketing and everything to do with the art of acting.

FOR DUDE,
who is so very good at this!

THIS BOOK HAS FIVE PARTS:

1. For Actors in Training: Acting Shakespeare

Part 1 is designed for college classes or independent workshops and includes a complete study of ten basic skills required to play Shakespeare's language truthfully. This section is designed for a training period of twenty to thirty weeks meeting four to eight hours per week. Actors may also use this material to self-teach.

2. A Demonstration of Teaching and Learning Skills

Part 2 is the diary of a workshop in which the author teaches the skills. A group of ten actors participate in the forty-hour, twenty-session workshop. Their questions are included, along with the author's teaching strategy.

3. For Secondary Schools and Community Theatres: Reading Shakespeare Aloud

In part 3, some of the skills from part 1 are condensed for high school English or drama teachers and their students and are also useful for reading groups.

4. For Professional Actors and Coaches: The One-Day Brush Up

For the actor preparing an audition or a role—or the coach or director brushing up—part 4 is a quick review of four essential skills.

5. Resources

A collection of exercises, an annotated list of selected successful and not-so-successful film and video performances, a bibliography of some excellent books, a glossary of terms, and the index.

Bait the hook well! This fish will bite.
MUCH ADO ABOUT NOTHING, II, iii

Contents

Emphasis in Actor Training • The Realistic Actor • The Classical Actor • The Film Actor • Are These Skills Difficult to Learn? • Know Thyself • Identifying Common Mistakes • The Big "Character" Mistake • What Goes Wrong? • Why the British Seem Better at This • Two Approaches to Training • Better Training • What Are the Special Skills? • What About Meaning? • What If These Skills Are Too Difficult? • To Summarize

Ten Basic Skills • Required Text • What is Blank Verse? • What is a Regular Blank Verse Line? • What Are Feminine Endings and Elision? • What is a Short or Shared Line? • What is a Rhymed Couplet? • What Are Scansion and Stresses? • How Do I Select the Breathing Points? • What is a Caesura? • Text Study Seems Academic: Does It Matter?

I will arm me, being thus forewarned.
HENRY THE SIXTH, PART 3, IV, i

Preface to the Second Edition

Since the first edition of *Clues to Acting Shakespeare* was published six years ago, I've been asked hundreds of questions about techniques for teaching specific skills. Questions like, "How do you get the actors to apply all of these skills at once?" and "Is this the best order in which to teach the skills?" The simple and most useful way to answer the questions is with this second edition.

Part 2 is a completely new section. In the fall of 2005 I taught a forty-hour, twenty-session workshop to ten actors and recorded it. The actors, all in their twenties, had four to ten years of experience with realism or musical theatre, but almost no background in acting heightened text. Our agonies and triumphs are all recorded here, as are all of their questions and my answers.

Every one of these skills is designed to prepare the actor for rehearsal. The techniques used here illustrate one way to teach the skills, but certainly not the only way. This works for me, and some of it may work for you. Use what you can; ignore the rest!

Acknowledgments

To CICELY BERRY, for the published account of her work with the Royal Shakespeare Company, a huge debt is gratefully acknowledged. She has shared her discoveries brilliantly through her acting and voice books, notably *The Actor and the Text* (Scribner's, 1988), which is one of the best books on acting ever written.

Together with thousands of other actors, directors, and coaches in America, I am grateful to John Barton for producing his invaluable *Playing Shakespeare* text and accompanying videos (Methuen, 1984).

I am indebted to Kristin Linklater, especially for her *Freeing Shakespeare's Voice* (Theatre Communications Group, 1992), Delbert Spain's study, *Shakespeare Sounded Soundly* (Capra, 1988), Edward S. Brubaker's *Shakespeare Aloud* (Author, 1976), Robert Cohen's *Acting in Shakespeare* (Mayfield, 1991), and Patsy Rodenburg's *The Need for Words* (Routledge, 1993), all of which in their different ways affirmed what I have been doing the past thirty years.

Special thanks to Penguin Books for permission to quote from *The Complete Pelican Shakespeare* (Alfred Harbage, General Editor).

My gratitude is expressed to the following persons who read the manuscript and made invaluable contributions: Don Perkins (Actor, New York and Williamstown Theatre Festival); Patricia Norcia-Edwards (Rutgers University, M.F.A. Program); Joel Fink (Roosevelt University, M.F.A. Program, Chicago, and the Colorado Shakespeare Festival); Bonnie Raphael (University of North Carolina at Chapel Hill, M.F.A. Program); Sandy

Robbins (University of Delaware, M.F.A. Professional Actor Training Program); Harris D. Smith (University of Nebraska, M.F.A. Program); Scott Hayes (Florida State University, Asolo Theatre Conservatory, M.F.A. Program); Fred Goodson (Director and Elmira College Theatre Program Chair, New York); Charles Leader (Actor and Chair, Kansas City Community College Theatre Program); Leslee Caul and Michael J. Smith (Central Washington University Theatre Program); Jennifer Bennett (Actress, Washington); Nedra Dixon (Actress/Director, New York); Wendy Waterman (Tisch School of the Arts, New York University, Collaborative Arts Project); Jon Kerr (Pierce College, Washington); Laurie Kash (Sunset High School Drama Program, Beaverton, Oregon); Clint Pozzi (Actor and Drama Director, Meadowdale High School, Seattle); Nola Boughton, Robert Pierce and Anna Thorpe (Conroe High School, Texas); Zoe Climenhaga and Miriam Climenhaga (Bisbee Community Theatre and Cochise College).

Special thanks to actors David Plant, David Shoup, Kerri Van Auken, Keith Edie, and David Foubert, who helped introduce the manuscript to readers; to Nance Bracken for the graphics; and to Jen Huszcza, video librarian at the New York Public Library for the Performing Arts. Special thanks to Neil Freeman, University of British Columbia and editor of the modern-type *First Folio Editions* of Shakespeare. Together with the persons listed above, eleven teachers in a 1999 summer workshop made wonderful suggestions for part two. My thanks to Chris Carey (Huntington High School, Oregon), Katherine Carey (Eastside High School, Covington, Georgia), Hendrea Ferguson (Newberg High School, Oregon), Jim Fewer (Marshfield High School, Coos Bay, Oregon), Brian Hanson (Choteau High School, Montana), Leeann Mueller (Tenino High School, Washington), George Obermiller (West Valley Junior High School, Washington), Chris Pierson (Port Townsend High School, Washington), Jay Thornton (Enumclaw Junior High School, Washington), and Kate Wilson (Olympic College, Washington).

Special thanks and appreciation are expressed to Allworth Press publisher Tad Crawford, my editor Nicole Potter, her editorial/production assistant Katie Ellison, and their staff, whose excellent work on the book makes me look better!

And finally, my thanks to the several hundred actors and actors in training who I've had the pleasure to coach in "acting Shakespeare." You are too many to name, but you know who you are! Those hours were both a great pleasure and a special privilege for me, and I hope they were for you!

Condemn the fault, and not the actor of it.
MEASURE FOR MEASURE, II, ii

Introduction

It shall do you no harm to learn.
ALL'S WELL THAT ENDS WELL, II, ii

THE INTENTION of this book is to help the working actor discover and use specific skills for acting Shakespeare. There are many books *about* acting Shakespeare, but most deal with historical, philosophical, or personal approaches to the characters. They offer interpretations of these characters that are often drawn from actual performances (e.g., Antony Sher's *Year of the King*). But for the working actor struggling with blank verse, only a few of these books are of "immediate" or practical value. Several voice studies that illustrate the union of Shakespearean text and developed vocal skills are the most useful.

When preparing to act a role, the actor must learn to handle the language of the specific play so that the character will be truthful in both intention and presentation. Heightened language, as in Shakespeare's plays, can be difficult, and failure to handle it effectively will quickly destroy an otherwise well-intended characterization. Therefore, the actor must train the voice and then learn specific *skills* to handle this language. Once these skills have become practice, books that talk *about* acting Shakespeare are very helpful for character research and analysis.

That few books are available to help the working actor gain the skills necessary to handle verse is not surprising. A coach or director cannot write about this process until he or she has worked with hundreds of actors and discovered successful techniques.

I have had the privilege to coach the skills presented in this book to several hundred professional and student actors. These actors, mostly

American, *taught me* that what they needed most were skills to handle the language, especially the verse, as those skills would allow them to play characters truthfully. Most of these actors expressed confidence about character intention and development (the skills that are the core of realistic actor training), but were uncomfortable with the idea of playing their characters while speaking verse. Most of these actors were amazed (and then delighted) to learn that with Shakespeare, the character is discovered *through the verse.*

Therefore, when coaching Shakespeare, one must always begin with the practical skills required to speak the text. The scope of this book is limited to that study. Techniques to develop the character that emerges from correctly speaking the text are the subject of other books, many of which are listed in the bibliography. *Character study must always follow language study.* With Shakespeare, the reverse spells disaster, as I will clarify in these pages.

This book is primarily for actors who intend to play Shakespeare but whose training is based on realism. Because that specific training rarely considers blank verse, you, the actor, are probably missing a few skills. These skills must be identified and learned so that your work with Shakespeare can be successful.

When using this book, professional actors should turn immediately to part 4, page 217, the "Professional Actor's One-Day Brushup" for a quick review of skills you probably already know. Actors in training or professionals who want more detailed study should begin with part 1. Secondary teachers, reader groups and community theatre groups should begin with part 3, page 175, and refer back to part 1 as necessary.

Some of the realistic acting skills that you apply to Chekhov, Williams, Miller, Wasserstein, Mamet, or the dialogue in most films are important and applicable to acting Shakespeare. For example, once you've trained your voice, *playing your action to achieve your objective* is still the most important acting skill. But some of the others, like reading the subtext or emotional memory recall, are less important than the language when playing Shakespeare.

Special skills required to play Shakespeare must be *added to* or *replace* what you've already acquired. The differences are not in motives, actions, personalities, relationships, or conflicts (the ingredients of character and plot), but in the requirements of the language.

Two excellent studies on acting heightened text and acting realism are, respectively, Cicely Berry's *The Actor and the Text* and Constantine Stanislavski's *An Actor Prepares.* The subjects are often similar and share many common truths, yet certain skills are very different and will be identified in this book. While nothing needs to be changed in either

Berry or Stanislavski and every actor should master what each teaches, these exceptional works share a common problem: Their great depth of information can confuse and discourage the reader. The confusion is especially evident among American actors who attempt to master unfamiliar techniques for acting Shakespeare through Berry's book, unless they are fortunate enough to have an excellent coach who is familiar with the skills. Without a personal coach, or with a coach who is learning along with the actor, how does the actor trained in realism prepare to learn these many new approaches to acting?

Clues to Acting Shakespeare clarifies the specific preparation and identifies the skills required to act heightened text—to move from Chekhov to Shakespeare—to adjust from one language structure to the other. Procedures for learning these skills are included. The skills also apply to acting Shakespeare's contemporaries, other verse drama like Molière or the Greeks, and to modern realistic text.

Advanced study should follow, beginning with *The Actor and the Text* and Barton's *Playing Shakespeare* book and video series. Correct vocal usage should be learned and practiced, using the techniques of Berry, Kristin Linklater, or Patsy Rodenburg. When you are ready for a much more detailed study of verse structure, refer to Delbert Spain's *Shakespeare Sounded Soundly.*

Clues to Acting Shakespeare will not deal with playing realism— for example, Stanislavski's methods, Meisner, Hagen, and so on— because it assumes the reader has experience in that field and is now taking the step to act heightened text.

I have spent nearly thirty years coaching "acting Shakespeare" at universities or private workshops and even longer directing his plays. This book has evolved into a summary of what actors have taught me over the course of these decades. I hope these "clues" simplify the process for you and help make the material accessible. Don't let Shakespeare's text frighten you. This greatest of writers wrote *for actors*, and discovering what you can do with this language is challenging, stimulating, all-consuming, rewarding, and great fun!

> *He was skillful enough to have lived still.*
> ALL'S WELL THAT ENDS WELL, I, i

PART ONE

For Actors in Training: Acting Shakespeare

Now name the rest of the players.
A MIDSUMMER NIGHT'S DREAM, I, ii

CHAPTER I

Common Understandings

Their understanding
Begins to swell, and the approaching tide
Will shortly fill the reasonable shore.

THE TEMPEST, V, i

B EFORE WE BEGIN work on the specific skills required to act Shakespeare, let's review and clarify some terms and approaches to acting. Answering these questions now will give us a common foundation for the exercises that follow.

EMPHASIS IN ACTOR TRAINING

The Realistic Actor

The term "realism" refers to realistic scripts that are written in prose, where dialogue reads like everyday speech. Included are most stage plays written after 1900 and nearly all film and television plays. "Realistic actor" refers to that individual who has studied the craft primarily to act realistic text by application of Stanislavski methods. "Realistic actor" may suggest an artist who has taken supervised voice study, but that assumption may or may not be true. At any rate, it would be unrealistic to assume that any actor proficient in realism would automatically be a skilled presenter of Shakespeare.

The Classical Actor

The phrase "playing Shakespeare" refers to the performance of plays written in heightened language. Heightened text follows specific rhythmic patterns and is usually filled with imagery. Included are most plays written prior to 1900. There are exceptions, like Chekhov, Strindberg, and Ibsen, who wrote realism. Generally, learning to handle Shakespeare's heightened language also gives the actor a solid foundation for playing Molière, Restoration comedy, Goethe, Rostand, and many others. As most of these plays are referred to as "classical," actors trained to perform them are often called "classical actors."

The Film Actor

Nowadays, we also have the "film actor." This additional category is necessary because many performers on film are certainly "actors," but they may or may not possess the training and skills that stage actors acquire. Actors, including persons identified as "stars," who work primarily on film or video may or may not have a trained voice, and may or may not be capable of a range of characterization.

These categories actually identify an actor's training and preparation to work in the profession. The profession itself has many forms—stage, classical stage, musical stage, dance, video, film, radio, spoken books, recordings, voice-over, sales shows, demonstrations, modeling, and so forth. Well-trained actors can work in most of the forms, whereas less talented or less trained persons might specialize.

In this book, our concentration is on performance of Shakespeare's plays for stage, video, or film. However, many of the skills required to perform this task successfully can be applied to acting realism and other performance opportunities—indeed, they should be applied whenever possible.

ARE THESE SKILLS DIFFICULT TO LEARN?

O, answer me! Let me not burst in ignorance.

HAMLET, I, iv

No, but they must be learned. When an actor trained in realism tackles a Shakespearean role without applying these special skills, the usual results are an affected voice and strained and unbelievable acting. Shakespeare's language controls the actor, rather than the actor controlling the language. The ability to play realism on film or stage does not translate to the ability to play Shakespeare.

But, since fine Shakespeare acting coaches are available, actors with some degree of talent can be successful at playing verse. When we observe unsuccessful performances, we are left to wonder: (1) Where were the coaches? or (2) Is that actor really without talent?

The skills required for success with Shakespeare, once explained, are not hard to recognize. For example, young actors in training are often shown film or video performances of Shakespeare's plays. These student actors can quickly articulate the reasons for good or poor performances.

Part 5 lists some selected film and video performances that contain interesting acting challenges and are well worth studying.

KNOW THYSELF

Now will I begin your moral, and do you follow.
LOVE'S LABOUR'S LOST, III, i

As a realistic actor approaching Shakespeare, you face specific challenges; therefore, you must know your starting point. If you are a *strong realistic actor,* you probably work somewhat in the following way: You develop a character through playing your action and discovery of subtext and objectives. You realize that your action has to be measured in the person from whom you want something. In the rehearsal process, you find ways to "use" the text to illustrate and play your actions. Speaking the subtext, especially in many modern plays, is, you realize, often as important as speaking the actual words. You have success with these techniques, your character dominates the language, and you control the situation. This approach gives you strength and believability.

If you are a *limited realistic actor*—perhaps with little or no training or an ineffective voice, without the natural skills required to be honest—you can't work within this framework, because you can't speak the subtext or play the action truthfully. You may have a "tin ear." That problem is usually compounded by an untrained voice and a tendency to apply sarcasm to each line reading.

I believe that the application of sarcasm is rampant amongst poorly trained American actors, and I'm sure you have heard it in the performances of others. For truth, personality is substituted, and for honest feelings, attitude. The actor colors the text with sarcasm, thinking the text needs coloring, and not knowing what else to do or how else to do it. Many actors with limited skills can be seen daily in videos and television programs. Trained actors and directors recognize this limitation. Untrained actors and directors (and producers and casting agents) think such actors are just fine—as long as they are marketable.

Whether you are a strong or a limited realistic actor, you can easily identify the skills required to perform Shakespeare. You must then determine for yourself if you can go beyond identification to the process of learning and applying these skills.

IDENTIFYING COMMON MISTAKES

Awake your senses, that you may the better judge.
JULIUS CAESAR, III, ii

The First Mistake: When a realistic actor approaches Shakespeare by asking, How shall I play this character? the first mistake has been made.

Instead, the actor must ask this question: What is this language doing and what is the action implied?

The Second Mistake: Assuming that a character can manipulate the language is the second mistake. In realism, you play the subtext and sometimes can establish your own rhythm. In Shakespeare, the meter and rhythm are set for you, and you must play accordingly.

The Third Mistake: Plunging right into character development is the third mistake. When studying a Shakespearean role, development of character is the third thing you do, not the first. The first is text analysis, and the second is speaking the language aloud; only then can you make choices about what the character is doing and saying.

The early development of character choices is a serious mistake made by nearly all actors (student or professional) who attempt to play a character that is written in heightened language. The reason for the mistake is understandable: Realistic actor training is based on methods to discover truthful character, so it is difficult to refrain from immediate character choices.

THE BIG "CHARACTER" MISTAKE

When reading a script, actors imagine characters and quickly search for actions to bring those characters to life. Text study can seem to delay the opportunity to play the character. Many actors don't realize that with heightened language, character discovery comes *through the text.* These actors believe that text study is an intellectual activity that has little to do with playing the role. When acting Shakespeare, that naiveté will spell disaster.

If you know some basics about music and decide you want to play the piano, how successful will you be if you don't learn the skills? If you want to play baseball, but prefer to ignore hitting and fielding practice, how good will you become? Without applying yourself to master the skills, how successful can you be at anything?

But once you become really good at something, skills move to the background and your mastery of the activity takes over. We refer to such a performance as "effortless." We, the viewer or listener, see no technique—only skillful results. How much effort does it take to make something "effortless?"

Unless you make the effort to discover what the language is saying and doing, and then have the skills to read that language correctly, your Shakespearean characterization will be unsuccessful. Regardless of the amount of time you put into development of the character, if you haven't first discovered what's in the words, your character cannot be completely engaging; the audience will not clearly understand you and won't quite believe what you are saying.

WHAT GOES WRONG?

Pause awhile
And let my counsel sway you in this case.
MUCH ADO ABOUT NOTHING, IV, i

Everything. But primarily this: When you develop character *first*, you then tend to "adjust" the language to fit what the character wants to do, and you say the lines "the way the character would say them."

This approach spells disaster, because you are deciding *how* to say the lines before you know *what* you are saying. This Stanislavski acting principle is especially true when acting Shakespeare: Know *what* you are saying and *why* you are saying it, and the *how* will take care of itself.

The importance of Stanislavski's advice is *amplified* with Shakespeare, because, when compared to realistic text, the *what* is much harder to determine. When reading a blank verse line, you have a greater chance of being entirely wrong in your interpretation of what is being said, in which case, nobody will have any idea what you are saying.

You may have noticed, when watching Shakespeare, that the British actors, especially on film, sound much better than the Americans. Are they better actors? No. Are they better at Shakespeare? Yes. They are better trained to handle heightened text.

WHY THE BRITISH SEEM BETTER AT THIS

Thus comes the English with full power upon us.
HENRY V, II, iv

We often hear the argument that American actors will be better at Shakespeare if they use a British accent. John Barton argues convincingly in his book *Playing Shakespeare* and the accompanying videotapes that skill in handling Shakespeare has nothing to do with accent. He also points out that, when comparing American and British accents, the American is probably closer to actual Elizabethan speech. The American sound is rougher, less refined, more authentic.

And yet, when Americans approach Shakespeare for the first time, both professional and student actors seem to add this vocal affectation. This application (or coloring) not only weakens the voice, it destroys all chance at truth and honesty of character. Use your best and strongest natural speaking voice when handling Shakespeare's language.

TWO APPROACHES TO TRAINING

The primary reason why British actors are better than American actors at playing Shakespeare is simply the method of training.

The British start actor training with voice and movement, plus scene and language study. Many American training programs, acting schools, and studios begin with inner motivation, self-discovery, and characterization. It can be argued that the American system of actor training should be reversed: Teach Shakespeare performance with its required skills first, then teach realistic acting technique.

If this reverse were realized, Americans would have an earlier opportunity to play Shakespeare, and there would be no difference between British and American actors. Then why don't we do it?

The reverse isn't practical for the American job market. Work for actors in America is 99.5 percent in realism and 0.5 percent in plays with heightened language. American children are raised on television and film, so they are familiar with realistic text and acting styles long before actor training begins. Except in studio work or school, an American actor might work an entire career and never have a shot at a Shakespearean role.

Dustin Hoffman, one of America's best actors, reached the age of fifty-one without ever having played Shakespeare. His opportunity came when he played Shylock in Sir Peter Hall's production of *The Merchant of Venice* in 1989.

Of necessity, the business side of acting attracts American actors to realistic training, which is where the roles are.

In England, the foundation of most regional theatres is the Shakespeare canon, and the plays are included in every season. His plays are also produced extensively at the various festivals in England and Canada and at the Royal National Theatre in London. School children perform the plays in grade school and see numerous productions. Most actor training programs are independent and not housed in universities, as they are in America. Most British acting coaches see Shakespeare training as mandatory. The classic repertoire of British drama is in heightened language. In England, an actor cannot avoid Shakespeare training; in America, the actor must search for it.

Recent trends in England, however, such as the job market in film and television and declining funding which leads to a declining number of classical stage productions, indicate that British actor training is showing an added emphasis on the American approach.

When rehearsing American actors for two Los Angeles Shakespearean productions in 1999, Sir Peter Hall was asked by the trade newspaper *Back Stage West* if he rehearsed longer than he would have in England.

A little more. But to tell the truth, the tradition is not in a healthy state in Britain now either, because there's not enough Shakespeare being done there, because drama schools don't teach actors something they're probably never going to do. So I don't even do a Shakespeare play in England now without two weeks of teaching before I start. It wasn't all that different here, just a bit longer. (Scott Proudfit)

The "classic" repertoire of American plays is realistic or musical. When the Stanislavski techniques emerged in the 1920s, they were absorbed within ten years into American theatres and schools. Extensive training in voice, movement, and script analysis are recommended in Stanislavski's writings. But his early disciples in America largely ignored these techniques and favored concentration on motivation, sense memory recall, subtext, objectives, the magic "if," self discovery, etc.—in other words, the basic tools these teachers and directors believed were required to act the realistic texts that American playwrights were writing.

BETTER TRAINING

Let your reason serve
To make the truth appear where it seems hid.
MEASURE FOR MEASURE, V, i

The simple reality is this: An actor trained in Shakespeare performance can easily adjust to realistic text for stage or film. On the other hand, most actors trained in realism, especially for film, have no idea how to adapt that training to Shakespeare. In fact, the actor's training can actually hamper success. Except for the practical side of "making a living," it would make sense to reverse actor training in America. Is acting a business or an art?

Experimenting with the reversed training procedure, I have coached a half-dozen or so groups in which beginning actors (about age seventeen) were mixed with professionals, many of whom had numerous Broadway and LORT (League of Resident Theatres) credits. In these groups, the professional actors performed "final projects" at a higher level, but they did not learn the specific Shakespeare skills any faster than the beginners. One can conclude that the skills are easy to identify and learn, and that other factors like voice training and experience determine the level of performance.

A few M.F.A. acting programs now concentrate training on classical text. I have no doubt that young actors could be trained even earlier and, if started with voice work and the skills required to play Shakespeare, would graduate better prepared for the entire range of job opportunities.

WHAT ARE THE SPECIAL SKILLS?

Assuming an actor has a trained voice, the skills needed to play Shakespeare truthfully are:
- Learning to phrase and support the language
- Having the freedom to speak while playing your action

The first skill is tied to analysis of text, the second to voice and character.

WHAT ABOUT MEANING?

It is not especially difficult to study Shakespeare's language and explain its common meaning. As understanding improves, the actor is able to "dig deeper" and find more possibilities. One's knowledge and skill at the moment of reading a text are always changing, and among writers, Shakespeare especially seems to change.

Each time we come back to take a fresh look at a speech, we're amazed at the new ideas Shakespeare somehow inserted into the text since our last reading! We also begin to realize that the layers are infinite and that we will always discover something new.

Once the actor has a trained voice, the goal is to discover what's in the language and speak freely. What's in the language is discovered by learning and applying some basic skills to the blank verse. If the listener is actively engaged, the actor is using the correct verse skills.

Some directors believe that there are no rules applicable to performing Shakespeare, but that idea is certainly untrue. Specific skills needed to handle the language must be thought of as rules. If the actor ignores these skills, most listeners do not understand what is being said and simply doze off. How long can an actor hold an audience that can't hear? The same is true if they can't understand, and all the work put into discovering the language and character will go unrewarded.

Discovering what the language means, and then having the skills to *speak* that discovery, is what separates actors from English professors. I've heard dozens of English teachers and professors read Shakespeare aloud, but the only ones I have heard read effectively are actor-trained. This problem reflects a misunderstanding about drama—plays are written to be spoken aloud. Speaking and acting skills are required for the listener to hear what the language is doing. Lacking these skills and still reading aloud is a sure way to confuse the listener.

As all actors know, an idea (or interpretation) in one's head doesn't transfer automatically to the audience's ears. That step takes special skills with any text, and Shakespeare is no exception. In fact, plays written in heightened text require far more speaking skills than realistic plays.

Director Peter Brook coined a wonderful phrase applicable to unclear actors and confused listeners: *"The trouble with Shakespeare is that it goes on without you."*

WHAT IF THESE SKILLS ARE TOO DIFFICULT?

Sir, I am too old to learn.

KING LEAR, II, ii

Who would attempt to sing an aria in public without first learning something about voice and music? To handle the technical challenges in the aria, the singer must have the instrument (the voice) and training (the skills). One could certainly sing the aria and ignore the composer's notations, but then the listener is cheated out of hearing the music's real possibilities. The performance is less than satisfactory, because the material has been "adjusted" to the singer's limitations. Untrained listeners, of course, don't know the difference.

"Adjusting" the material to fit personal strengths and weaknesses is what some actors do all the time. We usually refer to these performers as "personalities" rather than actors.

Philip Bosco, the fine American character actor, remarked in an interview about preparing to act Shakespeare in *In Theatre* magazine that "fame doesn't give you talent." An actor may have a pleasing personality on film and be paid a lot of money, but may not be equipped with the essential skills, especially a trained voice, to handle Shakespeare or other classics.

If an actor without correct preparation accepts a Shakespearean role, the necessary procedure is to secure a coach and learn the skills. Simultaneously, the actor must develop the voice to handle the language.

Shakespeare's plays are often cut or "arranged" for specific situations. These changes are the director's or producer's production choices, but not usually language changes. Refrain from rewriting Shakespeare's language to accommodate your personal vocal limitations as, for example, you might transpose a song to better fit the vocal range of a singer.

Instead, develop your skills to act what the language requires. If you are not willing to learn the skills, avoid Shakespeare, spare the audience the boredom, spare yourself the bad acting, and don't insult the author.

TO SUMMARIZE

O Lord, I could have stay'd here all the night
To hear good counsel: O, what learning is!

ROMEO AND JULIET, III, iii

What we want to do, then, is handle the language so that the audience clearly understands the character's intentions. We know that the more skillful we become at speaking the language, the more the audience will be involved.

Now let's begin on the specific skills.

USEFUL IDEAS TO REMEMBER:

CHAPTER 2

The Basic Skill Set for Working with Heightened Language

THERE ARE TEN basic skills required to play Shakespeare. Some are identical to the skills required to act realism.

TEN BASIC SKILLS

1. Play your action and achieve your objective.
2. Stay in the moment, listening, not thinking ahead.
3. Use scansion, phrasing, and the caesura.
4. Support the thought all the way through the line. The end of the line is often as important, or more important, than the beginning.
5. Breathe at the correct places.
6. Let the words be the expression of your thoughts. Do not think, then speak. Speak what you think when you think it.
7. Understand the speech structure and rhythm.
8. Play the antithetical words, phrases, and thoughts. Use the caesura to help you. These skills will clarify your phrasing and prevent you from rushing.
9. Use analysis to understand all words and thought patterns.
10. Love the imagery.

These skills will be studied one by one. All actors know that skills are to be mastered and "forgotten," then revisited during rehearsal. In performance, the moment and the action must take over. Most actors would rather be "involved in the moment" than engaged in the "chore" of text study. Not surprisingly, then, it is more difficult to learn the skills and apply the discipline needed to practice them than it is to forget the skills and allow the moment to take over.

From the above list, number 1, "play your action," and number 2, "stay in the moment," are the same skills used in acting realism. We won't spend time reviewing them.

So pause awhile . . .

REQUIRED TEXT

At this point, you need to choose two sections of Shakespearean text: (1) a monologue in blank verse (not prose) and (2) a sonnet. Ten or twelve lines are enough for the monologue, and these can be cut from a longer monologue. Pick a sonnet you enjoy.

Your selections will probably be regular lines—ten syllables in each—but you may have to adjust to feminine endings or short or shared lines. Rhymed couplets are fine. Scan the lines, mark the feet and stresses, note the elision, circle the caesuras, the breathing places, and the words that break the rhythm.

I just used a series of words and instructions that you may not understand. Before I explain the ultimate exercise, "kick the box," we'll take a detour and learn these terms. You'll soon be on your feet and working aloud.

WHAT IS BLANK VERSE?

My tongue could never learn sweet smoothing word.

RICHARD III, I, ii

Simply stated, it is unrhymed verse usually written in lines of ten syllables. This line structure is called *iambic pentameter*. An *iamb* is a foot (or word) of two syllables, the first unstressed and the second stressed.

An *iambic pentameter* is a line of verse that consists of five metrical feet—in this case iambic feet, so we have ten syllables per line.

Here's a blank verse line from *Hamlet*, spoken by Horatio about the Ghost, with the feet separated and the stresses marked: ∪ for unstressed syllables; / for stressed.

Horatio: It beck / ons you / to go / a way / with it (I, iv)*

---

*All line quotes are taken from *The Complete Pelican Shakespeare*, Alfred Harbage, General Editor. New York: Viking Penguin, 1977.

Walk around and think of your foot falling "heel toe, heel toe, heel toe, heel toe, heel toe," and count five feet with ten "syllables." The "heel" is unstressed and the "toe" is stressed. The stresses in verse are often defined "dee dum dee dum dee dum dee dum dee dum." Keep walking and substitute "dee dum" for "heel toe." That's the rhythm of blank verse.

Blank verse was developed by Shakespeare and his contemporaries in the late sixteenth century and is usually considered the written form closest to actual English speech. You speak blank verse all the time, usually without realizing it. For example, "What do you want to do this afternoon?" and "Let's go to town and buy an ice cream cone" are two lines of blank verse! Converse for awhile in blank verse, and write out a few original lines of your own.

Use this space to write a few lines of original blank verse:

WHAT IS A REGULAR BLANK VERSE LINE?

A regular line is comprised of ten syllables with alternating stresses: "Dee dum dee dum dee dum dee dum dee dum." In a regular line, the stressed syllable is always the second syllable of each foot. This definition will lead us to suspect that there may be lines which are not "regular." That is true and, in fact, is a key to how Shakespeare's language works. He will change the regular rhythm and catch the listener's ear. Learning to recognize these changes and handle them convincingly is a key to speaking this language. We'll work on that soon. The blank verse form is used in modern daily life and in classical dramatic text and poetry. Invent a few more blank verse lines for practice.

> *I pray you mar no moe of my verses*
> *with reading them ill-favoredly.*
> AS YOU LIKE IT, III, ii

WHAT ARE FEMININE ENDINGS AND ELISION?

A blank verse line is sometimes spoken with eleven syllables rather than ten. The final syllable is not stressed and remains soft. The most famous line in Shakespeare illustrates the added syllable, the "dee" without the "dum," as Hamlet contemplates action.

Hamlet: To be, or not to be—that is the question. (III, i)

In this blank verse line, there are eleven syllables. The final syllable, the feminine ending, is a soft and unstressed syllable. The line scans like this:*

$$\cup \; / \quad \cup \; / \quad \cup \; / \qquad \cup \; / \quad \cup \; / \quad (\cup)$$
To be, / or not / to be— / that is / the ques / tion:

*Some actors prefer: $/ \; \cup \quad \cup \; / \quad (\cup)$
/ that is / the ques /tion

I 4

To recognize the feminine ending, you must count the syllables in the blank verse line. If you count eleven and notice that the final syllable would not be stressed—like "tion," "ing," or "en,"—you have a feminine ending. If you count eleven (or perhaps more) syllables but note that the final syllable must be stressed, you cannot use the feminine ending. In this case, use elision—contracting two words or syllables into one, like "I'll" from "I will"—to establish ten syllables.

In the following example, in which Hamlet speaks to Horatio with an eleven-syllable line, Shakespeare has already elided a two-syllable word into one, but the reader must elide another word, as "man" is stressed and would not make a feminine ending.

Hamlet: Horatio, thou art e'en as just a man.   (iii, ii)

Note "even" is already elided to "e'en" and pronounced as one syllable. The actor must elide "Horatio" to "Horat'o," pronounced as three syllables. Now the line can be spoken in ten syllables with correct rhythm.

$$\cup\ /\ \cup\ /\ \cup\ /\ \cup\ /\ \cup\ /$$
Hor a / t'o, thou / art e'en / as just / a man.

Elision is used frequently in Shakespeare. Here are more examples. In the first, Shakespeare provides the elision:

Gloucester: As flies to wanton boys are we to th' gods;   (iv, i)

Note that the fifth foot has three syllables, even with "th'gods" elided. This is acceptable and does not harm the meter.

$$\cup\ /\ \cup\ /\ \cup\ /\ \cup\ /\ \cup\ /$$
As flies / to want / on boys / are we / to th'gods;

In the following examples, the actor must determine the elision:

Lady Macbeth: He brings great news. The raven himself is hoarse

(i, v)

Elide "raven" to "rav'n," spoken as one syllable; however three sounds in the third foot also works.

$$\cup\ /\ \cup\ /\ \cup\ /\ \cup\ /\ \cup\ /$$
He brings / great news. / The rav'n / him self / is hoarse

Caesar: Nor heaven nor earth have been at peace to-night.   (ii, ii)

Elide "heaven" to "heav'n" spoken as one syllable.

$$\overset{\smile}{\text{Nor}} \overset{/}{\text{heav'n}} / \overset{\smile}{\text{nor}} \overset{/}{\text{earth}} / \overset{\smile}{\text{have}} \overset{/}{\text{been}} / \overset{\smile}{\text{at}} \overset{/}{\text{peace}} / \overset{\smile}{\text{to}} \overset{/}{\text{night.}}$$

Ghost: Cut off even in the blossoms of my sin.   (I, v)

Elide "even" to "e'en," spoken as one syllable.

$$\overset{\smile}{\text{Cut}} \overset{/}{\text{off}} / \overset{\smile}{\text{e'en}} \overset{/}{\text{in}} / \overset{\smile}{\text{the}} \overset{/}{\text{blos}} / \overset{\smile}{\text{soms}} \overset{/}{\text{of}} / \overset{\smile}{\text{my}} \overset{/}{\text{sin,}}$$

To elide or not to elide can be a confusing choice. If no help is available, choose the way that sounds best to your ear, while keeping the rhythm.

As clear
As morning roses newly washed with dew.
THE TAMING OF THE SHREW, II, i

WHAT IS A SHORT OR SHARED LINE?

A short line consists of fewer than ten syllables. If the line is finished by the following line, usually spoken by the next speaker, it is a shared line. If not finished by the next line, the missing syllables are probably a direction from the author instructing the actors to take a pause before continuing.

For example, here's Bassanio in *The Merchant of Venice* begging Portia's forgiveness for the "lost" ring. His speech ends with a short line which she finishes with her first line. Then she ends her speech with a short line which he finishes. Generally the actor who finishes a short verse line has a quick cue to keep the rhythm.

Bassanio: Portia, forgive me this enforced wrong;
            And in the hearing of these many friends
            I swear to thee, even by thine own fair eyes,
            Wherein I see myself,—
Portia: Mark you but that!
            In both my eyes he doubly sees himself,
            In each eye, one. Swear by your double self,
            And there's an oath of credit.
Bassanio: Nay, but hear me   (v, i)

Here is another example. In Juliet's second of three exits in the balcony scene in *Romeo and Juliet*, she first speaks a short line which he finishes, then a short line which is unfinished and certainly calls for a pause as he watches her leave. Does the pause call for a kiss?

Juliet:	Tomorrow will I send.
Romeo:	So thrive my soul,—
Juliet:	A thousand times good night! *(exits)*
Romeo:	A thousand times the worse, to want thy light! (ii, ii)

In the first two lines, his "So thrive my soul" finishes her "Tomorrow will I send." His second line, "A thousand times the worse, to want thy light!" is a regular verse line, and therefore it is not intended to complete her unfinished second line.

So there is an unfinished two feet after "A thousand times good night!" A four-syllable pause to be filled—a "dee dum dee dum." How? A kiss? A cross to the door and turn back? A cross and run back? A cross and thrown kiss? A hand clasp? A hand kiss? Just an exit? Your choice.

Farewell, farewell! One kiss and I'll descend.
ROMEO AND JULIET, III, V

WHAT IS A RHYMED COUPLET?

Just what it sounds like. Here are examples from *A Midsummer Night's Dream,* in which all of the verse rhymes and dozens of rhyming couplets can be found.

Helena:	O, that a lady, of one man refused,
	Should of another therefore be abused! (ii, ii)

Another:

Hermia:	So far be distant; and, good night, sweet friend.
	Thy love ne'er alter till thy sweet life end. (ii, ii)

Play the rhyme, don't try to cover it up. There is great pleasure in speaking and hearing it.

You will notice that your sonnet, and all of the other sonnets, ends with a rhyming couplet.

I have spoke the truth.
ALL'S WELL THAT ENDS WELL, V, iii

WHAT ARE SCANSION AND STRESSES?

Marking the soft and stressed syllables in a blank verse line is called scanning the line, or scansion. In a regular blank verse line, the second syllable of each foot is stressed, as shown on page 15. Shakespeare, however, achieves effects by creating irregular lines. In the following example, lines 1, 2, and 4 are usually considered regular, while line 3 is irregular. These are the opening four lines in *Romeo and Juliet*.

> Chorus: Two households, both alike in dignity,
> In fair Verona, where we lay our scene,
> From ancient grudge, break to new mutiny,
> Where civil blood makes civil hands unclean.   (*Pro*)

Using regular scansion, in the third foot of line 3, the word "break" would not be stressed. For the sense of the line, however, your common sense tells you that the verb "break" is more important than the preposition "to," so the stresses are inverted and the line scans like this:

$$\cup \ / \quad \cup \ / \qquad / \ \cup \ \cup \ / \ \cup \ /$$
> From an / cient grudge, / break to / new mut / i ny,

The third foot is called a trochaic foot, or trochee, as opposed to an iambic foot. The first syllable is stressed and the second unstressed, and the rhythm is broken. With just a little practice, you will learn to recognize irregular stresses and words that break the rhythm.

HOW DO I SELECT THE BREATHING POINTS?

It's easy to know when to breathe in Shakespeare; it's hard to make yourself do it. Breathe at the natural stops—the punctuation points—and not at the end of a verse line simply because, on paper, it looks like the end of a line. In verse, many lines are *enjambed*, which means the "thought" implicit in the line runs on from one line to the next without a break (or punctuation). In the above four lines from the *Romeo and Juliet* prologue, each line ends with punctuation, and you can breathe comfortably. But end-of-line breathing is usually *not* the case. In the following example, select the breathing points.

> Mercutio: O, then I see Queen Mab hath been with you.
> She is the fairies' midwife, and she comes
> In shape no bigger than an agate stone
> On the forefinger of an alderman,
> Drawn with a team of little atomies
> Over men's noses as they lie asleep.   (1, iv)

Notice the enjambed lines. You would not take a breath after lines 2, 3, or 5. Circle the correct breathing points—after "O," "you," "midwife," "alderman," "asleep"—and memorize them at the same time you work on and memorize text. You will discover that breathing correctly actually helps you memorize. While inhaling physically, you mentally "inhale" your next line. While exhaling physically, you "exhale" the line. This technique is studied in more detail in chapter 5.

WHAT IS A CAESURA?

Pronounced si-zhoor´-ə, it is a "sense" pause, usually in the middle of a blank verse line. Some verse lines contain punctuation, others do not. On the ones that do not, a sense pause is almost always present. Mark it like this: //.

A sense pause does not mean a breath pause. Don't breathe at the caesura unless the breath is planned and necessary.

Look again at the lines of Hermia and Helena in the rhyming couplet section on p.17. In each case, their first line contains punctuation and their second line does not. In each second line, we can insert a caesura.

Helena: Should of another // therefore be abused!
Hermia: Thy love ne'er alter // till thy sweet life end.

Note the elision by the author of "ne'er" from "never," creating a one-syllable word. Shakespeare sometimes elides consonants, although elision of vowels is more common.

By using the caesura, the lines are broken into separate phrases. Separate phrases identify separate thoughts. Identifying thoughts clarifies the lines. We'll work more on phrasing and caesura in chapter 3.

TEXT STUDY SEEMS ACADEMIC: DOES IT MATTER?

The red plague rid you
For learning me your language!
THE TEMPEST, I, ii

Text study matters, because the structure matters. Compared to music, the structure is the notation. Compared to baseball, the structure is the hand-eye coordination. You've got to put it together if you're going to hit the ball.

USEFUL IDEAS TO REMEMBER:

Scansion, Phrasing and Caesura

IN THE PREVIOUS chapter, we defined each of these terms. Now we'll look at them in greater detail.

SCANSION

Here is our simple modern-day blank verse line scanned. Each two syllables comprise one foot, and the soft and stressed syllables are marked.

> ⏑ / ⏑ / ⏑ / ⏑ / ⏑ /
> Let's go / to town / and buy / an ice / cream cone.

Here's a better line from *Romeo and Juliet*.

Romeo: But soft! What light through yonder window breaks?   (II, ii)

Break the line into feet:

> But soft! / What light / through yon / der win / dow breaks?

Mark the stresses:

> ⏑ / ⏑ / ⏑ / ⏑ / ⏑ /
> But soft! / What light / through yon / der win / dow breaks?

When you read the line, place emphasis on the stressed syllables: "soft," "light," "yon," "win," "breaks." With your hand, beat out these stressed words or syllables on the table or chair. Read the line a few times by beating out and *over-stressing* the five stressed words or syllables, then forget the scansion and read the line naturally.

If you've beat out the rhythm with your hand and emphasized the stressed syllables, you will discover that when you "forget" scansion and read the line more naturally, you automatically give a slight emphasis to the stressed words. Your goal is to achieve naturalness and honesty, but to do so by stressing the correct words.

For the Shakespearean line to be truthful, it is necessary to play the correct stresses. Let's test this idea by reading a line incorrectly. Here's the opening line from *The Merchant of Venice.*

Antonio: In sooth I know not why I am so sad.   (I, i)

          ᴗ / ᴗ /   ᴗ / ᴗ / ᴗ /
In sooth / I know / not why / I am / so sad.

If we follow the scansion, the stresses are "sooth," "know," "why," "am," and "sad." Read the line instead by stressing "In," "I," "not," "I," "so" and see what you get. That's probably not what you want!

> *For anything so overdone is from the purpose of playing.*
> HAMLET, III, ii

So pause / awhile ...

Now you need a pencil, not a pen. Put this book down and mark the scansion in your monologue and sonnet. Then read them aloud a few times, hitting the stressed syllables. Overdo it. Pound it out. You can pull back to realism later.

By overdoing, you discover meaning and "problems." Are there problems? Likely there are, so let's find them. For example, is there a stress that seems wrong? Or is there a line that won't scan to ten syllables? Trust your common sense, and remember that Shakespeare obtains much of his effect by inverting stresses, which changes the rhythm of the line. He will also write eleven syllable lines, sometimes with feminine endings, and, on occasion, lines of twelve to fourteen syllables. Here are examples that may be similar to your material.

Remember the *Romeo and Juliet* line from chapter 3?

Chorus: From ancient grudge, break to new mutiny,

The line scans like this:

$$\breve{\;}\;/\quad\breve{\;}\;/\quad\;\;/\;\breve{\;}\quad\breve{\;}\;/\quad\breve{\;}/$$
From an / cient grudge, / break to / new mut / i ny,

An action verb like "break" actually breaks the rhythm and creates a trochaic foot. Here's another example, as Juliet speaks to the Friar:

Juliet: Conceit, more rich in matter than in words,
            Brags of his substance, not of ornament.   (II, iv)

The line scans like this:

$$\breve{\;}\;/\quad\breve{\;}\;/\quad\breve{\;}\;/\quad\breve{\;}\;/\quad\breve{\;}\;/$$
Con ceit, / more rich / in mat / ter than / in words,

$$/\;\breve{\;}\quad\breve{\;}\;/\quad\breve{\;}\;/\quad\breve{\;}\;/\quad\breve{\;}\;/$$
Brags of / his sub / stance, not / of orn / a ment.

"Brags" breaks the rhythm. Often trochaic feet are found in the first foot of a line. The third foot is also popular, as in "break" above.

Here are regular lines and then a twelve-syllable line. Puck speaks to the Fairies in *A Midsummer Night's Dream*:

Puck: The King doth keep his revels here tonight.
          Take heed the Queen come not within his sight.
          For Oberon is passing fell and wrath,
          Because that she, as her attendant, hath
          A lovely boy, stolen from an Indian King.   (II, i)

Four lines scan as regular, but in line 5, which has twelve syllables, we must elide twice—because "king" is not a feminine ending—and also discover a trochaic foot.

$$\breve{\;}\;/\quad\breve{\;}\;/\quad\breve{\;}\;/\quad\breve{\;}\;/\quad\breve{\;}\;/$$
The King / doth keep / his rev / els here / to night.

$$\breve{\;}\;/\quad\breve{\;}\;/\quad\breve{\;}\;/\quad\breve{\;}\;/\quad\breve{\;}\;/$$
Take heed / the Queen / come not / with in / his sight.

$$\breve{\;}\;/\quad\breve{\;}\;/\quad\breve{\;}\;/\quad\breve{\;}\;/\quad\breve{\;}\;/$$
For O / ber on / is pass / ing fell / and wrath,

$$\breve{\;}\;/\quad\breve{\;}\;/\quad\breve{\;}\;/\quad\breve{\;}\;/\quad\breve{\;}\;/$$
Be cause / that she, / as her / at tend / ant, hath

$$\breve{\;}\;/\quad\breve{\;}\;/\quad/\;\breve{\;}\quad\breve{\;}\;/\quad\breve{\;}\;/$$
A love / ly boy, / stol'n from / an In / d'an King;

22

We have elided "stolen" to one syllable ("stol'n") and "Indian" to two syllables ("In-d'an"). "Stol'n" also breaks the rhythm. Now the line works.

Here are a few examples of feminine endings. In the first four lines of *Sonnet 58*, note that lines 2 and 4 have feminine endings:

> That god forbid that made me first your slave,
> I should in thought control your times of pleasure,
> Or at your hand th' account of hours to crave,
> Being your vassal bound to stay your leisure.

The lines scan like this:

$$\cup \ / \ \cup \ / \ \cup \ / \ \cup \ / \ \cup \ /$$
That god / for bid / that made / me thus / your slave,

$$\cup \ / \ \cup \ / \ \cup \ / \ \cup \ / \ \cup \ / \ (\cup)$$
I should / in thought / con trol / your times / of pleas / ure

$$\cup \ / \ \cup \ / \ \cup \ / \ \cup \ / \ \cup \ /$$
Or at / your hand / th'ac count / of hours / to crave,

$$\cup \ / \ \cup \ / \ \cup \ / \ \cup \ / \ \cup \ / \ (\cup)$$
Be ing / your vas / sal bound / to stay / your leis / ure.

Note the elision in line 3.
Here's Iago in *Othello*:

Iago: And what's he then that says I play the villain,   (II, iii)

The eleven-syllable line scans like this:

$$\cup \ / \ \cup \ / \ \cup \ / \ \cup \ / \ \cup \ / \ (\cup)$$
And what's / he then / that says / I play / the vil / lain,

The "lain" of "villain" would not be stressed, so we know it's a feminine-ending line.

So pause awhile ...

In your monologue and sonnet, mark all words that break the rhythm, circle all feminine endings, elide as necessary, and check your initial scansion.

You discover changes in the rhythm by applying scansion and trusting your common sense. When the rhythm changes, play it. Once you are comfortable that your monologue and sonnet are correctly scanned, move on to "phrasing."

PHRASING

Phrasing means to break the verse line into individual thoughts. If you take any Shakespearean speech or sonnet, the obvious phrases are separated by punctuation. Paraphrasing Webster, for our purpose, a "phrase" is a group of words that create a thought on which the mind can focus momentarily, and which can be preceded or followed by a pause. As most actors know, it is easier to mark the phrases than it is to handle them vocally.

Here's an example in which most of the phrases are clearly marked by punctuation. In *Julius Caesar*, Brutus responds to Cassius's hint that Caesar has become too powerful.

Brutus:	That you do love me I am nothing jealous.	(1)
	What you would work me to, I have some aim.	(2)
	How I have thought of this, and of these times,	(3)
	I shall recount hereafter. For this present,	(4)
	I would not so (with love I might entreat you)	(5)
	Be any further moved. What you have said	(6)
	I will consider; what you have to say	(7)
	I will with patience hear, and find a time	(8)
	Both meet to hear and answer such high things.	(I, ii) (9)

In lines 6–9, notice the phrases not separated by punctuation.

Here are those lines plus the next five. Caesuras (//) have been inserted to mark those phrases not already separated by punctuation. Some actors prefer to circle the phrases. Notice that the final four lines have no punctuation at all.

Brutus:	What you have said //	(6)
	I will consider; what you have to say //	(7)
	I will with patience hear, and find a time //	(8)
	Both meet to hear and answer // such high things.	(9)
	Till then, my noble friend, chew upon this:	(10)
	Brutus had rather be a villager //	(11)
	Than to repute himself a son of Rome //	(12)
	Under these hard conditions // as this time	(13)
	Is like to lay upon us.	(14)

The last is a "short line," calling for a pause or completion by the next speaker. In this case, Cassius finishes the line with "I am glad ..."

Why bother to mark the phrases? Your goal is to know the phrasing of the line so that you can (1) separate the thoughts, (2) play one phrase against another, which is called antithesis, (3) allow a thought to continue to the next line, as needed, and (4) identify your breathing spots, just like singing.

Shakespeare uses antithetical words, phrases, or thoughts in nearly every speech. To handle this language, you must master playing antithesis, and this mastery begins with phrasing. For the actor, antithetical words, phrases, or thoughts provide clear insight into the meaning of the text. Antithesis is the subject of chapter 8.

So pause a while . . .

Mark or circle the phrases in your monologue and sonnet. Now your scansion is nearing completion. Next add the caesuras.

> *Thus did he answer me, yet said*
> *I might know more hereafter.*
> CYMBELINE, IV, ii

THE CAESURA

> *Nay, I'll speak that*
> *Which you will wonder at.*
> ALL'S WELL THAT ENDS WELL, IV, i

The caesura, the short sense pause marked //, does many things:
- It allows the words preceding it to "sink in" before the listener must deal with more words
- It places focus on the word or phrase following it, giving that word or phrase special emphasis
- It slows the language down
- It separates phrases, which are often the character's thoughts, and allows the listener to hear them one at a time

When you run thoughts together, the audience is usually lost.

As with most rules, once learned they become automatic. Where caesura is concerned, use it thoroughly in rehearsal and preparation, as the use will force you to separate your thoughts. Then remove the caesuras, except where absolutely essential for audience understanding of a word or thought.

When the phrases are identified and the caesuras then removed, you will likely handle the line in such a way that each thought has its own emphasis and energy, and is clearly expressed without the pause. Using that pause in rehearsal, however, will guide you to the places where the thoughts separate.

Consider Richard's opening soliloquy in *Richard III*:

Richard:　Now is the winter of our discontent
　　　　　Made glorious summer by this son of York;
　　　　　And all the clouds that lowered upon our house
　　　　　In the deep bosom of the ocean buried.　　　　　(i, i)

We know that most verse lines without punctuation will take a caesura, usually somewhere in the middle. Arguably, you could place caesuras anywhere that thoughts change, or where you want to set up a word or phrase. Here is the same speech with lots of caesuras—far too many for performance.

Richard:　Now // is the winter // of our // discontent //
　　　　　Made // glorious summer // by this // son of York;
　　　　　And // all the clouds // that lowered upon our house //
　　　　　In the deep bosom // of the ocean // buried.

Your Richard will not need these pauses, and indeed, the pauses will tend to make the speech jerky and indulgent. But each represents something special that is happening in the language. When you remove the pauses, following your discovery period in rehearsal—surely you must remove most of them for performance—you will automatically do something vocally or physically to clarify the possibility of each thought.

Ah, to be blessed with a strong voice and to have trained it! You will need it now as you remove the pauses, and yet, you must play each idea clearly and individually so that it reaches the listener's ear.

Most verse lines lend themselves to at least one caesura. Some already have the thoughts separated by punctuation, and additional caesuras may not be necessary. But the very structure of the blank verse line lends itself to division of thoughts and to "setting up" important words or phrases. Use the caesura, but don't be tempted to retain it anywhere, except where it adds to the listener's understanding. Speaking the language with correct rhythm is much stronger than speaking with pauses inserted for emphasis. Most caesuras are for discovery, not performance.

Here is another example from the same play. To overthrow Richard, Richmond says to his troops:

Richmond:More than I have said, loving countrymen,
　　　　　The leisure and enforcement of the time
　　　　　Forbids to dwell upon. Yet remember this:
　　　　　God and our good cause fight upon our side;　　　　　(v, iii)

You might separate the thoughts like this:

> More than I have said, loving countrymen,
> The leisure // and enforcement // of the time //
> Forbids to dwell upon. Yet // remember this:
> God // and our good cause // fight upon our side;

Line 1: The thoughts are already separated by the author.

Line 2: Play both factors—"leisure" and "enforcement"—not just one, and don't play both as one. Also, don't breathe after "time," but you might take a very short caesura, because you want to set up and attack the active verb "forbids."

Line 3: The thoughts are separated by the author in the middle of the line. "Yet" is one of many transition words used by Shakespeare (some others include "but," "then," "when," "therefore," and "or"), and you can use "yet" to set up the next idea. Do that here.

Line 4: The two factors, "God" and "and our good cause," should not be run together as one. Use them to set up the final phrase.

You are now deeply into the skills required to play Shakespeare!

And skills are exactly what we're developing. We haven't begun to tap our brains to analyze the possibilities of each thought. And yet the language will start to make sense if we simply use these speaking skills. They allow the language to be heard in such a way that the ideas are emphasized, even if we don't know what all of the ideas are. These skills alone will take you a long way in Shakespeare performance and in cold readings. You're starting to allow the language to live.

Sir John Gielgud made this remark: If you were not quite sure of a very difficult speech in Shakespeare and you studied the punctuation and got it right, the sense would in some way emerge (*Acting Shakespeare*, 35).

> *Now I begin to relish thy advice.*
> TROILUS AND CRESSIDA, I, iii

So pause awhile ...

Take some time to insert caesuras into your monologues and sonnet. Once done, your basic scansion is complete and should include:

- Feet separation
- Stresses marked
- Words and feet that break the rhythm (trochees) circled
- Phrases marked or circled

- Caesuras marked
- Feminine endings and elisions noted
- Preliminary breathing points circled
- OED research on all words

Later we will add antithesis, analysis, imagery, and more detail on breathing points. But for now, continue on to "kick the box" and other skills.

USEFUL IDEAS TO REMEMBER:

CHAPTER 4

Support the Line and Thought

We'll begin these rites,
As we do trust they'll end, in true delights.

THE ACTOR MUST support the verse line all the way through to the final word. An exercise I call "kicking the box" teaches this skill.* I began using this exercise when I started working with actors on Shakespearean text some thirty years ago—kicking first an eraser (which was too small), then a sweatshirt (which was too soft), then a soccer ball (which nearly broke the windows), and then settling on a cardboard box one day when we had no eraser or sweatshirt or ball.

KICK THAT BOX!

Let's first review *why* this exercise is so important, then we'll practice it. In coaching "realistic actors" to handle Shakespeare, I have found that kicking the box is the most effective way to learn complete support of the verse line. This is the most basic and simplest of all the skills, and yet it is one of the most important. It is so important, because the natural speech of American actors is dramatically opposed to this necessary skill.

A line of our everyday speech looks something like this:

The emphasis and volume peak in the middle of the line, then fade away as if the speaker has lost interest in the thought or run out of breath.

In Shakespeare, the end of the line is equally important and many times more important than the beginning or middle, because it allows the thought implicit in the line to carry forward. As mentioned in chapter 2, many

---

*Cicely Berry, former voice coach for the Royal Shakespeare Company, mentions a similar exercise in *The Actor and the Text*, 179.

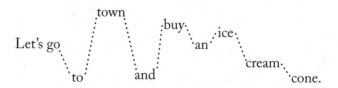

verse lines are enjambed, and the thought continues from one line to the next without punctuation or pause. In blank verse, the actor cannot afford to lose interest in the thought or run out of breath.

Kicking the box helps the actor support the final word or phrase and keep the thought from ending too soon.

We want to involve our entire body when speaking Shakespeare's language. Kicking the box helps the actor remain physically involved in the language.

> *For in such business,*
> *Action is eloquence.*
> CORIOLANUS, III, ii

Supporting the last word or syllable of the blank verse line is not easy and, once learned, is easily ignored. Physiologically, our diaphragm doesn't want to work that way. The muscle is "lazy" and prefers relaxation to tension. During voice training, actors learn to use the diaphragm to support speech. But even after training, many actors forget to "kick the box."

They forget for three reasons:
- The effort to read the line "naturally" and truthfully encourages us to fade out at the end
- We don't practice speaking blank verse on a daily basis
- Breath support becomes lackadaisical, so rather than support the ends of lines, it is easier to allow them to fade away like they do in our daily speech

Because our vocal muscles are uncomfortable with a change, any effort to support the ends of lines may at first seem strange or "overdone." But supporting is correct. If you don't support the end of the verse line, one can project that your Shakespeare will not be clear or truthful. The listener won't quite know what you are saying.

You need great physical energy to speak Shakespeare's verse, and kicking the box helps you to remember to use your body. Energy is a key to your success. Remember, Shakespeare's plays were written to be performed:
- Outdoors
- In broad daylight

- For large audiences
- With much of the audience standing for the entire play
- With people sitting on stage
- Amid concession sales, like a baseball game
- With birds flying around
- With the audience talking back to the actors

If you try speaking in that setting, you will discover immediately how much vocal energy is required.

Here's the kick-box skill and how to do it.
In this example, Romeo is speaking to Friar Laurence:

Romeo: Thou canst not speak of that thou dost not feel.   (III, iii)

Scan the line. Now speak the line in a "natural" way, allowing the final word "feel" to fade away. The line works to a degree. But now, circle the word "feel." Place a small cardboard box on the floor and stand by it. Speak the line, and when you get to "feel," kick the box. Don't kick on "not," and don't kick after "feel." Kick right on the *f* of the word.

It may help if you take a split-second pause (a caesura) before "feel," as this allows you to position yourself and the word, and to get your leg and balance ready to kick—then kick. Later, forget the pause. It's only for the exercise.

You will notice that the kick does two things—it gets your body physically involved in speaking the language, and it gets you to support the word "feel." The intent here is not to overplay "feel," not to shout it, and not to call great attention to it. You simply support it, as opposed to letting it fade out. However, for fun, try to over-stress "feel." Shout it. It's almost impossible to overdo it!

Your ear should tell you that the line means different things when you support or don't support "feel." If you don't support it, Romeo seems to be telling the Friar not to "speak of things." That information is in the first half of the line. If you do support "feel," Romeo may be reminding the Friar that he is celibate and has never felt the love of a woman, so how can he advise? That reading gives both actors much more to work with. Try it.

There are other interpretations of this line, of course, but you should see immediately the difference between supporting and not supporting the final word.

Not supporting makes the line a "general" comment—supporting makes it "specific." Remember Stanislavski's famous observation: "In general is the enemy of art."

EXERCISES FOR KICKING THE BOX

Kick the box on the tenth syllable of the blank verse line.
Here are the first four lines of *Sonnet 29*:

> When, in disgrace with Fortune and men's eyes,   (1)
> I all alone beweep my outcast state,   (2)
> And trouble deaf heaven with my bootless cries,   (3)
> And look upon myself and curse my fate.   (4)

First, try these two preliminary exercises:

1. Read the four lines, but pay no attention to the final words. Just let that final word of each sentence fall away, as we do in everyday speech.
2. Then read the four lines as if you've run out of breath before reaching the end of each line.

Having done that, put your cardboard box (size doesn't matter) in the middle of the room, and read the four lines again. This time, kick the box on the words "eyes," "state," "cries," and "fate." To do this successfully, you must prepare your body and your kicking leg in the space before the final word in each line; you must position yourself. If you don't prepare, you'll kick too soon or too late. So practice this until you have it perfectly. The box will be a mess, and you'll probably need a new one. (So that the lines make sense, don't forget to use the caesuras—probably after "Fortune," "alone," "heaven," and "myself.")

When doing the exercise correctly, you will notice many things. By "playing" the final word of each line, the line takes on new meaning. Also, the thought in the line is carried through the entire line. The thought then continues on to start the next line.

Because it takes breath support to handle the last word in each line, the air reserve held for that word actually helps support the *entire* line, which provides a double benefit.

When you support the final words, you will notice your diaphragm tighten, and the tension will feel a little uncomfortable. A more "natural" feeling would be to let these final words slide away gently and not to tighten the diaphragm. But that manner of speaking ignores correct vocal support.

When you kick the box on the last word of each line, notice how your entire body gets involved in the language. You want to breathe, and *can* breathe, after you kick—unless there is no punctuation. That breath helps you prepare for the next line. As you get better at this exercise, you'll discover that as you breathe *in,* your mind is grabbing the next line. As you breathe *out,* that next line is spoken. The procedure keeps repeating.

To check how much better the lines are now, read them again and let the last words fade away. Don't kick the box. Compare!

So pause awhile . . .

Practice this exercise with your monologue and sonnet. If you encounter a final word of many syllables, be disciplined. Kick only on the final syllable—not at the start of the word.

Here are the next two lines from *Sonnet 29*. Notice the final word in line 6:

Wishing me like to one more rich in hope, *(kick on "hope")*	(5)
Featured like him, like him with friends possessed, *(kick on "sessed")*.	(6)

You will also find that you can kick the box on any word that is followed by punctuation. For example, in line 6 above, you could also kick on the first "him." Normally we don't stress pronouns. In this case we might elect to give it a modest stress.

When the final phrase or word of a line is supported, the thought doesn't "end" until another person speaks. Even when a speech contains a period or semi-colon, continued support of the final word in each line keeps the listeners attentive—they know you have more to say.

> *I trust I may have leave to speak,*
> *And speak I will.*
>
> THE TAMING OF THE SHREW, IV, iii

When you allow the final word of the line to sag, it sounds like you've finished speaking. An imaginary "period" is heard. Then, if you begin talking again, the listener, who thought you had finished, must adjust. Nothing is keeping the thought going. You don't want that situation. You don't want the listener to "relax," but to stay attentive to what you are saying. Don't let 'em off the hook!

We don't want to abuse this exercise and overdo stress on the final syllable or word. Let your common sense and good ear be your judge. The intention is to support, not blast, and allow the idea to continue.

Supporting the final words keeps the listener hooked.

> *I bring a trumpet to awake his ear,*
> *To set his seat on the attentive bent,*
> *And then to speak.*
>
> TROILUS AND CRESSIDA, I, iii

MORE VALUES FROM KICKING THE BOX

Is it even so? Begin you to grow upon me?

AS YOU LIKE IT, I, i

Playing the final word of the line will help continue the thought to the next line.

From *The Merchant of Venice*, here is the first line of Portia's well-known "mercy" speech:

Portia: The quality of mercy is not strained;   (IV, i)

What's the line about? It is not simply about this thing called the "quality of mercy," but suggests that mercy cannot be obtained by *straining* at it.

(Where does the caesura go? Probably after "mercy.")

Read the line aloud and let "is not strained" drop away. Notice that the line seemed to be about "the quality of mercy" and something else, which was rather vague. It was vague for two reasons:

- It was hard to hear.
- The actor gave it no importance, so why should I, the listener, spend time with it?

As the next line is already coming to my ear, I have no time to deal with the "unimportant" phrase.

Now, read the line and play the condition of that quality called mercy—in other words, play the final three words of the line. Do this aloud. Voilà! Now the line is about something specific, namely that we don't achieve the quality called mercy by straining at it. And that is the thought in the line. If you don't play the entire line, you leave out the thought.

If your Portia allows me, the listener, to hear only "the quality of mercy (something)," I may continue listening, probably passively, but I'm not encouraged and challenged to do so. And what your character is saying seems loosely defined, not specific. On the other hand, if your Portia tells me that this "thing called mercy isn't obtained by straining," my mind jumps to the possibilities of that idea, and I want to hear what else you have to say—I want to hear the reasoning that supports your statement. Now, you've got me hooked actively, not passively. I want to hear the next line.

Here's the opening line to the same play:

Antonio: In sooth I know not why I am so sad.   (I, i)

Say the line aloud and allow "so sad" to fall away. What's the line about? It seems to be about something called "sooth" and "why" of something, or "not why" about whatever. Now, say the line aloud and play "so sad." What's the line about? (Caesura? Try it after "sooth" or "why.")

Here's a famous line:

Hamlet: To be, or not to be—that is the question: (III, i)

Do the same exercise, first allowing "the question" to fall away. Define what the line is about. Then play "the question" and define what the line is about. (Punctuation breaks up the phrases, so no caesura is needed.)

Together with supporting the final word of each line, you must also think about supporting *the entire final phrase of each line*. Here is the beginning of *Sonnet 92*:

> But do thy worst to steal thyself away,
> For term of life thou art assured mine;

Do the same exercise, speaking the two lines aloud and allowing "to steal thyself away" and "thou art assured mine" to fade out. (Be sure to make three syllables of "as-sur-`ed.")

Now, play the ending phrases and don't forget to kick the box on the final word of each line. (Don't forget to use the caesura—probably after "worst" and "life.") What are the lines about? Now we're dealing with someone wanting out (perhaps of a relationship) and the speaker asserting that this someone is, in the speaker's view, emotionally owned by him/her.

The study of analysis could be started here, and you can already see the marvelous opportunities for brain work with just these two lines. What are all the possibilities of this opening comment? There will be more analysis in chapter 9.

So pause awhile . . .

Now do this exercise aloud with your sonnet and your monologue and have someone check you for:
- Clearly playing the final phrase of each line
- Allowing the thought of the whole line to be released

You've now come miles on the road to playing Shakespeare!

To show our simple skill,
That is the true beginning of our end.

A MIDSUMMER NIGHT'S DREAM, V, i

_____

SUPPORTING REALISTIC DIALOGUE

Supporting the final word or phrase of the blank verse line is required for sense. This skill will also work with most realistic dialogue. Once you have learned this skill, apply it to all text. When working with prose, including Shakespeare's, you may be amazed to discover how frequently the final word or phrase of the prose line is the most important part. Modern writers are not using blank verse or placing a stress on the tenth syllable, but the idea of supporting the entire second part of the realistic line, if not the last word, will almost always work for you.

Here is Octavius's first speech in George Bernard Shaw's *Man and Superman*. Observe the final word and phrase of each line.

Octavious: But he had daughters; and yet he was as good to my sister as to me. And his death was so sudden! I always intended to thank him—to let him know that I had not taken all his care of me as a matter of course, as any boy takes his father's care. But I waited for an opportunity; and now he is dead—dropped without a moment's warning. He will never know what I felt.   (I, i)

Here is the opening speech of Arthur Miller's *A View From the Bridge*, spoken by the lawyer, Alfieri:

Alfieri: You wouldn't have known it, but something amusing has just happened. You see how uneasily they nod to me? That's because I am a lawyer. In this neighborhood to meet a lawyer or a priest on the street is unlucky. We're only thought of in connection with disasters, and they'd rather not get too close.   (I, i)

Except for the second sentence, note how supporting final words and phrases will work with this speech. As for the second sentence, we rarely want to emphasize pronouns or put a question mark on a question. Playing "me" would be wrong for both reasons. Supporting the phrase, "they nod to me," however, would be correct.

Here are two examples of Shakespeare's prose. First, the Duke in *Measure for Measure*:

Duke: The hand that hath made you fair hath made you good. The goodness that is cheap in beauty makes beauty brief in goodness; but
grace, being the soul of your complexion, shall keep the body of it
ever fair. The assault that Angelo hath made to you, fortune hath
conveyed to my understanding; and, but that frailty hath examples
for his falling, I should wonder at Angelo. How will you do to
content this substitute, and to save your brother?   (III, i)

Note how necessary it is to support the final phrase of each line, and how sometimes the final word also needs special attention.
Here is Sir Toby Belch in *Twelfth Night:*

Toby: Go, Sir Andrew. Scout me for him at the corner of the orchard
like a bum-baily. So soon as ever thou seest him, draw; and as
thou draw'st, swear horrible; for it comes to pass oft that a terrible
oath, with a swaggering accent sharply twanged off, gives man-
hood more approbation than ever proof itself would have earned
him. Away!   (III, iv)

Notice how the final word in the internal phrases and in the first complete sentence carries great importance. You would want to stress "bum-baily," "draw," both "swear" and "horrible," and, in the second complete sentence, the final phrase "that ever proof itself would have earned him." Of course, you would not stress "him." Stress pronouns only by specific choice and only when needed for the sense, which is seldom.

Most writers have their own style for dialogue, and some may intentionally "fade out" lines, like songs that don't know how to end. But you can't go wrong by keeping the idea of "kicking the box" close at hand. Test all of your realistic dialogue with this skill. Not only will the skill help you to sustain the thoughts, it will give you insight into the various meanings of the lines and teach you when to breathe.

> *See how apt it is to learn*
> *Any hard lesson that may do thee good.*
> MUCH ADO ABOUT NOTHING, I, i

USEFUL IDEAS TO REMEMBER:

CHAPTER 5

Practice the Breathing Skill

A SIMPLE TECHNIQUE to practice is this: Breathe at the natural stops, which are identified by punctuation marks. We could argue that the punctuation may be corrupt, so why follow it?

Pick any modern edition of Shakespeare (we're using *The Pelican Shakespeare*), and you have the punctuation that has evolved over four hundred years, often suggested by the world's most brilliant literary minds. That's a pretty good starting place.

Then trust your ear. If the punctuation seems wrong and your ear tells you it should be elsewhere, move it accordingly. The actor is ultimately in charge of the language and must speak with confidence.

YOU'VE GOT TO BREATHE!

Assuming the punctuation in our selected edition is acceptable, note what happens if you breathe "at random." Here are the first four lines of *Sonnet 143*:

> Lo, as a careful housewife runs to catch
> One of her feathered creatures broke away,
> Sets down her babe, and makes all swift dispatch
> In pursuit of the thing she would have stay.

If you breathe after "catch" simply because you're out of breath or because on paper it looks like the end of the line, the first two lines won't make sense. Try it, and you'll see that the first line "ends" if you breathe after "catch," and that it is not a complete sentence. This reading would jar the listener's ear. The second line becomes the beginning of a speech, ignoring the incomplete first line, and messes up the third line. Lines 1 and 3 are typical enjambed lines, because the thought continues without punctuation. The actor must play the thought, and breathe only when it is completed. Sometimes you can play two or more thoughts on one breath, but you should avoid breaking a single thought into more than one breath.

Tyrone Guthrie liked to say that any well-trained actor could speak seven lines of blank verse on one breath, in a large theatre, with clear diction and without rushing *(On Acting, 14)*. If you can't do that now, it's a good exercise to work on.

Read the first two lines in one breath (you can breathe after "Lo," if you wish), and note the sense. If you support "catch" (but don't breathe after it) and support "away," (and do breathe after it) the speech keeps moving forward—we know there is more to come.

(Don't forget to use the caesura—probably after "housewife," "creatures," and "thing.")

Here are the first two lines of *Sonnet 15*:

> When I consider everything that grows
> Holds in perfection but a little moment,

Again, don't breathe after "grows," although it might be followed by a caesura, because you need to set up "Holds" in the second line for sense.

The second line is not a "regular" blank verse line, because there is a stress on the first syllable, "Holds." How do we know that? Your common sense tells you that the verb "Holds" must be played, and that it would be silly to read the line with "Holds" unstressed and "in" stressed. Try it and you'll see. This line is an example of Shakespeare breaking the rhythm for effect.

Try the two lines taking a caesura after "grows" (but not a breath). Try it without the caesura. Trying to say "grows Holds" together isn't comfortable. It also destroys the active verb "Holds." Caesuras are often taken at special places where we might need a little pause to point up a word or thought, but don't need a breath. (Caesuras might be inserted after "consider" and "perfection," plus the extra caesura needed after "grows.")

Look at these lines in which Macbeth decides to kill Banquo and Fleance:

Macbeth:	To be thus is nothing, but to be safely thus—	(1)
	Our fears in Banquo stick deep,	(2)
	And in his royalty of nature reigns that	(3)
	Which would be feared. 'Tis much he dares;	(4)

And to that dauntless temper of his mind   (5)
He hath a wisdom that doth guide his valour   (6)
To act in safety. There is none but he   (7)
Whose being I do fear; and under him   (8)
My genius is rebuked, as it is said   (9)
Mark Antony's was by Caesar.   (III, i) (10)

This speech contains typical Shakespearean punctuation, as clearly as we can tell. We must remember that our versions of the plays were taken from actors' scripts. Different editions of the plays change the punctuation slightly.

The breathing points are the punctuation marks. Circle them, then read the speech and breathe at each mark. You will find that it is quite easy to speak from one breathing point to the next. The longest stretch is two and one-half lines.

Don't breathe after "Banquo" in line 2 or "nature" in line 3. But try it once to discover the problem. You will see immediately that the choice is wrong. Your common sense and good ear will tell you.

Don't breathe at the end of a verse line simply because it is the end of the line on paper. Unless there is punctuation, the end of the line isn't the end of the phrase or thought. Breathe at the end of the verse line only if there is punctuation.

Read these five lines, which have numerous punctuation points, and breathe at each natural stop (all of the punctuation points). Ariel, a spirit, greets his master, Prospero, who has sent for him, in *The Tempest*.

Ariel: All hail, great master! Grave sir, hail! I come   (1)
        To answer thy best pleasure; be 't to fly,   (2)
        To swim, to dive into the fire, to ride   (3)
        On the curled clouds. To thy strong bidding task   (4)
        Ariel and all his quality.   (I, ii) (5)

Did you cheat? *Read it a second time and make yourself breathe at all punctuation points.* You will notice that you don't need that many breaths.

You may be able to read the first line breathing only after "master" and the second "hail," thereby cutting two breaths. But don't cut them unless you don't need them. You probably would have used the breaths in the three-thousand seat original Globe Theatre, but won't use them in most modern theatres or for film. If you use breaths after "fly," "swim," and "fire," they may help you create images with each phrase, which may be appropriate for the character.

Trust your judgment. Your goal is to have a reserve of breath power available at all times and to be able to kick the box on the final word of a sentence. If you haven't enough breath to support the final word, you are not breathing correctly. Inserting more breaths into the lines is not the best solution (although it is one), because these added breaths break up the thought in the verse line in an unnatural way and may leave you gasping and unclear. If you need to insert a breath, do it where the phrasing allows and where it will add emphasis to what you just said or are about to say.

Your goal is to breathe correctly—to fill your lungs at each breathing point—and to avoid little gasping breaths that fill only one-third of your lung capacity. Take the time to breathe deeply, and then speak the line on the exhale. The words ride on air; just send them out.

> *Yet words do well*
> *When he that speaks them pleases those that hear.*
> AS YOU LIKE IT, III, V

Actors accustomed to realistic text often want to "enhance" that text with sounds, gasps, crying, whispering, pauses for effect, sighs, and "ahs." With heightened text, "enhancements" tend to destroy the rhythm of the line. When the rhythm is lost, the antithetical ideas and images are lost, and the audience listens only passively because they are not quite certain what you are saying.

For an excellent example of reading heightened text with great heart and commitment, correct breathing, and without breaking the rhythm with unnecessary pauses or character "enhancements," watch Kenneth Branagh speak the Saint Crispin's speech in act IV of his film, *Henry V*. It's perfection. Other similar examples are listed in part 5.

Embellishing the language with emotion because "my character would do this" will usually not work for you in Shakespeare. Your performance becomes indulgent, because you've lost *what* is being said in favor of *how* it is being said. Generally this direction works: If you need to cry, cry after the line, not on the line. Reason? We must hear the words first, then we can experience your sorrow without the irritation caused by a muffled and unclear line.

If you must whisper, and risk the irritation caused by the muffled line, do it so that everyone, including the back row, can hear and understand clearly.

You can even rant and rave with a powerful voice and great energy, and the audience will listen only passively if they don't know exactly what you are saying.

So pause awhile . . .

Here is a good rehearsal exercise. Clearly mark the breathing points in your monologue. Then read the speech aloud, and use up all of your air on each group of words from breathing point to breathing point—one breath, one thought. Make certain that you support the final words, but otherwise, empty your lungs between breathing points.

With this exercise, you will discover how much force and power you have available. It also implants in your mind the necessity to breathe. Use all of the air between breathing points, even if the line has only one word.

As you practice this exercise, you will begin to notice that taking the breath gives you the split second you need to grasp your next line. As you inhale physically, you also inhale mentally, so to speak, and grab the next line. Then out it comes on the next breath.

If it is your tendency as an actor to break up lines with "embellishments" for emotional effect, the above exercise may convince you that the only pauses you really need in Shakespeare are the breathing points. Keep the pauses intact, the words moving, and play the antithetical ideas against each other. You will discover that the application of too much emotion to heightened text does nothing but bury the meaning, so the audience stops listening.

As with all good acting, don't get ahead of yourself by thinking ahead. Stay in the moment, listen, respond. Don't anticipate or indicate. Realize that after you speak a line, your breathing skill allows you to mentally secure your next line, and this skill will help you develop the confidence to stay in the moment.

If you have three or four lines with no breathing points, try to conquer them. You will need a deep breath before you start line 1 and will need to control the release of your air, or you'll never make it through and surely won't have anything left for the important final word.

So pause awhile . . .

Try this example, as the Bishop of Canterbury tells King Henry V that, if he will attack France, the Church will supply him with the money needed for the campaign.

| Canterbury: | O, let their bodies follow, my dear liege, | (1) |
| | With blood, and sword, and fire to win your right! | (2) |

In aid whereof we of the spiritualty	(3)
Will raise your highness such a mighty sum	(4)
As never did the clergy at one time	(5)
Bring in to any of your ancestors.	(i, ii) (6)

Read the speech aloud and see if you can do lines 3–6 without a breath. If you can't make it, take a breath after "sum," but notice that the speech flows better without the breath. Note, too, that "spiritualty" must be elided to three syllables.

Try these lines of Chorus before Act IV in *Henry V.*

Chorus:	Now entertain conjecture of a time	(1)
	When creeping murmur and the poring dark	(2)
	Fills the wide vessel of the universe.	(3)
	From camp to camp, through the foul womb of night,	(4)
	The hum of either army stilly sounds,	(5)
	That the fixed sentinels almost receive	(6)
	The secret whispers of each other's watch.	(iv) (7)

Read the speech aloud, breathing only at the punctuation. Support all last words, especially "universe," "sounds," and "watch." Don't insert a breath after "dark."

Keep these simple clues in mind:

- The words ride out on the breath; just send them.
- Inhaling gives you a moment to grasp your next line.
- Breathe at every opportunity. If you cut a breathing point, do it intentionally because you don't need it.
- Strong breathing gives you power; lack of breath signals weakness.

Always read and work on Shakespeare aloud. This language is meant to be spoken, and much of the sense is discovered through speech. Shakespeare doesn't just work better aloud, it works *ten times better*! Therefore, when you work on the lines, use the opportunity to practice breathing and voice skills as well.

Once you can use these basic tools, you've come even farther on the journey to playing Shakespeare.

Ay, marry, sir, now it begins to work.
THE TAMING OF THE SHREW, III, ii

USEFUL IDEAS TO REMEMBER:

Practice the Speaking Skill

Now mark him, he begins again to speak.

JULIUS CAESAR, III, ii

Modern actor training in America emphasizes memory recall, playing the subtext, and character development. In many ways, this training makes words secondary to feelings. The actor nowadays tends to "reflect" on the thought, then express it by "handling" the words. The actor may manipulate the words to express the subtextual thought.

The moment required to reflect creates a pause. That "pause to reflect" may come at any time—before the thought, in midthought, or after the thought. The placement and length of the various pauses are based on how the character *feels* about the thought. During a "pause to reflect," the actor usually breathes and reflects, which makes it a different kind of pause than the no-breath caesura—which is a pause to *set up* a word or thought and is not intended to provide time to "reflect."

Today, this pause-to-reflect acting style dominates most films, stage productions of many realistic plays, and especially modern scripts, which call for great subtextual clarification. This technique is at the core of realistic acting.

A problem with this approach emerges, however, when the more important requirement of "playing your action" becomes secondary to "playing your feeling." Because the desire to play your feeling is so grounded in realistic actor training, even good actors often forget to play their action first.

When an actor allows the concept of "playing your feeling" to dominate, the end result is often indulgent acting. The result of indulgent acting is ponderous text, unrealized author intentions, and loss of audience.

SAY WHAT YOU THINK WHEN YOU THINK IT

With Shakespeare, you will be most successful if you
- Say what you think when you think it while...
- Playing your action

By "say what you think," I mean, cut out the moment of "reflection" on the thought and simply speak the thought. Don't think, then talk. Just think while you talk. In other words, act *on* the words, not *between* them.

Shakespeare's language is written so that the actor rarely needs to "reflect" to express feelings or reasoning, because characters say aloud what they are reasoning and feeling. In Shakespeare, the thought is not hidden in the subtext. What's to be said is right there on the surface.

For many actors, dealing with this concept is not easy. The dominance of subtextual acting in film is embedded in our minds. We hear most dialogue read with pauses and searching and poured-out feelings. If we've never tackled Shakespeare before, it is possible that all of our acting has been based on subtextual line readings.

Yet, to determine that language written hundreds of years ago might require different speaking skills than modern language is not really surprising. After all, if a good play, as Hamlet says, intends "to hold, as 'twere, the mirror up to nature," then both modern and Elizabethan writers will mirror their respective languages and speaking habits.

When Shakespeare's language was written, the concepts of "character" and "subtext" as we think of them today were unknown. In the sixteenth and seventeenth centuries, before Sigmund Freud and electronic media, people probably spoke feelings and thoughts more clearly than we do today. Writings of the period demonstrate that practice. In modern-day conversation, however, our tendency is often to disguise what we mean. We are taught as children to "be polite" and not to annoy others with what we really think or feel.

As the thought in modern plays is revealed more in the subtext (what you're thinking) than in the text (what you're saying), modern acting focuses on the skills required to find and speak that subtext. But Shakespeare didn't write that way.

As you study *what* and *why* a specific Shakespearean character is speaking, you will discover that the words are exactly the same as the thoughts. The character is saying exactly what he or she means. So you don't need to play the subtext. In fact, your work will be stronger if you forget acting subtext and, in doing so, remove the "reflective" pauses.

Certainly there are subtextual thoughts in Shakespeare. The point is that the thoughts are also in the language. If useful, of course, and if you are playing the language convincingly, you can work with whatever subtext seems necessary. But in doing so remember that Shakespeare put the thought into the spoken words. Your "subtext" will be a modern-day application; it may cause you to lose the rhythm, and your acting may become indulgent, ponderous, and unclear.

Answer every man directly.—Ay, and briefly.—Ay, and wisely.
JULIUS CAESAR, III, iii

WORKING WITH SUBTEXT

Here are some examples of speeches that could be broken up for subtextual reflection—so the character can "feel it"—or could be spoken *without* the reflection, in which case the character, without taking pause, says directly what he or she is thinking or feeling. See which way works better for you.

In *The Merchant of Venice*, Antonio is about to lose "a pound of flesh," and probably his life, to Shylock. Bassanio, who created the problem, has this to say:

Bassanio: Antonio, I am married to a wife
               Which is as dear to me as life itself;
               But life itself, my wife, and all the world
               Are not with me esteemed above thy life.
               I would lose all, ay, sacrifice them all
               Here to this devil, to deliver you.   (IV, i)

Read the speech through a couple of times for sense. Next, let's create some subtext. Be Bassanio and read the speech, playing these basic feelings about the situation. Play out each one.

1. Hate Shylock: Create a subtext which says, "I hate this man," and play the speech around that subtext.
2. Love your wife: Create a subtext around your great love for Portia and how tragic it would be to lose her.
3. Persuade Antonio of your love: Create a subtext that allows you to thoroughly assure Antonio that you would do anything for him.
4. Apologize: Create a subtext that says how sorry you are to have allowed this problem to develop.

Here are possible results of these four subtextual readings:

1. With this subtext, the speech is about your hatred of Shylock.
2. With this subtext, the speech is about *your* sacrifice, not Antonio's.
3. With this subtext, the speech is about the struggle within *you*, not what Antonio is facing.
4. With this subtext, the speech turns sentimental and indulgent.

Now just read the speech as it is written, adding nothing, but taking this moment to reaffirm your honest feelings to Antonio. Say what you think as you think it. Your action, "to reaffirm," is measured in Antonio and how he responds to you.

Isn't everything you need right there in the words? Is it necessary to apply subtext? Is it necessary to be extremely emotional for any reason? Is it necessary to take any pauses other than the natural breathing points?

Also notice that when playing any of the four subtext examples, you forget to *play your action.* You lose sight of your objective, because your concentration is on a subtextual *feeling.* The action is lost, because those feelings, when expressed, are all descriptive.

To hear and see some other examples, in part 4 are listed a few film and video performances that may be helpful. I've indicated in what way the various performances are successful. Some are brilliant, and these clearly illustrate the points we're discussing.

ACHIEVE YOUR OBJECTIVE

In *The Comedy of Errors*, Antipholus of Ephesus tries to inform the Duke about the ill treatment to which he has been subjected by his wife and others.

Ant/Eph: By the way we met
     My wife, her sister, and a rabble more
     Of vile confederates. Along with them
     They brought one Pinch, a hungry lean-faced villain,
     A mere anatomy, a mountebank,
     A threadbare juggler, and a fortune-teller,
     A needy, hollow-eyed, sharp-looking wretch,
     A living dead man. This pernicious slave,
     Forsooth, took on him as a conjurer,
     And gazing in mine eyes, feeling my pulse,
     And with no face, as 'twere, out-facing me,
     Cries out, I was possessed. Then all together
     They fell upon me, bound me, bore me thence,
     And in a dark and dankish vault at home
     There left me and my man, both bound together,
     Till, gnawing with my teeth my bonds in sunder,
     I gained my freedom, and immediately
     Ran hither to your Grace; whom I beseech
     To give me ample satisfaction
     For these deep shames and great indignities.   (v, i)

Read the speech through a couple of times for sense. Next, be Antipholus and apply the following subtextual possibilities.

1. Get vengeance: Convince the Duke how evil was this fellow, Pinch, and carefully describe all his characteristics.
2. Hate your wife: Create a subtext which places all blame on her.
3. Despise what happened to you: Create a subtext which allows you to feel sorry for yourself.
4. Seek sympathy: Create a subtext which draws sympathy from the Duke.

Here are possible results of these four subtextual readings:

1. In this reading, you completely lose track of your objective—which is not about Pinch.
2. In this reading, "he doth protest too much!"
3. In this reading, the action you are playing to achieve your objective is colored with whining and whimpering, and I soon lose interest.
4. In this reading, you are trying to guide the Duke's feelings, therefore playing the wrong action, which is to seek his reasoned justice, to which you are entitled.

Use the language to achieve your objective. Now you are Antipholus, so say what you think as you think it and reach for your objective. Know each action, and state clearly and emphatically what happened to you.

Don't dwell on Pinch, but use your memory of him to accent how you were treated, and move the entire first part of the speech to reach the line, "I was possessed." (That is your "proof" that your accusers are liars.) Your action is to reduce your accusers to liars—so reduce them.

Now, play the second part of the speech to reach the line "and great indignities." Notice, there are no full stops between "Then all together" and "great indignities." As quickly as you relate one thing, the next thing is on your lips. There is a great urgency to reach "give me ample satisfaction," and then the final line, which summarizes why you deserve that satisfaction.

Your objective is to obtain satisfaction—so obtain it. "Detours" from this action are not required. Your success is measured in what the Duke does when you finish.

Here are additional notes for working on this speech. If you set out to obtain satisfaction, you won't delay unnecessarily to describe Pinch, to seek sympathy, or for any other reason. If you select too much indignation, we lose interest; too much excitement and we lose the reasoning; too much anger and the emotion buries the words—and we don't hear your argument. Find the balance between your built-up frustration over what happened to you and your need to obtain satisfaction.

If you appear to be "mad," your accusers will appear to be right. You must use your reason to (1) prove your sanity by control of your actions, and (2) prove you are deserving of satisfaction. Balance your reason and your emotion to achieve your objective and allow your argument to be heard. Reach for your objective, and the action will pull you along without delay.

> *He has strangled*
> *His language in his tears.*
> HENRY VIII, V, i

> *I speak as my understanding instructs me...*
> THE WINTER'S TALE, I, i

USEFUL IDEAS TO REMEMBER:

CHAPTER 7

Working with Structure and Rhythm

Refer to the sonnet you have selected. To understand speech structure is only one of many reasons why you should work on sonnets. Notice how the sonnet develops. In fourteen lines, there is usually an opening statement or idea, followed by development of the idea, and a concluding thought. In the sonnet, the concluding thought is expressed in a rhyming couplet.

The *basic line structure* through which the thought is expressed is usually 4-4-4-2. Some sonnets do not have a full stop (i.e., period, question mark, exclamation point) until the end of the final line, and the main thought is carried for fourteen lines. Others have full stops after each four lines. The structure is determined by the way Shakespeare chooses to develop the thought.

SPEECH STRUCTURE

I pray, can you read anything you see?
Ay, if I know the letters and language.
ROMEO AND JULIET, I, ii

Shakespeare's speeches are structured much the same as sonnets. There is usually an idea stated and then developed, followed by a concluding or summary thought.

Since most speeches are in three parts, the actor can use the structure as a guide to performance choices.

The opening idea needs to be clearly stated, or the development will fall on deaf ears. The development section often includes the rich poetry, the imagery, and the antithetical thoughts, and can be the hardest part of the speech to make clear. Handle the conclusion with conviction.

The speech structure is such that one can cut a Shakespearean play to less than one hour by simply keeping the opening and closing of each speech and taking out the poetry, which is usually in the middle. What you have left is the action line without the richness.

So pause awhile . . .

Using your rehearsal material, break up the sonnet and the monologue so that you isolate the opening thought, the development, and the conclusion. Check your work against these two examples.

Here are a sonnet and a monologue, which will illustrate and compare speech structure. First the sonnet:

Sonnet 57

Being your slave, what should I do but tend	(1)
Upon the hours and times of your desire?	(2)
I have no precious time at all to spend,	(3)
Nor services to do, till you require.	(4)
Nor dare I chide the world-without-end hour	(5)
Whilst I, my sovereign, watch the clock for you,	(6)
Nor think the bitterness of absence sour	(7)
When you have bid your servant once adieu;	(8)
Nor dare I question with my jealous thought	(9)
Where you may be, or your affairs suppose,	(10)
But, like a sad slave, stay and think of nought	(11)
Save, where you are how happy you make those.	(12)
So true a fool is love that in your will,	(13)
Though you do any thing, he thinks no ill.	(14)

Lines 1 and 2 set out the thought and end with a full stop.

Lines 3 and 4 explain the thought. Then there is another full stop.

Lines 5–8 explore the thought; there is no full stop, and the exploration continues.

Lines 9–12 take the idea even farther, and end with a full stop.

Lines 13 and 14 summarize the reason for the problem that was pondered in the previous ten lines, after being set out in the first two.

A BRIEF DIVERSION

If you wish to work on this sonnet, here are some ideas. Don't get all sentimental. Instead, play the irony. Play the tongue in cheek, laughing at yourself for having gotten so deeply into this love affair that you excuse whatever your lover does.

There are other ways to read these lines, but this approach introduces you to the irony playable in the sonnets and cautions against sarcasm or sentimentality.

Sarcasm is always the *last* choice you should make for a line reading. Use it only if the character choice absolutely demands that the thought intended for the listener is sarcastic.

Oh, horrors! When we think back on the sarcastic acting style of the film industry of the 1930s through the 1950s, or if we listen to many modern soap operas or turn on prime time television or watch (and hear) any number of film stars read every line with sarcasm, we ask, "How did that happen to American realistic acting? It surely wasn't Stanislavski's intention!"

> *Who has read or heard*
> *Of any kindred action like to this?*
> KING JOHN, III, iv

Here is an example of speech structure in a monologue. Claudius, King of Denmark, speaks to Hamlet's friends Rosencrantz and Guildenstern.

King:	Welcome, dear Rosencrantz and Guildenstern.	(1)
	Moreover that we much did long to see you,	(2)
	The need we have to use you did provoke	(3)
	Our hasty sending. Something have you heard	(4)
	Of Hamlet's transformation—so call it,	(5)
	Sith nor th' exterior nor the inward man	(6)
	Resembles that it was. What it should be,	(7)
	More than his father's death, that thus hath put him	(8)
	So much from th' understanding of himself,	(9)
	I cannot dream of: I entreat you both	(10)
	That, being of so young days brought up with him,	(11)
	And sith so neighbored to his youth and havior,	(12)
	That you vouchsafe your rest here in our court	(13)
	Some little time, so by your companies	(14)
	To draw him on to pleasures, and to gather	(15)
	So much as from occasion you may glean,	(16)
	Whether aught to us unknown afflicts him thus,	(17)
	That opened lies within our remedy.	(II, ii) (18)

Line 1 is a standard greeting.

Lines 2, 3, and part of 4 point out that "we have a need" and a problem.

Lines 4 through part of 10 review the problem.

Lines 10 through part of 14 are an invitation.

Lines 14–18 are the command to Rosencrantz and Guildenstern to get to the bottom of the problem.

Speech structure may vary, depending on length and intention, but an awareness of the basic form will serve you well. In Shakespeare's speeches, you can usually ask the following questions and find answers:

- What is the speech about (or what is the thought)?
- What is the development?
- What is the conclusion?

Use your awareness of this structure to play your action and achieve your objective.

BREAKING THE RHYTHM

How "meter" differs from "rhythm" can be confusing for some actors.

Technically, meter is the measured arrangement of words into a specific pattern, which is, for us, lines of five feet (each a meter), with each foot comprised of two syllables.

Rhythm is (for us) the recurring pattern of strong and weak accents within the meter (the foot). Thus, here are five meters with recurring rhythm:

dee dum / dee dum / dee dum / dee dum / dee dum.

This explanation seems to work for actors: Meter is the written structure, rhythm is what we hear.

Of the many marvelous things about Shakespeare's language, one of the most unique is the effect achieved when he breaks the rhythm. As an actor, you've got to know when this change is happening, and you must play it accordingly. If you don't do so, the complete sense of the line is lost.

For example, notice the break in this rhythm:

dee dum / dee dum / dum dee / dee dum / dee dum.

There are hundreds of examples of breaking the rhythm, and once your eye (and ear) are searching, you'll soon identify them. Here are a few. From *Henry VI, part 2*:

| York: | How now? Is Somerset at liberty? | (1) |
| | Then, York, unloose thy long-imprisoned thoughts | (2) |

And let thy tongue be equal with thy heart.   (3)
Shall I endure the sight of Somerset?   (4)
False king, why hast thou broken faith with me,   (5)
Knowing how hardly I can brook abuse?   (6)
King did I call thee? No! thou art not king,   (7)
Not fit to govern and rule multitudes,   (8)
Which dar'st not, no, nor canst not rule a traitor.   (v, i) (9)

The meter is broken to start 5, 6 and 7, so the rhythm changes in each of these first feet to "dum dee." As an actor choice, in lines 4 and 5 you could argue that the rhythm of the first foot in each line would be "dum dum," with no unstressed syllable. In line 7, you could argue that every word is stressed. (In monosyllabic lines like this, watch for many stresses!) Know the possibilities, and make your personal choice.

From *Richard III*, Clarence speaks to his murderers:

Clarence: I charge you, as you hope to have redemption   (1)
           By Christ's dear blood shed for our grievous sins,   (2)
           That you depart, and lay no hands on me: (3)
           The deed you undertake is damnable.   (1, iv) (4)

The meter is broken in line 2 by "shed," which is an active verb that must be stressed, but is in the unstressed position. You need the verb, and certainly "for" (the other half of the foot) would not be the stressed syllable. So a caesura is taken after "blood" to set up "shed," which is stressed. (As an actor choice, once you stress "shed" you could also stress "for" to achieve a specific emphasis.)

The other three lines are regular, with line 1 having a feminine ending.

From *The Comedy of Errors*:

Duke: One of these men is genius to the other;   (1)
           And so of these, which is the natural man,   (2)
           And which the spirit? Who deciphers them?   (3)
Dromio S: I, sir, am Dromio; command him away.   (4)
Dromio E: I, sir, am Dromio; pray, let me stay.   (v, i) (5)

In line 2, "which" breaks the meter. In the Dromio lines, both "I's" break the meter.

So pause awhile ...

Scan your rehearsal monologue and sonnet for words that break the meter. Circle them. These are obviously important words and must be played. They are real clues to reading the lines.

> *Scan this thing no further; leave it to time.*
> OTHELLO, III, iii

USEFUL   IDEAS   TO   REMEMBER:

CHAPTER 8

$Practice\ Identifying\ Antithesis$

In the study of how Shakespeare's language works, nothing is more important than understanding antithesis. According to Webster, "Antithesis is the placing of a sentence or one of its parts against another to which it is opposed to form a balanced contrast of ideas."

For text awareness, you should not rely on your director. First, textual study is part of the actor's job; to know exactly what you are saying is part of the work. Secondly, American directors are often more interested in the visual element of a production than the textual. That approach, if not balanced with the time needed to thoroughly analyze the text, can spell disaster for the actors.

If you are working in a situation where the text is not being studied for antithetical words, phrases and thoughts, you need to work especially hard on your own. You might also seek private coaching or assemble a group of actors outside rehearsal and do this work. Without text study, your acting will fall short of your capability.

For the actor, discovering antithesis is both enriching and exciting. Discovery is not an academic exercise. Rather, it turns on the brain, and does so in such a way that it fuels emotion and spontaneity. Text study gives you confidence; it does not take away confidence. (That very thought is antithetical!)

Shakespeare read without playing the antithesis sounds generalized, and we all know what Stanislavski said about "in general." On the other hand, when you *play* the antithetical words, phrases, and thoughts, the meaning becomes specific.

Because you want your acting to be specific, seek opportunities for text study. Realize that each antithetical idea you dig out and play will make your acting stronger.

So pause awhile ...

ANTITHESIS: THE ACTOR'S FRIEND

Here are exercises in locating antithesis. In the first examples, the antithetical ideas are identified. Then there are examples to practice on your own.

For this second group of examples, the answers are hidden in the next two chapters. After digging out the antithetical ideas as best you can, turn to that help and compare. You may even find more examples than are identified. Also, for this work, five or six brains are usually better than one, and it's more fun. So get a pizza, put a small group together, and plunge in.

This procedure works well: First, read the speech aloud for general sense, then concentrate on two or four line sections. Read these lines aloud, and dig out the antithetical ideas. After you've finished, read the entire speech aloud, this time playing the discoveries, and listen for *even more* antithesis. For example, the first half of the speech might be antithetical to the second half, or an early line might be antithetical to a later line.

Once you believe that you've exhausted all possibilities, read the speech with the new discoveries, and compare to your first reading.

When in rehearsal, also be aware that any of your speeches may be antithetical to something said by another actor. See, for example, the speeches below.

This is all as true as it is strange.
Nay, it is ten times true, for truth is truth
To th'end of reck'ning.

MEASURE FOR MEASURE, V, i

Here is Romeo's first speech. He talks of love with his cousin, Benvolio, then notices that a street fight has taken place between the two warring houses.

Benvolio:	Alas, that love, so gentle in his view,	(1)
	Should be so tyrannous and rough in proof!	(2)
Romeo:	Alas, that love, whose view is muffled still,	(3)
	Should without eyes see pathways to his will!	(4)
	Where shall we dine? O me! What fray was here?	(5)
	Yet tell me not, for I have heard it all.	(6)
	Here's much to do with hate, but more with love:	(7)
	Why, then, O brawling love! O loving hate!	(8)

57

O any thing, of nothing first create!	(9)
O heavy lightness! serious vanity!	(10)
Mis-shapen chaos of well-seeming forms!	(11)
Feather of lead, bright smoke, cold fire, sick health!	(12)
Still-waking sleep, that is not what it is!	(13)
This love feel I, that feel no love in this.	(14)
Dost thou not laugh?	(15)
Benvolio: No, cuz, I rather weep.	(1, i) (16)

Here are some of the antithetical words, phrases, and thoughts. Perhaps you will discover others.

Lines 1/2: The phrases "gentle in his view" and "tyrannous and rough in proof" are antithetical. (The first idea is a pleasant anticipation; the second an unpleasant experience.)

Line 4: "without eyes"—"see pathways"

Line 6: "tell me not"—"have heard it all"

Line 7: "hate"—"love"

Line 8: "brawling — "loving"; "love" — "hate"

Line 9: "any thing"—"nothing"

Line 10: "heavy"—"lightness"; "serious"—"vanity"

Line 11. "Mis-shapen chaos"—"well-seeming forms"

Line 12: All four phrases.

Line 13: "Still-waking"—"sleep"; "is not"—"is"

Line 14: "love"—"no love"

Lines 15/16: "laugh"—"weep"

Also, the *thought* in line 13—"That's not what it [love] is"—is antithetical to the type of "love" expressed in lines 7–12.

Now read the speech and play all the antithetical possibilities!

In an example from *Henry V*, here is the King's prayer before the battle at Agincourt.

King:	O God of battles, steel my soldiers' hearts;	(1)
	Possess them not with fear! Take from them now	(2)
	The sense of reck'ning, if th' opposed numbers	(3)
	Pluck their hearts from them. Not to-day, O Lord,	(4)
	O, not to-day, think not upon the fault	(5)
	My father made in compassing the crown!	(6)
	I Richard's body have interred new;	(7)
	And on it have bestowed more contrite tears	(8)
	Than from it issued forced drops of blood:	(9)
	Five hundred poor I have in yearly pay,	(10)
	Who twice a day their withered hands hold up	(11)
	Toward heaven, to pardon blood;	(12)

And I have built two chantries,   (13)
Where the sad and solemn priests sing still   (14)
For Richard's soul. More will I do: (15)
Though all that I can do is nothing worth,   (16)
Since that my penitence comes after all,   (17)
Imploring pardon.   (IV, i) (18)

Here are some of the antithetical words, phrases, and thoughts.
Lines 1/2: "steel"—"fear"
Lines 3/4: "sense of reck'ning"—"pluck their hearts"
Lines 8/9: "bestow'd"—"issued"; "tears"—"blood"
Line 14: "sad and solemn"—"sing"
Line 16: "all"—"nothing"
Also, the thought—"think not upon the fault"— (lines 5 and 6)—is antithetical to the thought—think on all of this penitence and award us victory (lines 7–18).
Here is Olivia encouraging love from Viola in *Twelfth Night:*

Olivia: O, what a deal of scorn looks beautiful   (1)
          In the contempt and anger of his lip.   (2)
          A murd'rous guilt shows not itself more soon   (3)
          Than love that would seem hid: love's night is noon.   (4)
          Cesario, by the roses of the spring,   (5)
          By maidhood, honor, truth, and everything,   (6)
          I love thee so that, maugre all thy pride,   (7)
          Nor wit nor reason can my passion hide.   (8)
          Do not extort thy reasons from this clause,   (9)
          For that I woo, thou therefore hast no cause;   (10)
          But rather reason thus with reason fetter,   (11)
          Love sought is good, but given unsought is better. (III, i) (12)

Clarification note: "maugre" means "despite," and "fetter" is something that confines: (Webster: "boredom puts fetters upon the imagination.")
Antithetical text includes:
Lines 1/2: The idea that scorn, contempt, and anger can be beautiful on the lip is antithetical.
Lines 3/4: "murd'rous guilt"—"love"; "shows"—"hid"; "night"—"noon"
Line 7: The thought "I love thee so" is antithetical to the thought "mauger all thy pride."
Line 8: "wit nor reason"—"passion"
Line 12: "sought"—"unsought"
Also, the thought expressed in lines 1–4—"you hide your love behind scorn and pride"—is antithetical to the thought expressed in lines 5–8—"my love is unhidden and freely expressed."

And in lines 9–12, the thought—"you deny the passion of love"—is antithetical to the thought—"but I'm giving myself to you."

From *Richard III*, here is Queen Margaret (whose husband, King Henry VI, has been killed by Richard) condemning Queen Elizabeth, who succeeded her.

Margaret:	Decline all this, and see what now thou art:	(1)
	For happy wife, a most distressed widow;	(2)
	For joyful mother, one that wails the name;	(3)
	For one being sued to, one that humbly sues;	(4)
	For queen, a very caitiff crowned with care;	(5)
	For she that scorned at me, now scorned of me;	(6)
	For she being feared of all, now fearing one;	(7)
	For she commanding all, obeyed of none.	(8)
	Thus hath the course of justice whirled about	(9)
	And left thee but a very prey to time,	(10)
	Having no more but thought of what thou wast,	(11)
	To torture thee the more, being what thou art.	(IV, iv) (12)

If you study this entire speech you will discover that these lines, taken from the middle, are antithetical to the lines that preceded them. This speech also contains these antithetical ideas:

Line 1: "Decline"—"now"
Line 2: "happy wife"—"distressed widow"
Line 3: "joyful mother"—"one that wails"
Line 4: "being sued to"—"humbly sues"
Line 5: "queen"—"caitiff"
Line 6: "scorned at me"—"scorned of me"
Line 7: "feared of all"—"fearing one"
Line 8: "commanding all"—"obeyed of none"
Lines 9/10: "course of justice"—"prey to time"
Lines 11/12: "what thou wast"—"what thou art"

So pause awhile . . .

Do these next examples on your own. After finishing, dig around in chapters 9 and 10 and find my listing of the antithetical words, phrases, and thoughts. Perhaps you found more possibilities.

In *The Taming of the Shrew*, here is Petruchio speaking to Kate after he has dismissed the tailors and plans to travel to her father's home in old clothes.

Petruchio:	Well, come, my Kate; we will unto your father's,	(1)
	Even in these honest mean habiliments.	(2)
	Our purses shall be proud, our garments poor,	(3)
	For 'tis the mind that makes the body rich;	(4)
	And as the sun breaks through the darkest clouds	(5)
	So honor peereth in the meanest habit.	(IV, iii) (6)

In *Richard II*, here is the King alone in prison shortly before his death.

Richard:	I have been studying how I may compare	(1)
	This prison where I live unto the world;	(2)
	And, for because the world is populous,	(3)
	And here is not a creature but myself,	(4)
	I cannot do it. Yet I'll hammer it out.	(5)
	My brain I'll prove the female to my soul,	(6)
	My soul the father; and these two beget	(7)
	A generation of still-breeding thoughts;	(8)
	And these same thoughts people this little world,	(9)
	In humors like the people of this world,	(10)
	For no thought is contented.	(v, v) (11)

Also from *Richard II*, Bolingbroke condemns Exton, Richard's killer, after having wished the murder done.

Bolingbroke:	They love not poison that do poison need,	(1)
	Nor do I thee. Though I did wish him dead,	(2)
	I hate the murderer, love him murdered.	(3)
	The guilt of conscience take thou for thy labor,	(4)
	But neither my good word nor princely favor.	(5)
	With Cain go wander through the shade of night,	(6)
	And never show thy head by day nor light.	(v, vi) (7)

Note: Line 6 follows the *Folio*. The Pelican edition prefers "through shades of night."

In *As You Like It*, the shepherdess, Phebe, is in love with Rosalind, who is disguised as a man and has rejected her.

Phebe:	Think not I love him, though I ask for him;	(1)
	'Tis but a peevish boy; yet he talks well.	(2)
	But what care I for words? Yet words do well	(3)
	When he that speaks them pleases those that hear.	(4)
	It is a pretty youth; not very pretty:	(5)

	But, sure he's proud, and yet his pride becomes him.	(6)
	He'll make a proper man. The best thing in him	(7)
	Is his complexion; and faster than his tongue	(8)
	Did make offense, his eye did heal it up.	(9)
	He is not very tall; yet for his years he's tall.	(10)
	His leg is but so so; and yet 'tis well.	(11)
	There was a pretty redness in his lip,	(12)
	A little riper and more lusty red	(13)
	Than that mixed in his cheek; 'twas just the difference	(14)
	Betwixt the constant red and mingled damask.	(15)
	There be some women, Silvius, had they marked him	(16)
	In parcels as I did, would have gone near	(17)
	To fall in love with him; but, for my part,	(18)
	I love him not nor hate him not; and yet	(19)
	I have more cause to hate him than to love him;	(20)
	For what had he to do to chide at me?	(21)
	He said mine eyes were black and my hair black;	(22)
	And, now I am rememb'red, scorned at me.	(23)
	I marvel why I answered not again.	(24)
	But that's all one: omittance is no quittance.	(25)
	I'll write to him a very taunting letter,	(26)
	And thou shalt bear it. Wilt thou, Silvius?	(27)
Silvius:	Phebe, with all my heart.	(28)
Phebe:	I'll write it straight;	(29)
	The matter's in my head and in my heart;	(30)
	I will be bitter with him and passing short.	(31)
	Go with me, Silvius.	(III, v) (32)

In this speech, you will find an antithesis not found in the previous two examples.

When lines have no antithetical thoughts, check to see if any ideas are antithetical to something spoken by another person. Note this example from *The Merchant of Venice:*

Bassanio:	This is no answer, thou unfeeling man,	(1)
	To excuse the current of thy cruelty.	(2)
Shylock:	I am not bound to please thee with my answer.	(3)
Bassanio:	Do all men kill the things they do not love?	(4)
Shylock:	Hates any man the thing he would not kill?	(5)
Bassanio:	Every offense is not a hate at first.	(6)
Shylock:	What, wouldst thou have a serpent sting thee twice?	(IV, i) (7)

In lines 2 through 7, the idea in each line is antithetical to the next line. You will find many similar exchanges in Shakespeare. Watch for them and play them accordingly. (There is nothing in the answer key about this example.)

You will find many lines and short speeches with no antithetical words, phrases, or thoughts—just straightforward dialogue. In these cases, use the scansion and kick the box.

As a final example, let's look at one sonnet. The sonnets are rich in antithetical words, phrases, and thoughts. They are also rich in imagery, which we will consider in chapter 10.

Sonnet 15

When I consider everything that grows	(1)
Holds in perfection but a little moment,	(2)
That this huge stage presenteth nought but shows	(3)
Whereon the stars in secret influence comment;	(4)
When I perceive that men as plants increase,	(5)
Cheered and checked even by the selfsame sky,	(6)
Vaunt in their youthful sap, at height decrease,	(7)
And wear their brave state out of memory:	(8)
Then the conceit of this inconstant stay	(9)
Sets you most rich in youth before my sight,	(10)
Where wasteful Time debateth with Decay	(11)
To change your day of youth to sullied night;	(12)
And, all in war with Time for love of you,	(13)
As he takes from you, I engraft you new.	(14)

You will discover wonderful antithetical words, phrases, and thoughts in this remarkable sonnet, some of which are included in the answer key.

Hath that awakened you?
Ay, but not frighted me.

THE TAMING OF THE SHREW, V, ii

So pause awhile . . .

Before moving on, take your monologue and sonnet and work out the antithetical words, phrases, and thoughts. It's more fun if you have a few people work with you and have someone check your readings after you've added the antithesis.

USEFUL IDEAS TO REMEMBER:

CHAPTER 9

Text Analysis

By the pricking of my thumbs,
Something wicked this way comes.

MACBETH, IV, i

T HE SKILLS WE'VE been working on are part of "analyzing a text." Each of the following skills is a form of analysis:
- Scanning the lines
- Locating where the rhythm breaks
- Using elision and the feminine ending
- Identifying short or shared lines
- Noting caesuras
- Marking the breathing spots
- Supporting final words and phrases (kicking the box)
- Discovering and separating phrases
- Not running thoughts together
- Stressing the antithetical words, phrases, and thoughts
- Considering the speech structure
- Understanding the various meanings of each word
- Identifying the imagery

As each of these skills is critical to acting Shakespeare successfully, analysis is not an academic exercise. Only when analysis of the text is completed and the words are spoken aloud should an actor proceed to "character analysis."

ANOTHER DIVERSION

How is analysis tied to playing your action? With Shakespeare, once you know what the language is doing (rhythm changes, antithetical thoughts, etc.)

and what it is saying (meaning of all the words, etc.), achieving your objective by playing your action is the same as with realistic text.

There is this difference—in realism, the action you want to play may be buried in the subtext. In Shakespeare, the action is stated in the words themselves. We have returned to a point made earlier: You can't make character choices—including which action to play—until what the language is doing and saying is absolutely clear.

For examples, refer again to "Working with Subtext" on pages 53 to 56.

Complete analysis of a script or sonnet includes even more than the application of those skills that are designed to help us speak the text clearly. It also includes in-depth study of word meanings. Various words had different meanings in the year 1600 than they do now. The actor needs to know as closely as possible what the word meant to Shakespeare, for this will help determine what he intended the line to mean. Immediate sources for these meanings are *The Shakespeare Lexicon* (see bibliography) and the *Oxford English Dictionary* (*OED*). The *OED* will clarify the meaning of every word at the time of origin. Check every word in your monologue and sonnet to understand what the word meant in Shakespeare's time. Write the meaning in your text.

Knowing the various ways in which a word might be used leaves the actor freedom of choice. The character will choose the use of the word that helps play the action.

On the other hand, when an actor doesn't bother to dig out the possible meanings of a word and makes an early choice on what the word may mean, the character can become locked into that reading. The action, however, may lead in another direction.

Following is an example of "in-depth" study to determine what is being said in blank verse lines. From the point of view of simply interpreting words and phrases, we will do a basic analysis of *Sonnet 15*. For this analysis, footnotes from various editions, comments from scholars, and personal observations will be used. What each word means or could imply will be worked out.

Begin the text analysis of either scene dialogue or a sonnet by discovering what each word means. Most editions include footnotes that explain unfamiliar words or phrases, but the notes from various editions might differ. Consult at least three.

For analysis of scene dialogue, you will discover that there are hundreds of studies of each of Shakespeare's plays. Some of these are useful to the actor, and a few examples are listed in part 5. You should also be aware of a collection called the "New Variorum Edition," in which the words, lines, and ideas are fully annotated. Each page contains only a few lines of text and a few dozen lines of footnotes. Sometimes the opinions of eight or ten different scholars or directors are quoted.

For analysis of the sonnets, complete annotation is available in numerous critical studies. Two texts will be used here, and both are available to purchase for your personal library. Scholarly texts about the sonnets may seem complex at first. With practice, however, they become quite accessible. For the most part, they trace the usage of a word or phrase, and this can be helpful to the actor. Read through the following examples.

I should think this a gull, but that
the white-bearded fellow speaks it.
MUCH ADO ABOUT NOTHING, II, iii

DETAILED EXAMPLE

Sonnet 15

When I consider everything that grows	(1)
Holds in perfection but a little moment,	(2)
That this huge stage presenteth nought but shows	(3)
Whereon the stars in secret influence comment;	(4)
When I perceive that men as plants increase,	(5)
Cheered and checked even by the selfsame sky,	(6)
Vaunt in their youthful sap, at height decrease,	(7)
And wear their brave state out of memory:	(8)
Then the conceit of this inconstant stay	(9)
Sets you most rich in youth before my sight,	(10)
Where wasteful Time debateth with Decay	(11)
To change your day of youth to sullied night;	(12)
And, all in war with Time for love of you,	(13)
As he takes from you, I engraft you new.	(14)

First, review the footnotes to the sonnet provided in your text. Then, read the footnotes listed here, as provided in the edition we have used throughout this book, *The Pelican Shakespeare*, edited by Alfred Harbage, and as provided in the HarperCollins edition, *The Complete Works of Shakespeare*, edited by David Bevington. The edition also includes all research used for *The Bantam Shakespeare*.

THE PELICAN SHAKESPEARE	HARPERCOLLINS/BANTAM SHAKESPEARE
Line 3, *stage*—the world	Line 2, *holds in perfection*—
Line 4, *in secret influence comment*—	maintains its prime

Answers from page 61: line 3, "purses"—"garments" and "proud"—"poor"; lines 3/4, "garments poor"—"body rich"; line 4, "mind"—"body"; line 5, "clouds"—"sun"; and note that the thoughts in lines 5 and 6 are a simile, not an antithesis.

provide a silent commentary
by influencing the action
Line 6, *Cheered and checked*—
applauded and hissed or
nourished and starved
Line 7, *vaunt*—boast
Line 8, *brave*—splendid; *out of
memory*—until forgotten
Line 9, *conceit*—idea; *stay*—duration
Line 11, *wasteful*—destructive;
debateth—joins forces, fights
Line 14, *engraft*—graft, infuse new
life into, with poetry (Harbage,
1455).

Line 5, *as*—like
Line 7, *sap*—vigor; *at height
decrease*—i.e. no sooner
reach full maturity but they
(humans) start to decline
Line 9, *conceit*—notion;
inconstant stay—mutable
brief time (on earth)
Line 11, *wasteful... Decay*—i.e.
Time and Decay contend to
see who can ruin you fastest,
or join forces to do so,
debating between them the
best procedure
Line 13, *all in war*—I, fighting with
might and main (Bevington,
1619).

For critical analysis of *Sonnet 15*, the following selections are taken from four pages of notes in *Shakespeare's Sonnets*, edited with commentary by Stephen Booth, and a few examples selected from two pages of notes in *William Shakespeare: The Sonnets and A Lover's Complaint*, edited by John Kerrigan.

KERRIGAN: Line 3: *This huge stage presenteth naught but shows*. A renaissance commonplace; compare *As You Like It* 11, 7.138–40. 'This wide and universal theatre/Presents more woeful pageants than the scene/Wherein we play in'; and Jaques' reply, 'All the world's a stage...'

BOOTH: Line 4: This line is metrically unusual; it asks to be pronounced as a twelve-syllable, six-stress line, and sounds good when pronounced that way. [Note: As an actor reading this sonnet, you must choose between a twelve-syllable line or a feminine ending on "comment." You would probably ignore the twelve-syllable suggestion, elide "influence" to "influ'nce" and select the feminine ending.]

BOOTH: Lines 1–4: The quatrain moves in an appropriately orbital path. It begins with *I consider* and concludes with *the stars ... comment*; it travels far from its starting place and ends up far from its starting place, but, in a way, the quatrain returns to its starting point, because line 4 can activate the atrophied literal meaning of "to consider": "to look at the stars" (from Latin *cum* and *sidus, sider-*). Lines 3 and 4 are a complicated inversion of *I consider*.

KERRIGAN: Line 4: Renaissance astrologers believed that the *stars* affected men by pouring down an ethereal fluid; this they called *influence*.

BOOTH: Line 6: *Cheered* encouraged ("to cheer" did not yet have its modern and special theatrical meaning, "to shout applause").

BOOTH: Line 7: ...*at height decrease* having reached their prime, begin to decline *(height* describes the peak of an actor's career—or that of one of the heroes he plays; the full growth of a plant, and the highest point reached by a celestial body in its passage across the sky).

BOOTH: Line 8: And wear their splendid finery (*brave state*) beyond the time when anyone remembers them or the outdated fashions they wear.

BOOTH: Line 10: *Sets you,* places you, that is, evokes your image. *Rich in youth* (1) opulent, magnificent during the time of your youthfulness (*in* indicating duration); (2) possessed of abundance of youthfulness (*in* indicating that to which the attribute is limited); (3) richly clothed in youthfulness (*in* expressing relation to that which covers). (Booth, 155–157)

KERRIGAN: Line 12: *sullied night.* The contrast with *day of youth* suggests 'old age, with all its disfigurements' rather than 'death.'

KERRIGAN: Line 13: *all in war* battling with all my might. The poet replaces *Decay* as *Time's* antagonist (Kerrigan, 192–193).

> *Where did you study all this goodly speech?*
> THE TAMING OF THE SHREW, II, i

This research is part of your personal text analysis as itemized on page 73. Now, as you begin rehearsal, nothing is unclear and the choices are at your fingertips. We haven't yet studied imagery, but locating images is also part of your analysis and is the subject of the next chapter.

It may be comforting to know that, for the most part, analyzing sonnets is more difficult than analyzing dramatic text. The ideas and images are more compressed.

This type of analysis for each sonnet and play is available in much more detail in most libraries. Some of the research texts listed in part 4 can easily be added to your personal library.

Discovering the meaning of Shakespeare's language is a world unto itself. Once you enter into it and become excited about the riches hidden there, escape seems impossible. The wealth that you discover is transferred to your character, who, in rehearsal or performance, is supplied with rich, verbal treasures. To apply this type of analysis to your material takes only discipline and time.

So pause awhile ...

- Using the edition from which you took your monologue and sonnet, compile the footnotes or endnotes related to your material.
- Obtain at least two other editions of both the monologue and the sonnet, and compile those footnotes.

- Study the analysis of your sonnet from at least two different authors; you may have to choose between numerous interpretations.
- Read the entire play and various analyses of the play from which you selected your monologue.
- Be certain to check the OED for various meanings of each word.

But thou art deeper read, and better skilled.

TITUS ANDRONICUS, IV, i

USEFUL IDEAS TO REMEMBER:

Answer from page 61: line 2, "prison,"—"world"; lines 3/4, "populous"—"myself"; line 5, "cannot do it" to both "hammer it out" (also in line 5) and "compare" in line 6; line 6, "brain"—"soul"; lines 6/7, "female"—"father"; lines 9/10, "thoughts"—"humors." Antithetical ideas: he will no longer be alone if he can hammer out thoughts into people (the cell will become populous).

CHAPTER 10

Love the Imagery

I ONCE ASKED a fine professional actress what she thought was meant by imagery. She said, "In a text? Well, certain words allow me to draw pictures for the audience—put pictures in their minds. I think that is imagery."

Here is Webster's first definition of imagery: *The formation of mental images.*

The images in Shakespeare's language are expressions of the character's state of mind at that moment. Thousands of papers and books have been written about this subject, and you might want to study some of them at your leisure. For our purposes, remember this: Shakespeare's characters speak what they are thinking, and they communicate much of the time through imagery. That imagery is often a very strong clue to who the character is.

Shakespeare's characters use imagery far more than do the characters in modern plays. They *need* to express themselves through images. In Elizabethan times, the other characters, and the audience, grasped the images. All were on the same page. Nowadays, if you speak in images, much of the audience is likely to be left "in the dark."

Here are a few examples of imagery. In *Romeo and Juliet*, Juliet, a thirteen-year-old girl, uses nine specific images in only seven lines, as she impatiently awaits word of Romeo:

Juliet:	Gallop apace, you fiery-footed steeds,	(1)
	Towards Phoebus' lodging! Such a wagoner	(2)
	As Phaeton would whip you to the west,	(3)

And bring in cloudy night immediately. (4)

Spread thy close curtain, love-performing night, (5)

That runaways' eyes may wink, and Romeo (6)

Leap to these arms untalked of and unseen. (III, ii) (7)

Note the images:

Line 1: "fiery-footed steeds"

Line 2: "Phoebus' lodging" (Phoebus is Apollo as the sun god)

Line 3: "wagoner as Phaeton" (Phaeton is Phoebus' son)

Line 3: "whip you to the west"

Line 4: "cloudy night"

Line 5: "spread thy close curtain"

Line 5: "love-performing night"

Line 6: "runaways' eyes may wink"

Line 7: "Romeo leap to these arms"

In all likelihood, most of the Elizabethan audience understood these images. Surely the actors in the company were familiar with them. Nowadays, comparing something to Phoebus or Phaeton would hardly clarify the idea.

In this example from act III of *Henry V*, Chorus describes the scene of the King's departure for France.

Chorus: Thus with imagined wing our swift scene flies, (1)

In motion of no less celerity (2)

Than that of thought. Suppose that you have seen (3)

The well-appointed king at Hampton pier (4)

Embark his royalty; and his brave fleet (5)

With silken streamers the young Phoebus fanning. (6)

Play with your fancies, and in them behold (7)

Upon the hempen tackle shipboys climbing; (8)

Hear the shrill whistle which doth order give (9)

To sounds confused; behold the treaden sails, (10)

Borne with th' invisible and creeping wind, (11)

Draw the huge bottoms through the furrowed sea, (12)

Breasting the lofty surge. (III, i) (13)

… and continuing for a total of thirty-five image-rich lines. Here are the first:

    1. The "scene" flying as if on wings

    4. "the well-appointed king"

Answer from page 61: line 1, first phrase to the second phrase; lines 2/3, "wish him dead"—"hate the murderer"; line 3, "love"—"hate"—"murdered"—"murderer"; lines 4/5, "guilt of conscience"—"good word nor princely favor"; lines 6/7, "wander," "show"—"wander,"—"the shade of night"—"day nor light."

4. "at Hampton pier/Embark"
5. "brave fleet/With silken streamers"
6. "young Phoebus fanning"
8. "hempen tackle" followed by "shipboys climbing"
9. "the shrill whistle"
10. "treaden sails"
11. "invisible and creeping wind"
12. "huge bottoms" followed by "furrowed sea"
13. "breasting the lofty surge"

As a final example, look back at *Sonnet 15* on page 70, and let's concentrate on some of the images.
3. "huge stage"... "shows"
4. "stars... comment"
7. "vaunt in their youthful sap" (youth boasting); "height decrease" (aged bending)
8. "wear their brave state" (perhaps aged people wearing what is out of fashion; other possibilities as well)
10. "set you most rich in youth" (seeing the one you love in the richness of youth)
11. "Time... Decay" (an image which is probably different to each person)
12. "sullied night"
14. "engraft you new"

> *For by the image of my cause I see*
> *The portraiture of his.*
> HAMLET, V, ii

A well-spoken image should create an analogy, an identifiable likeness, in the listener's mind. Nearly every speech in Shakespeare contains images. Use them to help you play your action and achieve your objective.

An image-rich passage is active, not passive. In performance, it engages (or seduces) the listener to participate in the character's action. It is not sentimental, and if you read it too lyrically the listener will lose interest. The imagery must be active and move the action forward.

IMAGERY EXERCISE

With this exercise, the actor experiences what the audience will experience—the language, complete with images, coming at the ear. It is not enough for the actor to visualize an image and then use that visualization to help create an emotion to accompany the line reading, a technique which is commonly taught in realistic acting classes. *It is more important that the actor not indulge in applying an emotion, but learn to handle the image vocally so that the audience can experience it as well.*

To practice how to handle the image vocally, apply this exercise to any of Shakespeare's speeches. If a line does not yield an image for you, simply go on to the next line. Not all lines contain clear images.

Look at Chorus's speech from *Henry V* as shown on page 71. Read it aloud once for sense and for the listeners to hear how you read it. Then lie back on the floor, close your eyes, and have someone else read the speech to you—very slowly—without any emphasis or selection of important words. When you hear a word which invokes an image, raise you hand to signal the reader to pause. Concentrate on the image. When you have it in detail, lower your hand to signal the reader to continue—very slowly. Pause at the next image, etc. When you've heard all of the lines, stand and read the speech yourself aloud.

You and the listeners will notice many things. You will try to communicate to the listener the details of the images you have seen. Your articulation and control of the language will improve. You will slow down. You will develop a personal commitment to the images in the speech and a personal ownership of the lines. You will want to make them clear.

This wonderful exercise works every time. You can also use it for realistic text.

You may notice that speeches rich in imagery often have few antithetical words, phrases, or thoughts. Looking at Chorus's same speech, the antithetical words are limited to "motion" and "thought" in lines 2 and 3, "order" and "confused" in lines 9 and 10, and "furrowed" and "lofty" in lines 12 and 13. In Juliet's image-rich speech above, the idea of getting rid of light and bringing on night is antithetical, but there isn't much else.

As an actor, you love words that allow you to draw images. You want to paint pictures in the listeners' minds. Painting pictures helps you to establish who you are, where you are, and what you want. To help you paint those pictures, you won't find better images in dramatic language than Shakespeare's. Love and cherish them!

Answer from page 61-62: Here are only a few of the antithetical words, phrases, or thoughts. You should have no trouble picking out the others. Line 1, first phrase against the second phrase; line 2, "peevish boy,"—"talks well"; line 3, first phrase against the second phrase; line 4, "speaks"—"hear"; line 5, "is pretty,"—"not pretty"; line 6, "proud,"—"pride becomes"; lines 8/9, "offense,"—"heal" and "tongue,"—"eye." There are at least six more in the next twenty-two lines. But note—the second part of the speech, beginning with line 20, is antithetical to the entire first part of the speech. The character appears to reverse direction in the middle of her thoughts. We hadn't seen that reversal in any of the other examples.

O, woe is me
To have seen what I have seen, see what I see!

HAMLET, III, i

There are other skills you may want to learn for playing Shakespeare, but we won't study them here. The skills learned in this book prepare you for more advanced work. There are dozens of other exercises which, if practiced, will develop your skills, especially vocal.

Study Cicely Berry's book, *The Actor and the Text*, John Barton's *Playing Shakespeare* (with the accompanying videos), and Kristin Linklater's *Freeing Shakespeare's Voice* or Patsy Rodenburg's *The Need for Words, The Right to Speak* and *The Actor Speaks*. They will help you to improve your Shakespeare.

Do your language study before rehearsals begin, then the rehearsal process can be about character and relationships, as it should be.

A parting thought: no, not "parting is such sweet sorrow," but rather—

Speak the speech, I pray you, as I pronounced it to you, trippingly on the tongue. But if you mouth it, as many of our players do, I had as lief the town crier spoke my lines.   *Hamlet*, III, ii

There will be no such mouthing, I pray you…   (*WV*)

Thou speak'st
In better phrase and matter than thou didst.

KING LEAR, IV, vi

O, well done! I commend your pains,
And every one shall share i' th' gains.

MACBETH, IV, i

USEFUL IDEAS TO REMEMBER:

Answers from page 63: Line 3/4, "stage"—"stars" and "shows"—"comment"; line 6, "cheered"—"checked"; line 7, "vaunt"—"decrease" and "youthful"—"height"; line 12, "day"—"night" or "day" of youth"—"sullied night"; line 13, "war"—"love"—"takes"—"engraft." Note that the thought of lines 9–14 is antithetical to the thought of lines 1–8. The reader must set up the idea that "time wins every time," so that this thought can be contradicted with "however, my love is such that when time pursues you, my poem makes you immortal in youth."

PART TWO

A Demonstration of Teaching and Learning Skills

Very little pains
Will bring this labor to an happy end
KING JOHN, III, ii

CHAPTER 11

Session One

In this session: • Procedure • Selecting monologues and sonnets
• The OED questions and answers • Subtext • Verse or realism
• Shakespeare's limited appeal • Rhythm of blank verse
• First assignment

The Workshop: Ten actors, all in their early to late twenties and all living in the
Seattle area, are assembled in a workshop with the author as coach. We plan to work
together for twenty sessions of two hours each over a ten-week period—a total of
forty hours. Three of the actors have some background in acting Shakespeare, but the
other seven have never tried it. To begin our work, we assemble around a table.*

Coach: As usual, with Shakespeare, there's too much material, but we'll
get through a lot of it. Part 1 of this book, *Clues to Acting Shakespeare,* is
our guide. Each of the skills we want to work on is discussed here. We can
try to stick to the order in which the skills are presented, but that's not
always possible.

For example, one of you may have a line in your monologue that can't
be resolved without jumping ahead to a new skill. So when that happens,
we'll jump ahead. But we'll still revisit that skill when we arrive at that
section of the book.

Learning to speak Shakespeare's language is very much like baseball.
It's about fundamentals, and the more times you scoop up the grounder or
swing the bat, the better you become. So you can't visit any of these skills
too often.

*Actors are Kristin Calhoun, Bridgett Foley, Alex Garnett, Maggie Hillding, Ryan Holmberg,
Alicia James, Jerrod Neal, Amber Peoples, Emily Rollie, and Bride Schroeder-LaPlatney. For
their participation in the recording of this workshop, and for being good sports, my sincere
thanks!

Alex: What if we don't like baseball? *(General laughter.)* But I get your point.

Coach: And there's a second point we can also tie to baseball. You don't try to turn a double play until you can scoop up the grounder. So there is a kind of progression to learning these skills.

Alex: Do you need to follow it?

Coach: You could jump ahead to the last of the basic skills outlined in part one, which is imagery, but you'll be a great deal better at imagery if you can first dig out the antithesis, and you'll be better at finding antithesis if you can first phrase a line, and so on.

If you turn to page 12, you'll find a list of the basic skills we're going to work on. In our sessions together, we'll work on each of the skills. Then you apply that skill to your monologue. Each of you needs a monologue—twelve to twenty lines—something you like. Planning ahead, select something you can use as an audition piece for the next few years. You'll be spending many hours with this monologue, so you might as well get double mileage out of it.

Kristin: Can the women do men's monologues?

Coach: Sure, but it may not serve you as well for the double use—now, and later as an audition piece. But you can surely select one.

So here's the path. We learn the skills one by one, then each time you perform your monologue, you add a new skill. The other actors listen and everyone takes notes. We listen only for the skills we've learned to date. For example, after we've learned scansion and end-of-line support—the first two skills—you'll read your monologue and we'll listen for your use of those two skills. We'll point out where you missed using them and trust that next time you do the monologue, those spots will be fixed.

Your first assignment is to select a monologue and a sonnet. You won't perform the sonnet but you will perform the monologue, with all skills applied. After we've applied all of the skills to the monologue, I'll invite some people in to hear your work.

With your sonnet, apply the skills as we go along and write out the analysis, then hand it in at the end of the workshop. This will allow me to review an example of your written analyses.

At our next session we'll hear everyone's choices and determine whether these are good monologues to work on. For example, if the monologue uses both verse and prose, you're better off finding something else. All of the skills we'll be learning apply to verse, but only some apply to prose. Also, be certain your monologue has a beginning, a middle, and an end. Later, if you use it for an audition piece, you'll want that structure.

Once the monologue has been approved and we've completed any cuts or additions to the monologue, type it up—double- or triple-spaced—and bring a copy for each member of the workshop. The triple-spacing is to give you room to write down the analysis of each word, phrase, and line. You'll need that space.

Bridgett: What if we find it online and it already has some space?

Coach: I still want you to type it up. And you must not ask anyone else to do it for you. You must do it yourself. Anyone know why?

Emily: You won't miss anything?

Coach: Right. Every syllable, every comma, has to be accurate. You must identify them all. You can't "skim" blank verse. If you leave out one syllable of a blank verse line, likely the line won't scan correctly and you won't be able to figure out how to read it. But don't type until your monologue has been approved—which is the next session.

Bride: Are there ten skills?

Coach: About ten. That's the number used in this book, which is designed for people just starting to act Shakespeare. There is more advanced study available to you. Those works are listed in the bibliography.

Missing any of these sessions is a bad idea. If you must be absent, you should probably drop out now and take the workshop at another time. The reason is that we are constantly learning new skills, then applying them. If you miss a session, you miss a complete skill or two. It's hard to catch up.

Once you can apply these skills to Shakespeare's text, you will be able to speak it; people will not only listen, but they will also understand what you're saying. If they don't understand, you're not using one or more of the skills. One of my favorite lines about Shakespeare comes from Peter Brook: "The trouble with Shakespeare is that it goes on without you." What do you suppose that means?

Amber: People can't understand you?

Coach: That's one thing. Why can't they understand you?

Bride: You don't know what you're saying?

Coach: That's part of it.

Alex: Neither the audience nor you knows what you're saying.

Coach: That's pretty much it. Your mouth is working and words spew forth, but you don't know what they mean, so the audience certainly doesn't know, and Shakespeare keeps right on going—without you. We'll probably hear some of that in here. *(General laughter.)* This "going on without you" is a common ailment for actors who want to act Shakespeare by "natural talent" rather than learning the skills. We've probably all seen a good deal of that.

Because it's essential for you to know what every single word means— and not what you think it means, but what it probably meant to Shakespeare in 1600—you'll need to visit the library. Can you find one? *(A few chuckles.)* Anyone know what you're going to do there?

Kristin: Look up words.

Coach: Yes. Look up words. Look up every word in your monologue and sonnet except conjunctions and pronouns. But certainly all nouns, adjectives, and verbs. And there's a special place to look. It's called the *Oxford English Dictionary*—the *OED*. All twenty-six volumes. You'll find them in the reference room. *(General groans.)* Why the *OED*?

Emily: I know because I've used it before. It gives the historical origin of all words in English. So you can find when a word was first used, which sometimes was in a Shakespearean line, and what its original usage was—the meaning in the line. It goes way back before Chaucer, I think, so you can see what the word meant at that time.

Coach: Wonderful. With the *OED* you can figure out what your words meant to Shakespeare. For example, the Nurse's line when she brings word of Romeo and tells Juliet, "You have made a simple choice." Everyone probably thinks he knows what the word "simple" means, right? But guess what? To Shakespeare, it probably didn't mean "easy." It probably meant "ignorant" or even "stupid." Notice how that different meaning could easily change the way the Nurse reads the line. Instead of giving Juliet information, she provokes her. Much better for both actors to work with. You certainly don't have to read the line with the newly discovered meaning of "simple"—it's your choice. But now you have a choice. Choices are good, aren't they?

Jerrod: The more the better.

Coach: I think so. Wait until your monologue has been approved before visiting the *OED*. But if you're eager, you could start working on your sonnet right away.

Together with the skills, we also have a series of exercises outlined in the book. You'll find some in each chapter. The exercises help the actor to actually use the skills in various ways. We'll have time to do some of them; others you can do on your own or in a small group. These exercises come from the Royal Shakespeare Company, Cicely Berry, Kristin Linklater, Patsy Rodenberg, and others, including me. Most of them are well proven, so be confident in using them. They will do what they're intended to do.

For the next thirty minutes, we exchange knowledge about Shakespeare's life and times, and I offer a short lecture about the plays, their plot origins, their publishing, their history, and claims to their authorship.

Alicia: To me, Shakespeare sounds so real. You don't realize the actor is speaking in verse.

Coach: How do you suppose that happens, that we don't realize the actor may be speaking verse?

Alicia: The actor knows how to speak the language.

Coach: Which is exactly what we're going to do in here. And after we learn those skills, if the audience can't understand your Shakespeare, it's probably not the author's fault. *(General chuckles.)*

Ryan: You have to know what you're saying.

Coach: And if you don't, how in the world will the listener know what you're saying?

To know what you're saying, and then knowing how to say it, require that you go through a series of steps. These are the skills that allow you to know what the language is doing and saying.

None of this has anything to do with character. Don't think yet of character. Because an interesting thing happens when you apply the skills to the language. You come to discover your character. Your character is the person who needs to say what these words mean.

Ryan: What about the character's subtext? In most plays you find out right away what the character wants and go from there.

Coach: In Shakespeare, and in many classic plays, the characters simply say what they are doing, where they are, what they want. The actor does not need subtextual ideas to figure out these wants. We have no documentation to show that writers or actors in the sixteenth and seventeenth centuries ever used terms like "subtext" or "motivation." These are concepts from the late nineteenth century and early twentieth century.

Can you use subtext when acting Shakespeare? Well, sure. It's hard to be an actor today and not think about subtext. But when you use it, remember that you're inserting a modern idea into classical language. Does the language need it? If it helps, use it. But use it after you know what the language means.

At this point the actors want to know why Shakespeare is considered the best writer of the English language. Who decides what is best? In this discussion, we talk about art, cars, poetry, novels, music, architecture, food, etc. What makes A better than B better than C, etc.? A consensus is reached that a standard of excellence can be established for most things, including writing plays. It is that which others are measured against.

Coach: More questions? Let's get all of our concerns on the table.

Bridgett: I'm not sure how Shakespeare can be the standard if it has no subtext.

Coach: You're deeply involved with subtext because realism is so filled with it and you're filled with realism. But realism, as we know it, is a twentieth-century development. You all know of Stanislavski's work with subtextual acting, but he developed that because of what the playwrights were writing. These characters tended to disguise what they wanted to say or do, and their language became more realistic by comparison to its predecessor, so the actor finds the truth in the subtext rather than the text. But the contemporary theatre of Shakespeare's time was language based—we refer to it as "heightened language"—and the characters said what they were doing and thinking. As an actor, you can use subtext when acting Shakespeare, but not to the degree that it interferes with the needs of heightened language.

Writing with subtext doesn't guarantee that the writing is superior. It's not a measure of quality. We would all agree with that, right? *(The actors all do.)* Nor does using heightened language ensure that the writing will be high quality. But the centuries have proved that Shakespeare's heightened language is the best that can be found in English—and it was written without subtext as we know it today.

Ryan: What about plots?

Coach: If you consider the Shakespeare plays you already know, you can probably name three plots in each of them. Many modern plays, however, have only one plot. One plot written in realistic language is probably easier to act, direct, and produce than three plots in heightened text. That doesn't mean modern writers don't have a language style. Consider Mamet, who is contemporary today and 180 degrees from Shakespeare, and yet has a strong language style.

Amber: Why do so many people not like Shakespeare?

Coach: I think it's because they can't understand it. Consider us in this room—most of you are in the theatre business itself and are having your first real, in-depth study of Shakespeare. For most people, a couple of weeks of *Romeo and Juliet* or *Macbeth* in high school English are about all they ever get. English majors in college will surely be familiar with Shakespeare, but not even all of them will be required to do any comprehensive analysis. Few people actually study, and therefore understand, Shakespeare.

Then consider how many actors are really trained to speak this language—speak it so that an audience can understand it. When you start asking around at various theatres where you work, I don't think you'll find very many. Actor training today simply isn't based on classical language.

So you will hear a lot of bad Shakespeare, and it will grind on you like chalk on the old chalkboard or somebody singing flat. It will drive you mad. And because so many of the skills required to hear or speak Shakespeare apply to realism, you will start to hear hundreds of poor line readings on television or film, on the radio, and in the theatre. You will start to hear emphasis on the wrong word, ends of lines falling off, pronouns stressed, questions marks used on lines that are already questions, antithesis missed, ignorance of imagery—oh, the poor authors.

Bride: Why don't all actors learn this?

Coach: They should. But learning the skills we'll be working on requires effort and discipline. Many actors prefer to rely on "natural talent"—sure death when doing Shakespeare. So ignorance of what you could learn is a major block, as is laziness. A bigger block, however, is probably the lack of opportunity to perform it. "If there are no jobs, why study it?" some say. I can answer that for them. You study it because it's acting—and you apply whatever you learn here to any kind of material. It can only make you better.

But many actors don't want to go to the *OED* and look up their words. They say, "Oh, I know what that means." What a mistake. They have no idea what the word meant to Shakespeare, and when an actor discovers that meaning it almost invariably changes the line reading for the better. The actor's job is to thoroughly understand the material—to know precisely everything he says and why. It's dangerous to rely entirely on your director. He or she may not want to look up the words either.

An interesting thing is that it's easier to learn these skills than to use them as a character. You'll have these skills in no time and can use them for the rest of your lives. But the hard part is speaking the language as the character, and not allowing the language to control or dominate you—which is what usually happens in bad Shakespeare. Once you have these skills, you know your character's language. Now you have a chance to create a truthful character. Notice that I said "have a chance," because it is not guaranteed that you can create a truthful character, even when you know the language. But at least you have a chance.

Consider the actor who tries to create a character and has no idea how to handle the language or what the language is doing. The character will stumble over the language or not clarify it for the listener. That's why we learn how to handle the language first, then work on character. When working on your character and his relationships to other characters, as an actor you don't want to be burdened by the language. That will really mess you up. You want the language to be natural. Sorry is the actor who "shoots from the hip" with Shakespeare's language.

Bride: Where do we even start with this material?

Coach: If you were a musician with an instrument, how would you learn to play it? Probably by learning how to read music. The same with Shakespeare. We want to learn how to read blank verse. That's where we'll start.

Kristin: I've heard about iambic pentameter.

Coach: Everyone stand up and walk with me. *(They do.)* As you walk, say "heel-toe, heel-toe, heel-toe," etc. Now change "heel-toe" to "dee-dum, dee-dum, dee-dum, dee-dum, dee-dum." The "dee" is soft and the "dum" is stressed. As you can see, one foot is dee-dum, soft then stressed. This is called an "iamb," from the Greek word, *iambos,* for foot. Put five of these together and you have five feet, five *iambs.* The word "pentameter" describes putting the five iambs together. "Penta" is a prefix that means "five," as in pentagram. Iambic pentameter. That's one blank verse line. Not so scary, huh?

Jerrod: Got it.

Coach: We're ahead of ourselves a little, and will do more of that next time.

Alicia: Some people say Shakespeare has to be heard, you can't just read it.

Coach: It was written to be heard, wasn't it? Not just read. In Shakespeare's time, the audience members would never be able to get a copy of the script to read the play. There were only a few copies made of each complete play. So not only is Shakespeare better when heard, it's *ten times* better!

If you lie in bed with a huge book of Shakespeare's plays on your chest and try to read one of them to yourself, you'll be asleep by the end of the first scene. So right up front, remember this: When you work on your monologues, work on them out loud. Go out in a field or wherever you have to go and speak aloud and on your feet. You need to use your muscles and you need to hear the language. It doesn't do much good to mumble it to yourself while you watch television. You have to be on your feet, doing it aloud.

Bridgett: It still scares me, trying to do this. I mean, he was a genius.

Coach: No doubt he was a genius, but he was also an actor, and he wrote for actors. The theatre was his profession, playwriting and acting his means of livelihood. I think you'll lose your fear.

Kristin: And there's the language—strange to us.

Coach: Sure. The closest we come to verse is maybe the study of a few poets in high school and college, like Emily Dickinson. Here's an analogy to food. Suppose you're having dinner at another home and the hostess places in front of you a very strange-looking meal with a name you can't pronounce and a slightly funny smell. How many of you are eager to plunge in and try this dinner? *(Laughs, and one hand, Amber's, goes up.)* You think, "I'm not sure this is for me." Because it's different we immediately think it might not be good.

Alicia: I did a Shakespearean scene at a community college once and found it very easy to memorize.

Coach: I believe most actors will agree with you. There's a rhyme and a structure—like learning the lyrics to a song. You do that rather quickly, I'll bet.

We're running out of time. For next time, read the first two chapters, and find a monologue you might like to work on. We'll read the monologues aloud and see if they'll work for you. Then we're going to work on blank verse—how to scan it and how to support it. And I'll talk less and get you working more. Be sure to bring your *Complete Works of Shakespeare* as well as our acting text. Thanks for a great opening session, and see you next time.

CHAPTER 12

Session Two

*In this session: • Blank verse structure • Creating blank verse
• Irregular feet • Scansion • Elision • Feminine endings • Trochees
• Selecting monologues • Second assignment*

Coach: Before we read your monologues today, let's take a few minutes and work on blank verse itself. What is blank verse? Well, it's nothing more than the English language written in ten syllable lines. Let's use our own feet and walk like blank verse, just like we did last time. If you walk heel-toe, heel-toe, heel-toe, heel-toe, heel-toe you've just walked a line of blank verse.

(Everyone is up and walking.)

Let's say it out loud while we walk. Heel-toe, heel-toe, etc. *(Everyone does.)*

Now let's change heel-toe to dee-dum, dee-dum, dee-dum, dee-dum, dee-dum. *(Everyone does and keeps walking.)*

Now let's make the dee, or heel, soft and the dum, or toe, stressed. Speak it that way as you walk about. *(Everyone does.)*

Now you have the rhythm of blank verse. Five feet, ten syllables, in each foot the first syllable is soft and the second is stressed. That kind of foot is called ...

Alex: An iamb—Greek, *iambos*, for foot.

Coach: So five of those iambs give you penta iambs, thus the term "iambic pentameter"—which is a term describing the form blank verse is presented in. Everyone now has the feel of the rhythm, so let's sit down and open our complete works to a page that contains both blank verse and prose. For example, look at page 280 in the Pelican edition of *Much Ado about Nothing*, or act I, scene i in the other editions that some of you have, and note the two dialogue styles. *(Everyone opens to that page of MAAN.)* What do you observe?

Bridgett: Verse lines are shorter.
Coach: They appear that way, don't they? Can anyone explain it?
Amber: Ten syllables.
Coach: Sure. At ten syllables you have a regular blank verse line, so you go to the next line. But notice that often there is no punctuation at the end of the line. That line keeps going into the next line, and so on. If we count the number of words in a line, for example from period to period, verse lines can be just as long as prose lines—they just look different. And that's because of the ten syllables. When you hear fine actors read blank verse it sounds no different than prose.

This is what Shakespeare and his contemporaries discovered. That the English language is best expressed in blank verse. It's the way we speak naturally. It's not poetry, but it can contain poetry. It doesn't have to rhyme, but it can rhyme. Since Shakespeare's time, no other author has been able to duplicate the perfection of his blank verse. Not only can he express his work in ten-syllable lines, but he makes the second syllable of each foot the more important syllable. If you don't think that takes genius, try it for yourself. Let's all speak some blank verse.

Everyone makes up blank verse lines and says them aloud. There are lots of laughs: "The mucus in my nose is running down." "I sure do hope the Sonics win tonight." "I got out of bed to take a shower." "I hate being put on the spot like this." We then try to redo the lines so that the second syllable in each foot is the more important, and have many more laughs.

As I mentioned earlier, this language is called "heightened text." Most realism you hear today is not heightened, as it has no real rhythmic structure. However, you might look at some of Blanche's speeches in Williams' *A Streetcar Named Desire.* That may be as close as realistic playwrights come to heightened text.

Before the actors arrived, I had placed two sections of information on the eraser board—a collection of six lines of verse, and a listing of terms with scansion symbols. The lines are:

1. Let's go to town and buy an ice cream cone.
2. Thou canst not speak of that thou does not feel.
3. What light through yonder window breaks?
4. The quality of mercy is not strained;
5. Horatio, thou art e'en as just a man;
6. To be, or not to be—that is the question.

The terms are:
1. iamb   [∪/]
2. trochee   [/∪]

3. anapest   [∪∪/]
4. dactyl   [/∪∪]
5. pyrrhic   [∪∪]
6. spondee   [//]

However, for iamb I wrote [/∪], and for trochee, [∪/].

Coach: Now let's look at the eraser board and see how to scan the lines. Breaking the line into feet and stresses is called "scansion," and with scansion we can read how the line is structured. Look at the first line, which is not Shakespeare's.

> Let's go to town and buy an ice cream cone.

The first foot is "let's go," so we divide it right there with a diagonal line. We mark the other feet the same way. A regular line in Shakespeare starts "dee-dum," so we mark it with a soft stress and a hard stress like this.

> ∪ / ∪ /   ∪ / ∪ /   ∪   /
> Let's go / to town / and buy / an ice / cream cone.

Often Shakespeare changes from a regular line to an irregular, but we'll get to that shortly. After you've marked the scansion, you read the line by stressing the stressed words—go, town, buy, ice, cone. Now beat it out on the table or on your leg. *(Everyone beats out the rhythm, hitting something on the "dum.")* This puts the rhythm into your muscle memory and it will stay there.

Now let's change the scansion. *(I put stresses over "cream" and "to." We experiment with reading the line as marked, then conclude that we should not stress "to" but might stress "cream," giving it the same importance as "cone.")*

Now the next line. Who wants to do it? *(Jerrod walks to the board and marks the scansion:)*

> ∪   /   ∪   /   ∪ /   ∪   /   ∪ /
> Thou canst / not speak / of that / thou dost / not feel.

It's a regular line, so we work on the stress that must be placed on "feel" and how much stress it can handle. We take turns reading the line and increasing the stress on "feel" with each reading. We continue until we're shouting the word, which would usually be too much stress, and we begin to realize the importance of the final word in the blank verse line.

Coach: Usually we wouldn't place that much stress on the final word, but the example points out the immense importance of the final word in a blank verse line.

The next line, which Bride works, also regular, is: "The quality of mercy is not strained;" and she scans and reads it, realizing that "strained" has to be stressed but won't take as much as "feel." She also discover why this is a harder line to scan: The words themselves sometimes divide into more than one syllable. "Quality" itself is three syllables and "ity" is a complete foot because it contains two syllables. Strained is a long word but it's only one syllable.

Coach: Now that we've scanned these three lines, do you know how we can tell if we're right? Try reading the lines and stress the unstressed words: thou, not, of, thou, not. And in the other line: the, it, of, cy, not. *(Everyone tries this and we get lots of laughs.)* That's so awful it's good!

Now say those two lines naturally. *(All try.)* Make them even more natural—no effort at stresses—try whispering them. Do them quietly into a microphone. *(All try this and discover.)* Notice what we hear. Even whispering, if you've once beaten the stresses into your system, you will automatically read the line correctly with just the slightest stress on the important words.

Alicia: Wait a minute. Something doesn't seem right. You've written up there that an iamb is "stress/soft," but that isn't what we're doing.

Coach: Good! You caught it. Everyone see what the problem is. I tried to fool you by messing up the first two terms, "iamb" and "trochee." But you caught me at it.

Please go up and rewrite iamb correctly, and redo trochee. *(Jerrod does.)* The iambic foot is written soft/stress and an inverted foot, called a "trochee," is written stress/soft. We'll soon find a trochee. Look at the next line.

What light through yonder window breaks?

Who wants to work it? *(Bridgett attempts to mark the scansion, then stops.)*

Bridgett: Something's fishy here. I don't know how to get five feet.

Coach: What's the matter?

Emily: We're missing a foot. Is it finished by another line?

Coach: That could be a good guess, but it's not what happens here. Somebody check the line in the book—*Romeo and Juliet. (They find it.)* What's the problem?

Emily: There's more to the line.

Coach: Right. I didn't write down the first two words of the line. See what they are?

"But soft!" Now can you mark the five feet? *(Bridgett adds the two words to the beginning of the line, then scans it.)*

Now we have ten syllables. If you don't get five feet and ten syllables, something is irregular. And Shakespeare does this all the time, but he didn't do it here. Everyone beat out the rhythm of the line. *(All actors practice reading the line with huge stresses and then very naturally, always beating out the rhythm.)*

You have to do this with every verse line you ever tackle in Shakespeare. And we haven't even started looking up the words. For example, what did "quality" mean to Shakespeare? What did "strained" mean—and "soft" and "breaks"? When you know what the words meant to Shakespeare your original use of the word will change. And, of course, we haven't yet done phrasing and breathing, which come next. We have done two skills—scansion and end-of-line support. Except we still have to kick the box.

Kristin: What happens when he works backwards?

Coach: Do you mean a trochee?

Kristin: Yes, when he reverses the stresses.

Coach: Amazing you should ask that right now—because look at the next line.

Kristin: I already saw it coming. That's why I asked the question!

Coach: Way ahead of me already. Someone read the next line. *(Kristin goes to the board. She reads the line.)*

> Horatio, thou aren't e'en as just a man.

Coach: Go ahead and mark the scansion. *(She does.)* How many feet do you have?

Kristin: Six.

Bridgett: Five.

Coach: Before we answer, someone do the next line. *(Amber marks the scansion.)*

> To be, or not to be—that is the question.

Coach: How many syllables? *(All say "eleven.")* How many syllables in the other line? *(Most say "eleven." Some say "ten," some say "twelve.")* The first thing we do with a blank verse line is count the syllables. If we don't get ten, the next thing we do is check out the last syllable. Notice the difference in the last syllable of these two lines.

Emily: "Man" has to be stressed. But "tion" in "question" doesn't have to be.

Coach: Right, because we don't pronounce "question" as quesTION. So the "tion" is a feminine ending—a soft ending that is spoken but not stressed. You will find many feminine endings in Shakespeare—like "en" in "heaven," "ing," "er"; these endings, spoken softly, do not affect the rhythm.

Now write the word "e'en" and the word "even." *(Kristin writes these words on the board.)* Now write the word "elision." What does this say to you?

Kristin: This is like a contraction. He changed a two-syllable word into a one-syllable word by contracting two syllables into one.

Coach: Right. Now if Shakespeare had not elided "e'en," how many syllables are in the line?

Amber: Twelve.

Coach: Now we have a six-foot line. But Shakespeare took it to eleven syllables; now we have to take it to ten. What else can we elide? Working backwards, "a man" has to be your final foot, and "as just" is a foot. So somewhere in the first part of the line we need to elide a syllable.

Emily: In "Horatio."

Coach: Try it. *(Kristin works out an elision to read the name with three syllables, "Ho-ra-sho.")* Now we have ten syllables. Mark the elision with an inverted "u" over the "i"—meaning you won't pronounce the "i." Now mark the scansion and beat it out. *(She does.)* Now you know the structure of the line. In rehearsal you can say the line depending on your impulse, your motivation to speak it, but whatever that is, the structure of the line will be correct.

Say the line as if Horatio is being a complete ass to you. *(She tries a reading.)* Good. Now as if Horatio is being very kind to you. *(She tries a reading.)* Good.

And so on—depending on your motivation. But each time, the line has its correct words stressed. We need to get the stresses and rhythm correct before we look for motivation—or character choices. They will fall together later.

Now, does everyone see what we've done? We've used a Shakespeare elision and one of our own creation. Now let's go back to the most famous line in Shakespeare and mark the scansion. *(Alex does.)* And mark the feminine ending with parentheses around a "u." Read the line the way you've written it, which is like a regular line. Some actors prefer to read the fourth foot not as "that IS" but as "THAT is"—an inverted foot. Try it both ways. *(He does.)* What do you think? *(Everyone comments.)* Is it a trochee or isn't it? Well, it's your choice. It's an actor choice. You're the one who has to make it work, so make your choice and do it your way. But if you change it, do it knowingly—do it as a choice, not because you didn't know any better. Don't shoot from the hip. Work out the scansion, then read the line the way you elect to scan it.

Generally you're going to find trochees in the first, third, or fourth foot. If a line starts with a verb, the first foot is nearly always a trochee. If the third foot starts with a verb, it will be a trochee. Pretty soon scansion will be second nature to you, and you will trust your own judgment. We'll be doing the monologues many times and will pick out the trochees.

Note the terms again and put them where you can get to them easily—iamb, trochee, anapest, dactyl, pyrrhic, and spondee. You might have one or more of these in your monologue. So next we'll read the monologues, then kick the box, which will solidify the second skill—which is end-of-line support. You now have the first skill—how to scan a line. And we also know that we have to look up the words. Like "question," for example; why didn't Shakespeare use "problem" or "issue"? You need to know that. Let's take a break then read the monologues.

The following approach to monologue selection works for me: I ask the actors to have their complete Shakespeare in front of them. They take turns reading monologues they want to work on. Everyone follows along. We discuss the merits or problems of each speech, including its usefulness as an audition piece.

Kristin chose A Midsummer Night's Dream, *act II, sc ii,* Hermia, *from "Help me, Lysander ..." We reject this because Hermia is looking for a character who isn't there and we believe Kristin can find something better. After cutting the brother's line, we accept* Measure for Measure, *act III, sc i,* Isabella, *from "Oh you beast ..." for her:*

Isabella: O you beast,
               Faithless coward, O dishonest wretch!
               Wilt thou be made a man out of my vice?
               Is't not a kind of incest, to take life
               From thine own sister's shame? What should I think?
               Heaven shield my mother played my father fair,
               For such a warped slip of wilderness
               Ne'er issued from his blood. Take my defiance,
               Die, perish. Might but my bending down
               Reprieve thee from thy fate, it should proceed.
               I'll pray a thousand prayers for thy death,
               No word to save thee.
[Cut Claudio line.]
               O, fie, fie, fie!
               Thy sin's not accidental, but a trade;
               Mercy to thee would prove itself a bawd,
               'Tis best that thou diest quickly.

For Alicia, we accept Henry VI, part 3, *act I, sc i,* Queen Margaret, *from "Enforce thee..." after working out pronunciation of the names. We cut the first line and decide to begin with "I shame to hear thee speak," as starting a monologue with a question can be weak. Starting with a strong statement that catches our ear is much better.*

Queen Margaret: I shame to hear thee speak. Ah, timorous wretch,
                  Thou hast undone thyself, thy son, and me,

And giv'n unto the house of York such head
As thou shalt reign but by their sufferance.
To entail him and his heirs unto the crown,
What is it but to make thy sepulcher
And creep into it far before thy time?
Warwick is chancellor and the lord of Calais;
Stern Falconbridge commands the narrow seas;
The duke is made Protector of the realm;
And yet shalt thou be safe? Such safety finds
The trembling lamb environed with wolves.
Had I been there, which am a silly woman,
The soldiers should have tossed me on their pikes
Before I would have granted to that act.
But thou preferr'st thy life before thine honor;
And seeing thou dost, I here divorce myself
Both from thy table, Henry, and thy bed
Until that act of parliament be repealed
Whereby my son is disinherited.

Emily chooses Twelfth Night, act II, sc ii, *Viola, from "I left no ring with her..." We reject this because I warn the group that the monologue has been overused as an audition monologue, so it can't really be used in professional auditions. We had earlier agreed that these monologues should be prepared for later use in the professional world.*

Also, looking at this monologue we discover many differences in the six editions the actors are using. Both words and punctuation differ. We set the Pelican edition as "official" and all monologues are to be checked against it for specific spellings and punctuation.

Emily decides she really wants to work on the "I left no ring with her..." speech and none of the actors in the workshop has heard it before. (I realize again how much older I am!) However, before the next session Emily has decided not to do the "ring" monologue and instead selects Twelfth Night, act I, sc v, *Viola, from "I see you what you are ...." We select this after cutting some lines and inserting a bridge phrase. Later we add an Olivia and put some of the lines back in.*

Viola: I see you what you are; you are too proud;
            But if you were the devil, you are fair.
            My lord and master loves you. O, such love
            Could be but recompensed though you were crowned
            The nonpareil of beauty.
[Cut Olivia, "How does he love me?" and the next nine lines.]
            If I did love you in my master's flame,
            With such a suff'ring, such a deadly life,

In your denial I would find no sense;
I would not understand it.
[Cut Olivia, "Why, what would you?"]
[Insert]   Yet would I
Make me a willow cabin at your gate
And call upon my soul within the house;
Write loyal cantons of contemn'ed love
And sing them loud even in the dead of night;
Hallo your name to the reverberate hills
And make the babbling gossip of the air
Cry out 'Olivia!' O, you should not rest
Between the elements of air and earth
But you should pity me.

For Ryan, we accept Titus Andronicus, act V, sc i, *Aaron, from "Even now I
curse the day…" after a discussion about playing the good in an evil character.*

Aaron: Even now I curse the day, and yet I think
Few come within the compass of my curse,
Wherein I did not some notorious ill:
As kill a man, or else devise his death;
Ravish a maid, or plot the way to do it;
Accuse some innocent, and forswear myself;
Set deadly enmity between two friends;
Make poor men's cattle break their necks;
Set fire on barns and haystacks in the night
And bid the owners quench them with their tears.
Oft have I digged up dead men from their graves
And set them upright at their dear friends' door
Even when their sorrows almost was forgot,
And on their skins, as on the bark of trees,
Have with my knife carved in Roman letters
`Let not your sorrow die, though I am dead.'
But I have done a thousand dreadful things
As willingly as one would kill a fly,
And nothing grieves me heartily indeed
But that I cannot do ten thousand more.

Coach: Aaron is obviously a villain, and quite evil. However, for the actor,
playing evil on top of evil creates one-dimensional characters, unless you're
playing "mellerdrama," which is already one-dimensional. So when you
choose villainy as an intention for a villain, or when you read a villain as a
villain, what we hear is attitude—or HOW you're reading becomes more

important than WHAT you're reading. When playing an evil character, look for what's good in him/her. If there is nothing, look for what gives the villain joy or satisfaction—both better choices than evil. We'll do more on this when we work on character. For now, you should concentrate on reading without interpretation. *(However, Ryan later dropped the workshop, so we were never able to hear a final monologue.)*

For Amber, we accept The Taming of the Shrew, act V, sc ii, *Katherine (called Kate), from "I am ashamed that women are so simple..." after correcting many differences in punctuation between her text and the official text. Because of the length of the speech, we decide to begin at "Such duty as the subject owes the prince..." and discuss the differences between women's positions in 1600s England and now.*

Kate: Such duty as the subject owes the prince,
     Even such a woman oweth to her husband;
     And when she is froward, peevish, sullen, sour,
     And not obedient to his honest will,
     What is she but a foul contending rebel
     And graceless traitor to her loving lord?
     I am ashamed that women are so simple
     To offer war where they should kneel for peace,
     Or seek for rule, supremacy, and sway,
     When they are bound to serve, love, and obey.
     Why are our bodies soft and weak and smooth,
     Unapt to toil and trouble in the world,
     But that our soft conditions and our hearts
     Should well agree with our external parts?
     Come, come, you froward and unable worms,
     My mind hath been as big as one of yours,
     My heart as great, my reason haply more,
     To bandy word for word and frown for frown.
     But now I see our lances are by straws,
     Our strength as weak, our weakness past compare,
     That seeming to be most which we indeed least are.
     Then vail our stomachs, for it is no boot,
     And place your hands below your husband's foot,
     In token of which duty, if he please,
     My hand is ready, may it do him ease.

For Alex, we accept Henry IV, part 1, act III, sc ii, *Prince Hal, from "Do not think so..." but elect to begin with "God forgive them..." for a stronger opening, dropping "And."*

Prince: God forgive them that so much have swayed
Your majesty's good thoughts away from me.
I will redeem all this on Percy's head
And, in the closing of some glorious day,
Be bold to tell you that I am your son,
When I will wear a garment all of blood,
And stain my favors in a bloody mask,
Which, washed away, shall scour my shame with it.
And that shall be the day, whene'er it lights,
That this same child of honor and renown,
This gallant Hotspur, this all-praised knight,
And your unthought-of Harry chance to meet.
For every honor sitting on his helm,
Would they were multitudes, and on my head
My shames redoubled! For the time will come
That I shall make this northern youth exchange
His glorious deeds for my indignities.
Percy is but my factor, good my lord,
To engross up glorious deeds on my behalf;
And I will call him to so strict account
That he shall render every glory up,
Yea, even the slightest worship of his time,
Or I will tear the reckoning from his heart.
This in the name of God I promise here;
The which if he be pleased I shall perform,
I do beseech your majesty may salve
The long-grown wounds of my intemperance.
If not, the end of life cancels all bands,
And I will die a hundred thousand deaths
Ere break the smallest parcel of this vow.

Bridgett chose The Two Gentlemen of Verona, *act II, sc vii,* Julia, *from "The more thou ..." We reject this because it's so reflective and lacks real action. We try act I, sc ii,* Julia, *from "Nay, would I were so ang'red with the same ..." because it has great fun and action.*

Julia: Nay, would I were so ang'red with the same!
O Hateful hands, to tear such loving words!
Injurious wasps, to feed on such sweet honey,
And kill the bees that yield it with your stings!
I'll kiss each several paper for amends.
Look, here is writ 'kind Julia.' Unkind Julia!
As in revenge of the ingratitude,

I throw thy name against the bruising stones,
Trampling contemptuously on thy disdain.
And here is writ 'love-wounded Proteus.'
Poor wounded name! My bosom as a bed
Shall lodge thee till they would be thoroughly healed,
And thus I search it with a sovereign kiss.
But twice or thrice was 'Proteus' written down—
Be calm, good wind, blow not a word away
Till I have found each letter in the letter,
Except mine own name; that some whirlwind bear
Unto a ragged, fearful-hanging rock,
And throw it thence into the raging sea!
Lo, here in one line is his name twice writ,
'Poor forlorn Proteus, passionate Proteus,
To the sweet Julia.' That I'll tear away—
And yet I will not, sith so prettily
He couples it to his complaining names.
Thus will I fold them one upon another—
Now kiss, embrace, contend, do what you will.

Coach: Next time, we'll get to the other three monologues. If your monologue has been approved, you should now type it up triple-spaced, check it against the Pelican edition, and bring a copy for each member of the workshop. See you next time. We got a lot done today.

CHAPTER 13

Session Three

*In this session: • End-of-line support • Caesuras
• Use the diaphragm • Kick the box • Third assignment*

Coach: Let's begin today by approving the final three monologues. Who's first?

For Bride, we accept Macbeth, act I, sc v, *Lady Macbeth, from "The raven himself..." but consider adding more. We look back to "Glamis thou art..." then cut six lines from that speech and continue from "Hie thee hither ...," cut the Messenger, and continue with "He brings great news" for the bridge to finish the monologue with "Hold, hold!" These lines are added before the "raven" lines to make a monologue of usable length.*

Lady Macbeth: Glamis thou art, and Cawdor, and shalt be
               What thou art promised. Yet do I fear thy nature.
               It is too full o' th' milk of human kindness
               To catch the nearest way. Thou wouldst be great,
               Art not without ambition, but without
               The illness should attend it.

[Cut five lines.]

               Hie thee hither,
               That I may pour my spirits in thine ear
               And chastise with the valor of my tongue
               All that impedes thee from the golden round
               Which fate and metaphysical aid doth seem
               To have thee crowned withal.

[Cut nine lines.]

He brings great news.

                    The raven himself is hoarse
That croaks the fatal entrance of Duncan
Under my battlements. Come, you spirits
That tend on mortal thoughts, unsex me here,
And fill me from the crown to the toe top-full
Of direst cruelty. Make thick my blood;
Stop up th' access and passage to remorse,
That no compunctious visitings of nature
Shake my fell purpose nor keep peace between
Th' effect and it. Come to my woman's breasts
And take my milk for gall, you murd'ring ministers,
Wherever in your sightless substances
You wait on nature's mischief. Come, thick night,
And pall thee in the dunnest smoke of hell,
That my keen knife see not the wound it makes,
Nor heaven peep through the blanket of the dark
To cry 'Hold, hold!'

Coach: Notice that there are six lines without punctuation in this speech. Tyrone Guthrie used to say that a good actor should be capable of speaking seven lines of blank verse in a large theatre without rushing and without a breath. *(All the actors want to try it but we don't have the time.)*

Jerrod chooses Othello, act I, sc iii, *Othello, from "Most potent grave and reverend seniors..." This doesn't really work. We discover that he has only read the first four scenes of the play and is unfamiliar with the better speeches in acts three, four, and five. The problem with the "most potent" speech is that it is primarily informative, not active, so it is not a good choice for an audition piece. We decide to read aloud act III, sc iv, from "That handkerchief. ..." in class, but we also reject that speech. We then look at act IV, sc ii, from "Had it pleased heaven. ..." We accept this, cutting Desdemona's line and ending at "never been born." Jerrod will read the whole play outside of class.*

Othello: Had it pleased heaven
To try me with affliction, had they rained
All kinds of sores and shames on my bare head,
Steeped me in poverty to the very lips,
Given to captivity me and my utmost hopes,
I should have found in some place of my soul
A drop of patience. But, alas, to make me

The fixed figure for the time of scorn
To point his slow unmoving finger at!
Yet could I bear that too; well, very well.
But there where I have garnered up my heart,
Where either I must live or bear no life,
The fountain from the which my current runs
Or else dries up—to be discarded thence,
Or keep it as a cistern for foul toads
To knot and gender in—turn thy complexion there,
Patience, thou young and rose-lipped cherubin!
Ay, there look grim as hell!

[Cut 3 lines.]

                                                O thou weed,
Who art so lovely fair, and smell'st so sweet,
That the sense aches at thee, would thou hadst ne'er been born!

For Maggie, we accept A Midsummer Night's Dream, act I, sc i, *Helena, from
"Call you me fair?" even though the opening line is a question.*

Helena: Call you me fair? That fair again unsay.
             Demetrius loves your fair. O happy fair!
             Your eyes are lodestars, and your tongue's sweet air
             More tunable than lark to shepherd's ear
             When wheat is green, when hawthorn buds appear.
             Sickness is catching. O, were favor so,
             Yours would I catch, fair Hermia, ere I go;
             My ear should catch your voice, my eye your eye,
             My tongue should catch your tongue's sweet melody.
             Were the world mine, Demetrius being bated,
             The rest I'd give to be to you translated.
             O, teach me how you look, and with what art
             You sway the motion of Demetrius' heart.

Coach: Now everyone has a monologue. The next assignment is to type up
your monologue triple-spaced, check all punctuation against the Pelican,
then make copies for everyone. Bring the copies to the next session, but
don't make any notes on the copies to be passed out. And now you can
consult the *OED*.

Let's begin on the second skill, even though we've already touched on
it. The first skill was scansion, which means to mark the feet and stresses of
the line, and find the trochees, feminine endings, etc. So after you type your
monologue, take your copy and begin marking the scansion. You'll likely

run into problems. There will be some difficult lines, so bring them to our next session and put them on the eraser board. We'll work out the scansion together. Difficult lines might have eight syllables, or thirteen, and you can't make them work. We'll have everyone assist to work them out.

Remember, the very first thing we do—which can be while doing the scansion—is to look up all the words so we know what everything means.

The next skill deals with the structure of blank verse—but this skill can be used in realism as well as blank verse. In blank verse, the end of the line is usually more important than the middle or beginning, and it must be supported. So supporting the end of the line is our next skill. Usually this skill is also true in realism. In modern speech we often don't hear the last words of a line. The problem is caused by our losing interest in what we're saying, our running out of breath, our clumping the point of the line into the beginning, or, as is often the case in some film and television, our extreme effort to be "natural" at the expense of language.

If we lose the end of the line in Shakespeare we run into problems. I need a volunteer to read the line. *(Kristin volunteers.)* We've done the scansion on the line "Thou canst not speak of that thou dost not feel," so read it stressing the first half of the line but then run out of breath so we can't hear the second half clearly. *(She does.)* What does the line say?

Kristin: You can't speak.

Coach: That's all we hear, but is that what the line is about? This line is Romeo speaking to the Friar after the Friar has advised him to forget about marrying this girl, Juliet. Well, obviously the Friar can speak, because he is speaking. Now read both parts of the line. *(She does.)* Now what do we hear?

Amber: You can't talk about something you don't understand.

Coach: Yes. The Friar is supposed to be celibate, isn't he? How can he advise? Now the line makes sense and both actors have ideas and actions to play. Trying to read the line "naturally," by allowing the end to fall, totally destroys the meaning of the line.

Amber: You could actually get away with yelling the word "feel," like we did last time. Maybe using just a little less stress.

Coach: Yes. Isn't it amazing how far she could go in stressing the word, and still the line works? So you see how important the end of the line is. Speak the next line.

(Kristin reads: "The quality of mercy is not strained;") Read it as badly as you can. *(She does, and it is wonderfully awful.)* What happens if you make it entirely emotional? *(She does.)* What do you hear?

Maggie: All you hear is the emotion, not the words.

Coach: Right. Now do it and let the second half of the line fade away. *(She does.)* Now what do you hear?

Bride: Something about mercy. I've no idea what.

Coach: Do you see how quickly you can lose your audience—and how Shakespeare goes on without you? You see how you can read the lines and the listener has no idea what you're talking about? Now read both parts of the line. *(Kristin does and we all hear the line correctly.)* Good. Now start stressing "strained." *(She does until it becomes horrible.)* "Strained" won't take as much stress as "feel" did. How much will it take? *(She reads the line until she finds a comfortable stress for "strained.")* Good.

Ryan: How do you know?

Coach: Trust your ear. It will tell you. You'll know. If you support the end of the line correctly, your common sense will guide you to the proper stress.

Now, here's a bonus mini-skill. You could have strengthened both of those lines if you had used a bit of a pause in the middle of them. We'll have more on this when we get to the next skill, which is phrasing, but for now, let's use the pause to help make sense of the these two lines. This is part of scansion. Write the word "caesura" on the board. *(Kristin does.)* This is a sense pause. A little pause that you use to set up what you're going to say or to emphasize what you just said. It's not a breathing pause. *(I speak to the group using a lot of caesuras in my sentences and they quickly understand.)* Just like this *(pause)*, you use caesuras *(pause)* all the time. You set up the listener to hear what you're going to say. Mark a caesura with two diagonal lines. Look at the "mercy" speech. Where might the little pause come?

Kristin: After "mercy."

Coach: Right. That tiny pause after "mercy" allows the audience to keep up with you. You say something—"The quality of mercy"—then you tell them what you're talking about—"is not strained." Try it. *(Kristin does, with a caesura after "mercy.")* Good, but what did you forget to do?

Kristin: I was thinking about the caesura so I forgot to support "strained."

Coach: Yes. Try again? *(She does, and uses both skills.)* Everyone hear it?

Alex: Do you mean we have to walk and talk at the same time? *(Laughs.)*

Coach: And we've just started—there are at least ten things you have to do at the same time. *(Groans.)* We learn them one by one, and as we learn them we apply them to our monologues. We'll all listen to your monologue the first time to hear whether your scansion is correct and whether you're supporting the ends of the lines. The first time we won't be listening for anything else. Does that help? *(Mumbles.)*

Do you know why you forgot to support the end of the line, even though we just did the exercise?

Kristin: I wasn't thinking about it?

Coach: Partly that, but mostly because we never support the end of the line in our everyday speech and you were just being natural. To support the end of the line requires muscle work from our diaphragm—a muscle that is as lazy as our other muscles, until you prod it into action. You have to work the muscle, and it's easier not to. If you're going to support the end-of-the-verse line, the diaphragm has to kick in. Let's try it. *(We all hold our hand like a claw up against our diaphragm and say the "feel" line, really stressing "feel." It's easy to notice how the diaphragm tightens and "kicks in.")*

That's what you have to do with this kind of language. You have to use the diaphragm and you have to support the end of the line. That's why untrained actors doing Shakespeare can be really bad—because they aren't using this simple skill. Heightened text requires vocal energy. The end of the line is an important part of that energy.

You can also use the caesura to set up words. One of you suggested putting a caesura before "strained." There's no rule that says you can only have one pause per line. Try it. *(Kristin does.)*

Emily: Doesn't seem to work as well as after "mercy." Seems like too many pauses.

Coach: Yes, your ear is telling you that and you're probably right. But I liked that we tried it. We need to find out what works. In another line the second pause just might work. You'll have to test and see.

Now, for your monologue the scansion needs to include marking the feet, marking the stressed and unstressed syllables, and identifying inverted feet or trochees, feminine endings, elisions, and caesuras. Remember, if the stress on a foot doesn't come out right, you probably have a trochee. Questions? *(There are none.)* Let's take a break, then get back on our feet.

Coach: *(After the break.)* Now we need to kick the box. This exercise will drill into our bodies the need to support the end-of-the-verse line. Let's spread out into groups of two or three with some distance between you. Here's a box for each group. *(I distribute medium-sized cardboard boxes that have been tightly taped shut.)* What we're doing is using our body to help speak the language and forcing ourselves to support the end of the line.

Take the first line on the board: "Thou canst not speak of that thou dost not feel." You'll kick the box on the "f" of "feel." Not earlier and not later. Those who played soccer will find this very easy. So kick the box back and forth. *(The actors love doing this. All do it for awhile.)* As you continue, a secondary benefit of this exercise is the support it gives you for the entire line. For each group, the ones not kicking check the kicker. Make sure she kicks on the "f" of "feel." *(They do.)* Okay, now use the other foot. *(We get a lot of laughs as they do this more awkwardly.)* Is anyone picking up the benefit to you of doing this exercise?

Amber: It pumps up my juices.

Emily: I use my whole body.

Alicia: I remember doing this with you at another workshop. The prep required to get ready to kick involves the entire body.

Coach: And that's what is required to handle this language. Just for fun, let's kick on the wrong words. Some kick on "speak," some on "that," and some on "not." *(They do this.)* What happens?

Bride: We drop the end of the line. It loses importance.

Emily: On one of those I couldn't even hear "feel."

Coach: Now do it without looking at the box. Look at the person you're speaking to. *(All try this, to various degrees of success.)* What happens?

Bridgett: I missed the box!

Jerrod: I forgot the line.

Maggie: You lose some confidence, some energy.

Ryan: I kicked too early. I don't know why.

Coach: Change the kicking to the next line, "The quality of mercy is not strained;" and kick on the "s" of "strained." *(All do this for awhile.)* I'm going to try something new. Start with your back to the box. As you speak the line, time your turn so that you are completely in place for the kick, but not too soon or too late. *(All try this and eventually all get it.)* Sometimes you move and talk at the same time. *(Groans.)*

Alex: I'm not sure I can do that!

Coach: All find another line—use one from your monologue, and kick on the tenth syllable. What if there is a feminine ending?

Bride: Kick on the tenth syllable, not the feminine ending.

Coach: Right. Try it. *(All kick the box using lines from their monologues.)* Everybody comfortable with this exercise now? *(Lots of mumbles.)* Now write down the first two lines of your monologue, unless you already know them. Use one of the dry-eraser boards or just write them on a card you can carry. Check for feminine endings and be sure you have the scansion right. Now kick the box on two lines. You have a real box for the end of the first line, but after you kick it you must imagine it for the end of the second. *(All do this for awhile, kicking first the box, then just supporting the end of the second line without the aid of the box.)* Once you're confident with the first two lines, keep going on the entire monologue—do the rest of the lines.

Some do this, others work on the first two lines. It's very noisy, as all are working at the same time. But that doesn't matter, as each actor is concentrating on his or her material or helping the partner kick at the right moment. My main job is to get the actors to slow down so that they say every word clearly. They want to rush to the end of the line.

Coach: As you work on the monologue, determine the degree of stress required on the ending. The point of this exercise is not to suggest that the last word of the line is to be smashed. The exercise is to remind us to support, which, you remember, takes making the diaphragm kick in. As with all exercises, you use this to learn the material. Then you move on.

Let's all lie down on our backs. *(We all do.)* Let's say our monologues and keep the ends of the lines supported. Feel the diaphragm. *(They do.)* Now let's do them sitting up. Feel the diaphragm. *(They do.)* Now stand up and do the lines without kicking the box. *(They do, and they automatically support the final word of each line.)* Let's do them individually so we can all listen. *(They do two lines each for the others to hear.)* Do you all hear how the support of line one allows the idea inherent in it to continue to line 2? *(We work with the sense of the two lines, noting the idea that moves from line 1 to line 2. I remind them to add some caesuras, which they have forgotten to do. I also point out some of the important words that they must use when they develop the monologue.)*

Now, everyone read his or her first two lines standing on one foot. Hold on to your partner, or a box, or the wall or something. After the first foot, try it on the other foot. *(All do.)* Does it make any difference?

Maggie: None to me.

Coach: Does your focus shift to your feet?

Maggie: No.

Coach: No. Good. You can do your lines from almost any position—even the back of a horse—right? Are there any questions or realizations?

Amber: The exercise helps me find the rhythm of the entire line.

Bride: I just like it.

Coach: I know we've just started, but after you do this exercise you'll see how easy it is to memorize the lines. Now we have a second skill. Next we'll look at phrasing and breathing. So for next time, apply the first two skills to your monologue. Read the next two chapters. We got a lot done. See you next time.

CHAPTER 14

Session Four

In this session: • Review of sessions one, two, and three
• Using the skills in realism • Lines that are questions • Phrasing • Phrases within phrases
• Punctuation marks • Next assignment • Selecting sonnets • Scanning difficult lines
• Short lines • More on the OED

Coach: Let's review what we have so far as part of our scansion. *(Various actors name end-of-line support, feminine endings, identifying trochees, marking the hard and soft stresses, elision, and caesuras.)* Right now, one more thing about kicking the box, as related to prose rather than verse. The modern playwrights write in prose. But look on page 36, the first example of realism in the chapter. Somebody read the first line of Octavius, from Shaw's *Man and Superman. (Ryan does. He reads it naturally.)*

As you did not support the end of the line, the last phrase, let's do it again. *(He does, this time giving some support to the final phrase, "as to me.")* Can you all hear the difference? *(They do.)* Now, as you continue, put some support under any word that is followed by any punctuation mark. *(He reads the entire speech, supporting the last word in each phrase.)* Good, let's do Alfieri in Arthur Miller's *A View from the Bridge*, on the next page. *(Amber does. She supports the final phrase in each line.)* Good. What about the line with the question mark? "You see how uneasily they nod to me?" What's a basic rule to remember about question marks?

Bride: Don't put a question on a question because it's already a question.

Coach: Good. Just say the line. It's already a question. *(She reads the line again, this time without an upward inflection at the end.)* Good. Everybody hear the difference? *(They do.)* Of course, you can play a question mark if you do it by choice—if you think the line requires it.

Look at Shakespeare's prose in the next speech—Sir Toby Belch. *(Alex reads the speech. He doesn't allow the ends of lines to sag.)* Good. Now read it badly. *(He does, allowing the ends of lines to fade.)*

Ryan: I saw that production. In fact, I think I was in it. *(Laughs. Others acknowledge that they have also acted realism and allowed the ends of lines to fall way.)*

Coach: So consider this a little bonus from the Shakespeare workshop: When handling realism, you can use some of these same verse skills. What a bargain! Those of you currently in rehearsal for a realistic play, check your ends of lines and see if you're supporting them.

Today, before we refer to our monologues, I want to work on the next skill—it's actually on page 24 in chapter 3 of the book, some of which I already have on the board. Who wants to be the volunteer? *(Bridgett goes up.)* We're talking about phrasing. What is a phrase?

Emily: I read the chapter. It's an individual thought. It's an idea surrounded by other ideas, but it can stand alone.

Coach: And if the actor runs phrases together, the thoughts get run together, and the audience misses at least one and maybe both thoughts. So we look at the language and say, "Where does this break up?" Some actors mark phrases with caesuras while others circle them. It's hard to circle them in the book, so I used the caesura. But for rehearsal, I think circling is easier to see, and there's always the possibility that you may want to use a caesura at a place that isn't a phrase—like setting up an individual word.

Let's read Brutus's first four lines to the conspirators, on page 24, in chapter 3 of the book, beginning with, "What you have said I will consider." *(She does.)* Where do you think the first phrase is?

Bridgett: "What you have said I will consider."

Coach: Everyone agree?

Amber: No. I think it would be "What you have said."

Coach: Because "I will consider" is a new idea. *(Bridgett agrees that this is better.)* Yes, because Brutus is acknowledging that he has heard what they said, but now he's going to think about it. Please circle those phrases. *(She does.)* Now we have two phrases. So take the next line. *(She marks it.)* That's right: "What you have to say" and "I will with patience hear." Break the phrases up with a caesura and read it. *(She does.)* Notice how the break allows the listener to hear both ideas?

Bride: How long should that caesura be?

Coach: That's up to you, and the way you elect to play Brutus. It could be just the slightest bit of air, almost no space at all. Or it could be a reflection moment. That's what rehearsal is for, to find the answer to that question. All of the skills you learn are to prepare you for rehearsal. If you know what the language is doing before rehearsals begin, you can then use the rehearsal period to work on relationships and character, which is what rehearsal should be. If you already have your words, in rehearsal you can decide who the person is that uses them.

Maggie: And that's your character.

Coach: Right. We won't look at character yet. First we discover what the language is doing and what options it offers us. Then we use it to discover and play a character.

Let's do the next lines. *(Bridgett reads them and circles the phrases.)* Yes, "And find a time" is one, and "Both meet to hear and answer," and "such high things." Notice that if there is punctuation, you don't need a caesura, because the punctuation already allows you to pause. Now read the entire speech, using the phrases. *(She does, and it makes sense.)* What about "meet"—how do we know how Shakespeare is using the word?

Alex: We're going to look it up in the *OED*.

Coach: Right. Because you don't want to assume you know the answer. You may be surprised. Let's read the speech again and give you a hypothetical situation, to help you slow down and think with each phrase. These guys come to you with a scheme to hold up the 7-Eleven, and you have the only car. You don't want to offend these guys, but you're also not sure you want to get involved. Read it with those thoughts. *(She does.)* Now, for a few minutes, everybody walk about and work on this speech, using the phrases. But first, what is a simple technique when using phrases? Any phrase, set within a line, how do we handle it?

Bride: Say it how it's written.

Coach: But how is it written? Try the line.

Bride: "Till then, my noble friend, chew upon this." Just like that.

Coach: What is the phrase inside the line?

Bride: "My noble friend." *(She reads the line again.)*

Coach: What did she do?

Bridgett: Her voice went down.

Coach: She used a slightly different pitch with "my noble friend," setting it aside, so to speak. You can also look at it this way: She put "then" and "chew" on the same note, but lowered "my noble friend," thus making something different of the inside phrase.

And notice what you can do with "my noble friend." Say the line to a person you don't really trust. *(Bride does.)* Now to a person who is indeed your dear friend. *(She does.)* Now to a person known to you as courageous. *(She does.)* Because she has learned how to set aside the phrase, do you all see how her character can use that? *(All agree.)* All try it. *(They walk around, working on the speech with various degrees of success.)*

Alex: Would "chew" be a trochee?

Coach: Yes. Everybody see that? *(All do.)* Let's do the rest of the speech. Who will do it? *(Kristin goes to the board, reads the speech, and marks the phrases. We come to an agreement on the phrases.)* Notice the last line—called a short line. It is usually completed by the next speaker, as it is in this case, but it might be a short line that simply has a pause following it. Most people believe that's a direction from the author to take the pause, or to insert a physical action to fill the space, then continue the rhythm of the lines. Notice anything in the last four lines of the speech?

Kristin: Looks okay to me.

Maggie: There's no punctuation.

Coach: Right. Four lines without punctuation. When we get to our next skill, which is breathing, let's remember these four lines. Basically, you speak them without a breath. Anyone want to try? You need to get a real deep breath after "this"—then you can make it. And you must have enough breath left to support the end of the speech. *(Almost everyone tries and succeeds.)* Most of you rushed. Try again and realize that you have the breath and don't have to rush. *(All do.)* If you run out of breath, you can't support the end. Then you're weak. For an actor, strength comes from breath.

Jumping ahead, there are directors and coaches who don't believe you should breathe at the punctuation. They might tell you to breathe elsewhere. But for learning to handle the language, breathing at the punctuation points works. Later you can adjust, if it's necessary.

Amber: Should we breathe at every punctuation mark?

Coach: In learning the material, yes. That forces you to deal with each phrase, each idea, and forces you to keep breath power. But later, after you've learned the material, simply remove breaths you don't need. And you also may have to add some. But eliminate and add breaths by choice, not by shooting from the hip.

We'll do breathing skills next time. But planning ahead, as you begin memorizing your speech, mark and memorize your breathing points at the same time. Then you'll never run out of breath. Now, we have phrasing as our third skill. For next time, read chapter 5 on breathing. But now, before we check out our sonnets, which we haven't done yet, let's all get on our feet, walk about, and work some more on the Brutus speech, playing all the phrases. *(All work on this for some time, then a few read the speech aloud with correct phrasing. Then we take a break.)*

Coach: *(After the break.)* Let's look at our sonnets, see what you've selected, and hear you read them through once just for sense. *(Everyone identifies his or her sonnet. They select numbers 120, 30, 75, 65, 14, 107, 27, 78, and 29. One actor is absent. Everyone reads his or her choice aloud.)*

Notice that almost everyone forgot to kick the box, and we just worked on that skill. And notice that nobody has any idea what anyone is talking about. That's how difficult these sonnets can be. But for the most part, everyone went so fast that Shakespeare went on without us. You did not give us time to deal with the ideas of each phrase before you went on to the next one, and the sonnets are packed with ideas and images. We'll do imagery later. For now, type your sonnet—triple-spaced so that you have room for notes—look up your words, mark your scansion, and work out the phrasing. Then we'll read them again at the end of the workshop and you'll give them to me so that I can see your analysis work on something other than a monologue.

Often, a major mistake is not catching the listener with the first two lines. If I miss the sense there, how can I understand line 3, etc.? And notice that lines nine through twelve are usually the hardest to clarify. The rhyming couplet is usually lovely and easy to understand.

We take some time here to discuss a few of the thoughts discovered in the sonnets and to identify some very difficult phrases and lines. We also discuss the possible objects of the sonnets, Shakespeare's patron and his "dark lady." This leads to a discussion of patronage of the arts and how that works today compared to how it worked in Ancient Greek, sixteenth- and seventeenth-century France, and Elizabethan times.

Coach: As you probably know, Shakespeare dedicated his sonnets to a patron. In his time, patronage of an artist was a class act, with even the Queen supporting a troupe of actors—Shakespeare's company, actually. Does anyone know a patron of any artist today? *(Nobody does.)* I've known a few, and these were kept hush-hush. But in earlier times, in Greece, France, England, Germany, Italy, and other places, it was common to sponsor an artist.

Today, in America, sponsorship of artists is a rare thing, primarily delegated to state and federal funding. But the federal funding, the National Endowment for the Arts, is so strapped for money that the amount it allocates to each state each year—to support all of the arts in that state—isn't enough to build one military airplane. And there is always a group of conservative congressmen trying to deny all funding for the NEA. So the NEA has to fight just to get the pittance it does receive. It's not a healthy picture, so many deserving artists never receive the funding that would allow them to devote themselves to a project full-time. Oh, well, get me off my soapbox. Let's continue.

Please pass out a copy of your monologue to each other actor. *(They do.)* This is so we can easily follow your monologue as you begin work on it, and so we can take notes as we listen. The notes will be shared with you every time you do the monologue. On your personal copy you'll mark your complete scansion. That will become more and more complex as we add skills. So far you have three skills, plus their offshoots. All of that needs to be on your copy by our next workshop.

For today's workshop you were invited to bring any really difficult lines from your monologues, lines you just can't scan, and place them on the board. We'll work them out together. Does anyone have difficult lines? *(Most do.)* Then two or three people put their lines on the board. *(They do.)*

Everyone find the monologues from which these lines are taken, then we'll work them out. *(We all find the monologues and wait for the difficult lines to be written out.)* Now we have the lines, so let's work them out. From *The Taming of the Shrew*:

1.   And when she is froward, peevish, sullen, sour,

              And when she / is fro / ward, pee / vish, sul / len, sour,

We need an elision (or an anapest) for the first foot. Amber selects the anapest. From The Two Gentlemen of Verona:

2.   Injurious wasps, to feed on such sweet honey,

              Injur / ious wasps / to feed / on such / sweet hon / ey

The line has twelve syllables, so we elide "injurious" (to be pronounced "in-jur-yous") and use the feminine ending for "honey." Next, also from The Two Gentlemen of Verona:

3.   Except mine own name; that some whirlwind bear

              Except / mine own / name; that / some whirl / wind bear

The line has a trochee on the third foot and maybe a spondee on the second foot. From Measure for Measure:

4.   Die, perish. Might but my bending down

              Die / perish / Might but / my bend / ing down

The line has nine syllables, but the ending is regular, so the simplest solution is to stretch out "Die" a little and let it be the first foot. Next, from Titus Andronicus:

5.   Make poor men's cattle break their necks;

              Make poor / men's cat / tle break / their necks; (dee-dum)

The line has eight syllables and there are no one-syllable words that can be spoken as two syllables, so we read it as eight with a blank foot at the end. We suggest a brief action or pause to fill that beat because the short line is not completed by the next line.

Coach: Most directors believe that the missing beats call for an action that will continue the rhythm—you're missing a "dee-dum"—so take a moment to decide what you're going to say next—a natural pause.

Ryan: I think he might laugh to fill the foot.

Coach: That would fill the beat. Next time we'll put up the other lines people have, then we'll go on to breathing.

Be sure to look up all your words before you try to complete your scansion. Know what everything means. The good old *OED*! Is anyone using the online version?

Alex: Yes. I paid the $30 for the online version. It's ten times faster because you go right to the word rather than paging through a huge book.

Bride: I have a regional library card from home and found out that it gives me an automatic membership for the *OED*. My library subscribes, so I can use my library card number and get the online version.

Kristin: I like the books myself. You surround yourself with them and feel like you're soaking up all the words in the English language. It takes longer, but I enjoy it.

Coach: See you all next time.

Session Five

In this session: • Breathing • Lowering the voice
• More scanning of difficult lines • Next assignment
• First breathing exercise

Coach: Let's start with breathing, then we'll finish the difficult lines, then we'll come back to breathing again. I've put some lines on the board. Someone read them aloud. *(Alex does.)*

> Lo, as a careful housewife runs to catch
> One of her feathered creatures broke away,
> Sets down her babe, and makes all swift dispatch
> In pursuit of the thing she would have stay,

Look at Sonnet 143, in your books on page 38. Now, if you breathe at inappropriate times with verse, you muddle the basic meaning of the line. One of you read the first two lines and breathe after "catch." *(Emily does.)* Do you all hear what happens? *(They do.)* Realize that "catch" is still part of the thought of the first two lines, then new thoughts happen. Now read the first four lines but put a breath after "dispatch." *(Emily does.)* That doesn't work, does it? *(All agree.)* So how do we figure out where to breathe?

Observing their breathing technique is one of the pleasures of watching good actors work. We actually enjoy watching them breathe, and they might spit on certain words. By observing this, we realize that breathing does not cause delay. Nobody gets bored because an actor breathes. We're expected to breathe, and if an actor doesn't, he hasn't the vocal strength to get to the end of the speech. But young actors are often afraid to breathe. They think it takes too much time, or is unnatural, or whatever. So they take little gasps for breaths, filling about one-third of the lungs and requiring them to take another little gasping breath almost immediately.

One of you please read the four lines again, and this time breathe completely after "Lo," and after "away," and after "babe"—and take your time. *(She does.)* Do you mind that Emily takes time to breathe? *(We don't.)* After awhile, you learn how to breathe deeply and faster, but for your work here you should not try to go faster. You want to condition your body to breathe deeply. So do that and don't rush it. Take your time. Do it again, and breathe deeply, and as you breathe in air, "breathe in" your next line as well. Then send the line out on the exhaling breath. When she does this, something else will happen. See if you can hear it. *(She reads it again, with deep, unhurried breaths.)* What do you hear?

Maggie: Her voice got lower.

Coach: Yes. A great benefit from the exercise. Another good exercise is to force yourself to exhale all leftover air at the point where you're going to breathe so that you can practice inhaling to completely fill the lungs. You might get a little light-headed, so stop if that happens. *(Emily tries it with complete exhaling and deep inhaling at each breathing point.)* Any other observations?

Bridgett: For me, the breathing points kind of serve as pauses, so I had time to really hear what she just said before she went on.

Coach: A wonderful observation. Did everyone hear that? *(Some did.)* In a sense, you're thanking the actor for not going so fast that you can't get the image. The breathing also gives you the sense that the actor is in control, and is taking the time to feel the material, not rushing to the end. Remember the old Stanislavski statement that the actor must control the language, the language can't control the actor? We have a good example of that in this exercise.

You get a much more pleasant sound when your voice comes down, which it does when you breathe completely, which you do if you force yourself to exhale. So this is a good exercise.

Another observation while we're on this sonnet. Notice that the first eight lines are based around the idea that this happens, and this happens, and this happens, etc., until we get to line nine, when "So" answers "just as" from line 1. It's like eight lines are a huge phrase between "Just as" and "So." Does everyone see that? *(They do.)* This is a common structure in Shakespeare, so you need to be aware of how he completes a thought that might be started with "as" or "when" or "if." "But" and "yet" also set you up for changes, like reversals or completions of thoughts originated earlier.

That's a start on breathing. Now let's put the other hard lines on the board. *(Some do.)* From *Measure for Measure*:

6.   Heaven shield my mother played my father fair,

    Heaven shield / my moth / er played / my fath / er fair

This is a line with eleven syllables, so we elide "Heaven" to "Heav'n," spoken as one syllable. Now we have ten. From Othello*:*

7.   Steeped me in poverty to the very lips,
          Steeped me / in pov / erty / t'the ver / y lips,

Coach: We have eleven syllables. "Steeped," an active verb, has to be a trochee, right? *(All agree.)* "Lips" can't be a feminine ending, right? *(All agree.)* Working backwards, "The ver" and "y lips" might be two feet. If so, we have to get three feet from the rest of the sentence. What can we elide? *(All suggest "poverty," pronounced "pov'ty.")* But we could also do what?

We agree that "to the ver" could be one foot, as "t'the ver," kind of an elision of an anapest. Because many actors think "poverty" to be an important word to stress for the "sense" or meaning of the line, we settle on the elision of "to the ver."
  Everyone tries reading this line, and all want to drop "lips," a natural thing to do. But when they practice supporting "lips," the next line, which begins with "Catch me …," flows into the first much more clearly. An exercise here is to have the actor say the word "comma" after "lips," which helps him support "lips" and hear that the sense of the comma tells the listener there is more to come—which is what we want. Next, from The Two Gentlemen of Verona*:*

8.   Poor forlorn Proteus, passionate Proteus,
          Poor for / lorn Pro / t'us pass / ionate / Prot'us

Coach: The line has twelve syllables. You could read it with twelve syllables, which would work, but you could also do what?
Alicia: Elide "Proteus" both times. Say it "Pro-tus."

Bridgett selects this reading, but personally I would stay with the twelve syllables, as that works just fine. From Othello*:*

9.   Given to captivity me and my utmost hopes,

We work it out in this way:

Coach: What's the first thing we do?
Jerrod: Count the syllables.
Coach: So here we have thirteen syllables. And it starts with a trochee, "Given to."
What are our choices?
Bride: Working backwards, "my ut" and "most hopes" are two feet.

Bridgett: Let's elide "captivity" to "captiv'ty."
Bride: And elide "Given" to "Giv'n" for one syllable, so the foot is "Giv'n to." That makes "captiv'ty" work.
Coach: That puts a stress on "me," but in this case, we can stress the pronoun.
Bride: "My ut" isn't right—there's an "and" to deal with. An anapest or an elision.
We conclude with:

Giv'n to / captiv / ty me / an'my ut / most hopes,

From Henry VI, part 3:

10.   Had I been there, which am a silly woman,
          Had I / been there, / which am / a sil / ly wom / an,

This is an eleven-syllable line, but with a feminine ending. Next, a line also from Henry VI, *part 3:*

11.   Warick is Chancellor and the Lord of Calais;
          Warick / is Chan / c'llor and / the Lord / of Cal / ais;

This is a twelve-syllable line, but with a feminine ending. We elide "Chancellor" and have five feet.

Coach: If you find any other lines that don't work for you, bring them in and we'll work them out together. After the break, let's do more on breathing.
Coach: *(After the break.)* For next time, do the first eight lines of your monologue breathing deeply. Refer to the speech on page 39 of the book. Circle all the breathing spots, the punctuation points. Let's all read the *Macbeth* speech, taking the time to exhale completely and inhaling to fill the lungs. Take your time, and have full lungs for each phrase. *(Various actors read the speech.)*
    One note: on "reigns that"—"that" needs the same stress as "reigns." The breathing slows down the speech too much—but this is a rehearsal and sense exercise, not a performance exercise. Breathe through your mouth—you can fill the lungs much faster that way. Breathe deeply, and fill the lungs all the way down—not just the top half. Don't forget to kick the box. Because it's so pronounced and emphasized, do you find yourselves breathing along with the speaker? *(All do!)*
    Let's go to the Ariel speech, same page. There is lots of punctuation, so force yourself to exhale and breathe deeply at each point. You probably have an anapest in the line—"On'the curl," then "ed clouds"—so try it that

way. *(Various actors read the speech, breathing deeply.)* Is it too slow? *(All agree that the tempo only has to be picked up a little for performance, so the breathing only has to go slightly faster.)* When you breathe confidently, you automatically "send" the next line out to the listener, and you have great strength. Anything else?

Alex: Because of her bare middle, we can see how her diaphragm works. *(The actor reading is wearing low-riding jeans and a cut-off T-shirt, and all agree that we can see her working.)*

Coach: Right. You can see her muscles support the breath and the diaphragm kick in to support the ends of the lines.

Now, for a moment forget what we've said about breathing and just read the lines like the character might speak them. *(Some try it.)* Two things are happening. You're going too fast and your voices are going up in pitch, because you're not breathing confidently. You think performance immediately demands tempo. But haven't we already shown that the actor can take all the time she needs to breathe? *(All agree.)*

Let's work on our feet. *(We do.)* If you haven't memorized the first few lines of your monologue, bring a copy with you. Team up. The partner listens to the speaker and makes sure she breathes completely at all punctuation points. Take turns being the listener. Also put in caesuras as necessary. Partners should watch both the script and the actor. Make sure they're breathing correctly and confidently. Don't allow your partner to get away with filling the lungs only halfway. And notice how the voice comes down as you work with filled lungs. *(All practice this exercise for about thirty minutes. I walk about and listen to each group, correcting as necessary. It's noisy, but that doesn't matter.)*

Here's a note. When you get up here to do your first eight lines from memory, your tendency will be to rush. So don't be afraid to use up your air, which makes you have to breathe, which makes you slow down. You can use up your air on a one-word phrase or a four-line group of phrases. But use up your air. Besides, it's fun to do that. You can discover just how much air you have and how far it will go. Practice that for next time. You now have four skills, and you'll soon have more. Then we get to put them all together. *(Groans.)* Sure. See you next time.

CHAPTER 16

Session Six

In this session: • Breathing work
• Second breathing exercise • Third breathing exercise
• Next assignment

Coach: Let's finish up the breathing exercises, then we'll get to the use, or non-use, of subtext—chapter 6. Today, go up and read your first eight lines, breathing correctly. *(Kristin, presenting Isabella from* Measure for Measure, *goes first.)* Remember that this is a breathing exercise, not an acting exercise. *(She reads the speech.)*

Your voice has come down, and is very nice. However, you forgot to kick the box on almost every line. Next time? *(She agrees. Next is Bridgett doing Julia, from* The Two Gentlemen of Verona.*)*

You have good breathing and the voice is down. Again, though, you dropped the end of every line. *(We listen to Alicia, working on Margaret, in* Henry VI, part 3. *Her breathing is good, her voice has come down, and her speech is supported. Jerrod's breathing is good for* Othello, *but he tends to paraphrase.)*

Jerrod, you're missing a lot of words, and must get that fixed. Your memorization must be totally accurate or you'll be thrown off by a break in the rhythm. *Next we listen to Emily read Viola from* Twelfth Night:

Viola: I see you what you are; you are too proud;
             But, if you were the devil, you are fair.
             My lord and master loves you. O, such love
             Could be but recompensed though you were crowned
             The nonpareil of beauty.
             If I did love you in my master's flame,
             With such a suff'ring, such a deadly life,

In your denial I would find no sense;
I would not understand it.

Coach: I like that I can hear you breathing—you're using up your air and taking deep breaths. Your voice is coming down. Does it help that you're also a runner?

Emily: Oh, yes. I work on my Shakespeare when I'm running. I like to make the rhythms match.

Coach: Good. We have Kate, Lady Macbeth, and Prince Hal to go. *(Amber's voice is coming down for Kate, and her breathing is strong; Bride's breathing is excellent for Lady Macbeth; and Alex is solid with Prince Hal.)*

Coach: Bride, that was good handling of the five no-breath lines. *(All agree.)*

Bride: But I was pushing it. It'll get easier.

Coach: Right. Now, tell me what you have come to understand when practicing this skill. Does any of this help you for your future or for the realism you perform all the time?

Amber: I'm directing a short play, so in rehearsal last night I had all three actors do the breathing exercise. The play is realism, but after breathing at all punctuation points, they really slowed down—and they started to play the ideas in each phrase. It really helped us, and the actors understand the script better now.

Coach: They're hearing the different ideas. Now, if you have them circle their phrases and use the caesura, you'll hear another improvement.

Amber: I'm going to do that tonight.

Coach: Even with realism, many of these skills work.

Alicia: It seems to me that breathing gets so much easier.

Coach: If you watch some fine actors on film or video, you will notice how they breathe. For example, watch Kenneth Branagh do the famous *Henry V* speech. The camera is close, so you can see when he breathes and how deeply he does it. All take a look at it. You'll also hear it in Restoration comedy, Molière, *Cyrano*—any of the wonderful plays if they're performed by top actors. Check them out.

Emily: I really like how correct breathing brings the voice down.

Coach: I do too. Maybe you can all really think about that and start keeping the voice down all the time. You sound so much better when you do. You've all had other training in that, but it slips away, doesn't it?

They agree. Two of the actors are late, so we don't hear these two do the breathing exercise.

Coach: Now let's add some complexity to the exercise. I need help setting up chairs. *(All help.)* I believe this is a Cicely Berry exercise from the Royal

Shakespeare Company—the RSC. Place two chairs about six feet apart. The actor stands behind one chair and in two steps can cross to behind the other chair. The partner stays in front and checks the script and the breathing. Then trade places. Later we'll do this exercise with phrasing as well.

Here's how it works: From behind the first chair, say the words up to your first breathing point. When you reach that point, start moving and exhaling whatever breath you haven't used. As you arrive behind the other chair you should be inhaling, then speak the line as you get into position behind the second chair. Then exhale while crossing, inhale, and speak the next line. Continue through all of your lines. Establish the rhythm by speaking, exhaling/walking, inhaling, speaking, exhaling/walking, inhaling, speaking, etc. Going from chair to chair, you use the movement to rid yourself of excess air and to refill your lungs, simultaneously "inhaling" your next line as well. The movement forces you to take time to breathe and not rush into the next line, because you can't say the next line until you get behind the other chair.

Working in pairs, the actors practice this exercise until break time, about thirty minutes. I walk about, watching and correcting as necessary. This is an excellent exercise for both breathing and phrasing. When using it as a phrasing exercise, walk from chair to chair on every phrase, whether or not you have a breathing point.

Coach: If everyone's here, let's begin. You'll need scripts if you don't know your first eight lines. *(Most don't need scripts.)* By the way, this is the last session where you can carry your script. Now, everyone lie down. Lift your knees some so that your back is flat on the floor. Arms flat. *(All do, including me.)* Now, breathe through your mouth and feel the air go down into your lungs. It's rather cool and kind of makes a circle and comes back up. *(All try this.)* From this position, practice your monologue. Do the correct breathing, and start noticing what happens to your voice. Become as relaxed as you can. Don't work hard at it, just breathe, speak, exhale, breathe, speak, exhale—let it flow easily. *(All practice this for twenty minutes or so. I make sure nobody is straining. The goal is to keep this ease when they stand up.)*

Stop now. Notice how your voice support is coming from deep inside of you. Stand up and do the lines, trying to keep that sound and relaxation. *(All work at this.)* What do you notice?

Alex: Muscles are tighter when I stand up.

Bridgett: You get more self-conscious.

Alicia: It's just harder.

Coach: If you can't keep the prone feeling when you stand, go back down again and try it again. Try it until you're comfortable.

You might start to feel like the idea originates in your soul, so to speak, and it activates the vocal cords to speak it aloud. That's what you want your acting to do. You don't want this language to make you overact, work too hard, get confused, stumble, or give you any other problem. You want it to come from you. Each of you try to find the place inside of you where the ideas might originate—rather than in your head.

Here's a little exercise: I don't know if anyone else uses this and it may not be any good. But I can hear the difference when you use it. A volunteer. *(Alicia steps up.)* I want you to say your first line any way you wish—just breathe correctly. Then pause, locate a place of your choice inside of you, and make the idea in the line originate from that spot. Now say the line again. We'll listen to the difference. Go ahead and try. *(She does.)* We clearly hear a difference. *(All agree.)* You want your language to come from you, not to strain out from the vocal chords or the brain. Everyone work on this idea for awhile. It may be too vague a concept for some of you, and that's okay. But it's actually nothing but voice support. You can place your language ideas wherever they work best for you. *(They all work on locating more inner origins of the ideas and more relaxed use of the language and the vocal mechanism, which is essentially finding deeper support for the voice.)*

Now, each of you do two readings of a line—standing up or lying down—and we'll hear your new origin for the second reading. *(Each takes a turn, some lying down.)* This doesn't work for everyone, but when it does, we clearly hear it. Some of you feel you have to push it—not just allow the language to roll out on the breath. When that happens, both lines sound the same. But all of you are realizing that this language can come from you, can be yours and not some intellectual puzzle or exercise. If you can be in love with it, it will be more beautiful yet.

Work on this, and in one week be ready to do all twelve lines while applying all skills learned so far. *(Fake groans.)* Next time, more on phrasing and then subtext. See you then, and good work so far.

Session Seven

Coach: We haven't spent enough time on phrasing, so let's begin there today. Take out your monologues. *(Two have forgotten theirs and must borrow from others. I groan.)* So far, I don't think any of you have circled your phrases. So take a few minutes and circle all the phrases in your monologue. We want to be able to separate them. If you have a line you can't figure out, put it on the board and we'll do it together. *(They work on circling the phrases.)*

Amber: What about this line: "I am ashamed that women are so simple." Do I need two phrases?

Coach: You could do it as one, or you could break the line after "ashamed."

Bride: "Glamis thou art, and Cawdor, and shall be / what thou art promised." I see three phrases, or should it be four?

Coach: I think three would be enough.

Jerrod: "Had they rained all kinds of sores and shames on my bare head." I see either two or three.

Coach: Certainly break after "shames." The other would be a choice for you as the actor.

Emily: "Make me a willow cabin at your gate." I'd want to say that line as one phrase, but it could be two.

Coach: It could be two because first you're saying what you would do, then you're telling her where you would do it. So there are two phrases, but I agree with you. There could be no pause after "cabin," if that was your choice. On the other hand, there could be a caesura there. Your choice.

Now, using your first ten lines, let's work on our feet. Partner up and set up the chairs. *(They do.)* This phrasing exercise is not unlike the breathing exercise. From behind one chair, say your first phrase, then cross to the other chair and, when behind it, say your next phrase, and so on. Right now you don't need to concern yourself with the breathing, just concentrate on separating the phrases. Later we'll do both skills together. *(I demonstrate, using one of their lines.)* Your objective is to deal with the idea you're saying; then, as you're crossing, deal with the idea you're about to say. We could put the chairs a long way apart—then you would have lots of time to consider what you're about to say. And don't amble; go ahead and walk briskly from chair to chair. The partner holds the script and makes certain the speaker doesn't skip a phrase—or skip a cross. *(The actors work on this exercise.)*

Let's pause a moment. As you're moving to the next chair, make certain that you deal with what you're going to say. You'll notice a frustration comes into it. You want to speak sooner, the long delay between phrases forces you to wait to speak, and you can't speak because you haven't reached the other chair yet. That frustration is good. It makes you realize how much you want to get to the next idea. Later, when you eliminate the cross, you'll be able to use that. If you really want to experience the frustration, move your chairs about twenty feet apart, or just set other targets across the room and walk to those. *(They continue working on the phrasing.)*

Pause for a moment. I notice that sometimes you put a period at the end of a phrase, probably because you realize you can't say the next phrase right away. But only use a period if it's called for. Use the commas and support the idea in the phrase—let us know that there is more coming. That's one of the hardest parts of this exercise. If you have phrases that are all part of a larger idea, you have to keep the idea supported during the long pause between speaking phrases. Don't let the idea end if you don't intend to end it. For example, let's look at these lines from the *Twelfth Night* monologue:

> If I did love you in my master's flame,
> With such a suff'ring, such a deadly life,
> In such denial I would find no sense.

Notice the structure. We have an "If"—followed by this and this happens, then the conclusion to the "If," "I would find no sense." All of the phrases between "If" and "I" are part of the same idea—which is, "Your actions make no sense." So you don't want periods after any of the phrases.

If I did love you	(A caesura, maybe, but keep the idea going)
in my master's flame,	(The main idea, keep it going)
With such a suff'ring,	(An idea within the main idea, keep it going)
Such a deadly life,	(Another idea within the main idea, keep it going)
In such denial	(Another idea within the main idea, keep it going)
I would find no sense.	(Ties back to the first phrase and completes the idea.)

Coach: Is everyone clear on that? *(General agreement. They continue the exercise until each has worked with his or her monologue three or four times.)*

Good. Let's pause on that exercise now, and move on. Look at your monologue and decide how you can add the breathing skill to the phrasing. Move the chairs a little closer—some got spread out—so the breathing will work. We only want two steps to move from chair to chair. You breathe on the punctuation marks, which are usually also phrases, but you also move on phrases that aren't breathing points—like caesura divisions of ideas—and you don't breathe on those. So study your speeches and figure out what you have to do.

Remember to move on every phrase, whether or not it's a breathing point, and obviously move on all breathing points, as they will all be phrases. Partners, keep a sharp eye on the material and be certain the actor does both skills. No breathing simply because you're moving—breathe only at the appropriate places. *(The actors work on this exercise for about thirty minutes.)*

Alex: I can't find a motivation for moving on all of these phrases. *(Laughter.)*

Coach: That's because this is an exercise and has nothing to do with character. Remember, that comes later. All we're doing here is forcing ourselves as actors to discover all the ideas in the language and to breathe in such a way as to not disguise those ideas. Your character may elect to handle some of this differently—but in that case it's done by choice, not by accident.

Kristin: How much of this do we keep for performance?

Coach: I'm not sure I understand. How much of what?

Kristin: Of all these exercises and skills.

Coach: If you're an athlete, how much of your training techniques do you use in the game or event?

Kristin: Probably none of it. It just happens.

Jerrod: I played football. We had to run through all kinds of tires and ropes and things to make us learn to get our knees up, to keep our legs pumping. But those things weren't on the field during the game. We just learned the skill and then did it. Until we got tired. *(Laughter.)*

Coach: I think that's a good example. The techniques you're learning here will happen automatically. You won't be thinking about chairs six feet apart when you're playing a *Macbeth* scene. But you will be reading the lines so that the audience hears the various ideas put there by the writer. Your character will decide how she will handle the lines based on the needs of the scene, but however she handles them, the ideas will still be clear. Does that make sense? *(All agree that it does.)*

Alex: Will we ever get to character?

Coach: Only a little at the end of the workshop, when we're actually performing the monologues. Then we'll make a few choices. Mostly, character is for the next workshop and for other acting classes. There isn't any difference between developing a Shakespearean character and developing an O'Neill character—there's only the difference of the language. The Shakespearean character, regardless of the time and energy you put into it, will not be successful if you can't handle the language. (*There is some acknowledgment before they all return to the exercise.*)

You seem to be getting it, so let's each do a few lines. (*Taking turns, we all watch each person do a few lines of breathing and phrasing simultaneously.*) Good, especially when some of you had three or four phrases without a breathing point and were able to support the idea while moving. I notice one tendency. When concentrating on phrasing, often you don't breathe deeply—you take smaller, gasping breaths. You don't want to do that unless you choose to do it. But when you do breathe deeply, your voices are strong. And you also don't want to forget to support the ends of the lines, which many forget to do.

Now, we have to put these skills together with scansion and end-of-line support, and all of a sudden you're working with four skills for acting Shakespeare. Let's break.

Coach: (*After the break.*) Let's look at chapter 6 and try to decide why we don't apply a bunch of subtextual thoughts to the lines you're working on. A major concern here is this: In much modern acting of realism, and especially on film, large pauses are taken between thoughts to give the characters time to reflect and determine. On film, the camera can be close so that we can watch the actor's thinking process before he speaks. Onstage, we can't see that. So that's one reason why film-acting pauses don't work well onstage. But there's more. Actors often want to "enhance" the lines with pauses or sound effects, like "ahs" and "ummmms"—all of which take time and add beats to the line. Look on page 46. I'm talking about acting on the words—but in most film acting, so much is done between the words. That technique might work on film, but it kills verse.

The modern idea of subtext, as you know, grew out of realistic plays, where action was based on character motivation, and the character might not speak what he really means. But his meaning is under the words, or behind the words—it isn't just the words. And certainly, learning to play a realistic subtext became the great acting development of the twentieth century.

In Ibsen's *A Doll's House*, Nora offers a match to Dr. Rank, who wants to light his cigar, but we know he is in love with her. His response, "Thanks for the light," is not about the match, is it? Do you know the play? What is the line about?

Alicia: Thanks for what you've given me by being you.

Coach: Yes, it could be that. Quite a distance from a match. But Rank is speaking the subtext, and we hear the subtext, and we know what he means. He could, in fact, take a long pause while lighting the cigar, puff on it, look at her, then decide what to say so as not to say "too much." After all, she is married to his friend, so he must say carefully what he intends to say. Subtext is very useful here.

Shakespeare would not have done that. In this situation, he probably would have written Rank a speech about what she had given him by being her. He would have said what he intended to say, and likely would have said it with a verse passage that would require a certain rhythm to speak it and make it convincing.

I doubt that you'd want to do a modern play without using subtext. I can't think of any reason why you'd want to do that, or even how you could do it. On the other hand, there is probably no reason why you need subtext to do a Shakespearean play. Certainly you can use subtext if you wish, but the point is that you don't use it the way you'd use it in modern text.

Let's take Hamlet's "To be, or not to be—that is the question." The actor can use subtext to weigh the odds: *To act and get revenge, or not to act—what shall I do?* But if you take long pauses after each "be," as Rank might do before "Thanks for the light," the ideas become indulgent, bogged down, and passive. You've lost the language in favor of mood, and the mood is already in the language. By what he says we know what he's thinking. You don't have to "guide" us with long, reflective moments of thought; in fact, that approach will turn us off and put us to sleep. Hamlet reasons his way through the problem in the lines that follow.

Learning what the language is doing is the main reason why you must not jump to "How will I play this character?" when you take a classical role. If you say, "The hell with all that analysis—I'll use my natural talent and everything will come out fine," it won't. You cannot impose a character choice on the language in the beginning, making the language work a certain way because "that's how my character would say it." If you do this, the audience is listening to the "edge" you have imposed on the language, and not the language itself. Your "edge" has taken away the beauty of the language in favor of your quirks, actor tendencies, moods, attitudes, etc. It will end up shallow, and all of your work won't give you anywhere near the product you could have had. The audience will stop listening. I've seen so much bad acting of Shakespeare by actors who can do realism just fine. But they decide to play the role a certain way, which is the opposite of—what?

Maggie: Playing what the role requires.

Coach: A big difference, right? You can play a personality, especially on film. Rarely will it work onstage. Back to another realistic term. What is your objective?

Emily: Your goal—what you want to make happen.

Coach: And what is "playing your action?"

Emily: The things you do to get to your objective.

Coach: Right. Now let's look at page 46, the six lines from *The Merchant of Venice*, and work a subtext exercise.

The speech sets out to assure Antonio of Bassanio's love for him. Four actors are given imposed subtexts. They take some time to study their assignments. I then ask them to play their subtext to extremes, with lots of enhancements and pauses. (They do.) In each case, we find ourselves listening to an "attitude" rather than the words —hate Shylock, prove love for wife, persuade others of love for Antonio, apologize. Everyone plays a feeling rather than the basic action of the speech.

Coach: Remember, we don't want to play feelings, we want to play actions. Shakespeare's actions are pretty clear. You should be able to define the actions in your monologue clearly, and know your objective. What could be Bassanio's intention with this speech?

Emily: Maybe to retain Antonio's friendship?

Coach: Yes, we could play that. And what would Bassanio want from Antonio after saying these things to him? Remember, actions are measured in the other person. It's what the listener does that confirms for you if you have successfully played your action and reached some intention.

Maggie: He could hug him.

Coach: Good. Because that's a physical action from Antonio that follows the effort from Bassanio. It shows us that he reached Antonio and Antonio responded. What if Antonio had turned his back?

Bride: Then Bassanio was not successful with his intention.

Coach: Good. Actions and intentions are played in Shakespeare just like in realism, and their success is measured in the other person, just like in realism. Now, for a few laughs, everyone take the first four lines of his or her monologue and read them with an outrageous and imposed subtext. *(They do, and we laugh a lot.)*

I'm afraid sometimes directors can force such ridiculous interpretations of Shakespeare on an actor. Have you seen the film *The Goodbye Girl*? *(Nobody has.)* Watch it sometime, because in it the director forces a very effeminate interpretation on the character of Richard III, and the actor has to play it that way—to great humiliation. It's a nice example of imposing attitude on Shakespeare. All you can hear is the overly effeminate subtext applied to everything.

When you catch your partner slipping into an attitude, catch it and talk about it. For next time, we want to hear the speeches with the skills applied, and we want to be careful that attitude doesn't slip in. Later, when you develop a character, you can determine how you feel about the situations you are addressing in the monologue. You can ask, "What kind of character would say these words and want these things to happen?" And you've identified your character. See you next time.

CHAPTER 18

Session Eight

In this session • Review of skills
• First application of skills to monologues • Technique for giving notes
• Exposing weaknesses • Problems from realistic actor training
• Next assignment

Coach: Today we're about halfway through the workshop. We have a few skills left, then we need to work the monologues. Here's what we have so far—using the *OED*, scansion, trochees, other irregular feet, feminine endings, caesuras, elisions, end-of-line support, phrasing, breathing at the punctuation points, ignoring subtext. Let's set an order for the presentations. *(We do.)* Let's go through our monologues. Have someone hold your monologue to prompt you if necessary, but also know that if you need prompting, you may as well sit down. It's almost impossible to work on these skills if you're struggling over lines.

Everyone take out your copy of all the other monologues. *(They do.)* You'll be writing on these monologues, but use a pencil. You'll be using these copies many times. When another actor is presenting, those of you in the audience will listen for different skills and mark them on your copy of the monologue. To simplify this process, two people will listen for one skill. Everyone, take a number from one through nine. *(Nine actors are present in the workshop today.)* Number one will present her monologue first. While she is reciting, numbers two and three will listen for the scansion—stresses, trochees, feminine ending, elisions, etc. Numbers four and five will pay attention to end-of-line support; six and seven do the same with phrasing, while eight and nine will listen for the breathing. Note on the paper the places where you believe the actor did not fully commit to using the skill. Then we'll each give our notes. After we've given our notes to number one, number two goes up and number one takes her assignment. We rotate like that until everyone has presented and received his or her notes. Any questions? *(There are none.)*

Then let's begin with the first monologue. Stand over in the playing area. One of you is prompting as well as listening.

Kristin: I got it.

Coach: Good. Remember, this is not performance. This is an exercise for the actor to apply the skills that help us understand what the language is doing. No acting, please. Just gentle reading of the speech. Go slowly. We don't need any emotion yet.

Bridgett, doing Julia, stumbles all over her lines and I ask her to sit down after four lines. Kristin is next with Isabella and Bridgett takes Kristin's assignment, which is scansion. Kristin stumbles over her lines, so we stop.

Kristin: I really know this. I do it at home all the time.

Coach: I believe you, but are you working on it standing up and speaking aloud?

Kristin: No. Well, sometimes. But I'm also nervous.

Coach: For all of you, you don't know your words if you can't say them out loud. Does everyone understand what I mean? *(They do.)* Now, this is only an exercise. It's only a helper. I understand the nervousness, but if you can control it more, you'll gain more. Let's try again.

Kristin gets through the speech this time and we give notes. Each actor reviews skills with her, pointing out what she did and didn't do. She writes down the notes. The actors' notes are quite good. They are listening for the skills and they hear when the presenter misses something. We talk about their notes and explain why some scansion works, why the breathing works at certain points but not at others, what lines are supported, etc. Alicia goes up. She begins and I stop her. She isn't breathing and is already in performance mode.

Coach: Remember, this is only an exercise to see if you can use each of the skills. It's not about character or performance. All of that comes later. *(She begins again, but now is stumbling over her lines. She runs from the room. I call for the next actor.)* Folks, this is not supposed to be torture. It's simply an exercise. But do you know what's happening?

Emily: She was nervous.

Alex: She wasn't ready and just wanted to zip through it. Then you stopped her and it was all over.

Coach: I think "not ready" is probably the problem. When you trip over a word in blank verse, all of the rhythm is thrown off. Your mind realizes this and confusion is created. Sometimes you can get out of it, sometimes you just bog down. What's the answer to that?

Alex: To have the material down solid. You have to really know it.

Coach: Yes. You can't shoot from the hip. This language will expose you every time. And like we've said before, even if you learn it but don't take time to analyze and apply the skills, it will expose that you don't know what you're doing. So either it will expose you for being unprepared or it will expose you for being poor at acting Shakespeare. But you already know the solution to both of those problems.

Amber: Know the material solidly and apply the skills before you show it.

Alex: And before you create a character.

Coach: Easy, huh? *(Lots of laughs and groans.)* Well, you're going to gain tremendous confidence doing these skills. You will handle this language like it's your own, which is a goal; you will forget about us—we don't count; and you will just do the material ... and you will get very few notes. Then you'll be ready to move to character. Number four, are you ready?

Ryan gets through his Aaron monologue with two prompts. He stops to repeat many lines when he realizes he has missed something in the line, which is good. We go around and everyone gives notes.

Coach: Number five, are you ready?

Emily: Something I noticed. Everybody wants to do character immediately. Like, "Let's act." Like in realism.

Bride: Which is natural for anyone trained in realism.

Alicia has returned, but nobody acts as if anything unusual has happened. We accept that sometimes one has to run from the room. But later Alicia apologizes to the group for not being prepared, an apology that is well received. We don't dwell on it. She knows what to do before her next turn.

Amber: Some directors insist on many days or weeks of table work with the language, even with realism, before allowing you to get on your feet and start developing a character. But I suspect that around the table people are thinking "character."

Alicia: That's really hard not to do. The first time I read a script, I'm planning the character. It can change when I see what the other characters are doing, but I'm still planning it from the beginning.

Coach: It won't work with Shakespeare, or any classical language. So in here, where we're doing only Shakespeare, at some point you have to abandon your other tendencies and just work the language. The more you do this, obviously the more you'll find it easier. Actors who are really good at this can get 70 percent of the language on the first reading. They can move on to character and character relationships, the real purpose of rehearsal, quite soon. Once you're good at this, the language won't be in your way.

Alicia: I just wasn't ready. I'm sorry. But I'd like to try again so I can get the notes.

Bridgett: I'd like to try again, too.

Coach: Let's see how much time we have at the end of the session. Maybe we can do that. Number five, let's do yours.

Emily does her Viola monologue. She is more relaxed and concentrates on using the skills, going very slowly, and taking lots of time to breathe, which keeps her voice down. Everyone gives notes, many very useful. Some start picking up antithesis, which we haven't worked on yet. They are hearing it.

Coach: One of the nice things she did was have the confidence to breathe, and you could hear the benefits from that. Number six, are you ready? Are you relaxed, are you breathing?

Alex: I'm ready.

Alex does his Prince Hal monologue. He takes his time and breathes deeply, and everyone in the room is breathing with him! We acknowledge this and realize that it happens when you're working exercises like this. It is the impulse to help the actor along. The actors then give their notes. They also point out that he has applied an "attitude" to some of the material, something we don't want. Alex realizes he has done this and vows to remove it.

Bridgett: Some of us need to take a break. Hint, hint. (*We take a break before moving on to the last couple of monologues.*)

Coach: (*After the break.*) Number seven. Nice and slow, with lots of breathing.

Amber does her Kate monologue. She is well prepared and takes her time. Everyone gives his or her notes. The notes are becoming quite accurate and I am speaking less.

Coach: Number eight, go ahead. Notice that on days when we do the monologues, it takes the entire session. That leaves us only one session a week to learn new skills. So each time we learn a skill, you must get it applied to your monologue by the next session. Be sure to read chapters 7 and 8, and we'll get to antithesis next time.

Jerrod does his Othello monologue. Everyone gives his or her notes. We find an anapest in this speech and point out the foot that has three syllables in it. In these lines we also find an example of using "and" to point out two problems, rather than one. It's been my experience that actors often ignore the "and," even when it refers to two conditions.

Coach: Notice the "and" in the line, "All kinds of sores and shames on my bare head." Quite often actors slur over these "ands," but notice what it means. It means two things could have been imposed on him by heaven, not one, and he could have dealt with it. Watch for "ands" in your monologues and sonnets. Number nine, let's do it.

Bride does her Lady Macbeth monologue. Everyone gives his or her notes. She has one section of four-and-a-half lines without a breath, and runs out of air. But she vows she'll get a proper breath and won't run out of air next time. We work on how to put another breathing spot into that section, should it be needed. She also has a short line and will need to fill the extra feet with an action. She will check the Shakespearean pronunciation guide for one name. We also find an anapest in this speech.

Coach: Notice the "and" that Bride has—"Which fate and metaphysical aid doth seem / To have thee crowned withal." She's saying that two factors have confirmed that Macbeth will be king, not just one. That's huge for Lady Macbeth. There's no time for Maggie's monologue or to repeat Bridgett and Alicia, but we'll start with them next session.

Alex: And we'll continue to tear each other up. *(Negative reaction.)*

Coach: Does anyone really think that? *(Nobody does.)*

Alex: I was joking. This is really helpful.

Coach: Does everyone agree that this is helpful? *(All agree enthusiastically.)* I believe you'll all be better after this. And the notes were well taken and extremely helpful.

Amber: I know. I'll be much better when I apply these notes.

Coach: We'll see the next time we do the monologues! Don't forget to read chapters 7 and 8. See you next time.

Session Nine

Coach: Today let's start with Maggie's monologue, then Bridgett and Alicia again. After that, we'll move on to speech structure.

We first assign who will listen for which skills, then Maggie presents her Helena. She is well prepared and everyone gives notes. Bridgett and Alicia both repeat their monologues and get through them. The other actors give notes on what they heard or did not hear.

Coach: Again, try to remove the attitude and read from zero. Later you can determine who she is and what she feels. For working on the skills, try hard to stay away from character choices.

One of the hard things about Shakespeare's speeches is the discovery of how one line, perhaps early in the speech, ties in to another line, or group of lines, that is located much later in the speech. But if you don't tie them together, the speech will seem without focus, and that will be the actor's fault, not the playwright's. The Margaret speech has this challenge, as does the Othello speech. Notice Margaret's "Warwick is chancellor ... And yet shalt thou be safe?" There are phrases between the two lines, but the lines must tie together—as with Othello's "Had it pleased heaven ... I should have found in some place of my soul / A drop of patience." Again, many phrases are used between the original subject and the conclusion of the idea, but these two thoughts must tie together.

One of the notes was about descriptive words. You questioned Bridgett's handling of "bruising stones." She read the line stressing "stones" but not "bruising." On another line she did the opposite. At "loving words," she stressed "loving" but not "words." And she did that on "sweet honey," stressing the descriptive word "sweet." This speech is full of descriptive words.

Read the speech again and give equal emphasis to both the noun and its descriptive adjective. *(The actor tries this. Then the other actors read the speech and try to balance the descriptions with the nouns. After awhile they get it.)* Now check your monologue, and your sonnet, for similar problems and work them out. There's a danger that if you stress a descriptive word its noun will lose importance, as we just heard. But often we want and need to stress a descriptive word, so, in that case, stress both and it will work. Everyone understand? *(They do.)* Another note was about speaking the name "Julia." For scansion, it can't always be three syllables. How could it be pronounced?

Kristin: At one point it has to be Jul-ya to keep the rhythm.

Alicia: I remember that in a production of *Romeo and Juliet*, Romeo was pronounced Ro-me-o sometimes and Rom-yo at other times.

Bride: It's just elision, isn't it?

Coach: Yes, elision of a name is common in this language. Feel free to do it when necessary. Next week we're working on antithesis, and the time after that you'll be expected to present your monologue with all of the current skills, plus antithesis. Also, by next session, have your *OED* work completed. Know what every word in the monologue meant in its original usage. You will also see other usages, and your job is to choose one. I'll be selecting some words from each monologue and asking you what they mean.

Jerrod: Do we have to look up every single word?

Coach: Every word that might have been used in a different way. Never assume you know what a word means simply because you know the modern usage. We have some examples of how far afield this thinking can take you. Remember? *(They do.)*

Bride: I've found that the first use of some of my words was in a Shakespeare line, and in one case it was the line I was working on.

Coach: That would probably be one of the words Shakespeare invented.

Bride: Yeah! Cool.

Amber: What about when the editor has a footnote giving me the meaning of a word?

Coach: The editor has already gone to the *OED* and made a selection from among the various meanings listed. You can trust that information, or find out for yourself. I'm never comfortable assuming the editor made the same choice I might make. He or she probably didn't have to act the speech. The meaning of the word has to work for you. Make a good choice.

How many of the words you've looked up so far are being used like you thought they would be? Half?

Kristin: I'd say a little less than half.

Coach: So when we've listened to your monologue, you were guessing right on half of the words, but have since discovered another meaning for the other half.

Bridgett: Looking up the word "anger," I found it could mean being grieved, troubled, provoked, irritated, inflamed, flushed. In the line "Were I so angered with the same," I chose to use "troubled."

Coach: That's fine, but look at the difference if you used "provoked." And what about "inflamed," which is antithetical to "irritated"?

Bridgett: They seem to mean the same to me.

Coach: If you become inflamed by someone in a positive sense, what happens?

Bridgett: Maybe I'm hot for him.

Coach: But if you're irritated by the same guy?

Bridgett: Yeah, the opposite.

Coach: Inflamed, however, could also mean incredible wrath, couldn't it? Really worked up. I'll be interested to hear what choice you make.

Kristin: I had trouble with "played." "Heaven shield my mother played my father fair."

Coach: Is our first impression that she was faithful to him?

Kristin: Probably. But other choices are exhausted, worn out, treated, or performed—as in acting like a faithful wife.

Coach: I wonder what you will choose.

Kristin: I also was surprised by "slip." It's not something small, or a space you can sneak through. It means a scion or descendent. That helps clarify the line.

Emily: I had "nonpareil," which at first was simply unclear. But it means "a perfect example" or "epitome." I liked that.

Amber: "Boot" was unusual. It's not something to put on your foot, but means "to benefit." And "haply," in the same speech, does not mean "happily," it means "perhaps." Word definitions make a real difference in the sense of the speech.

Bride: In *Macbeth*, I was guessing on "battlements," which are entrances to a castle. I thought they were fortresses of some kind, but they're the actual entrances. So when Duncan enters the castle through Lady Macbeth's battlements, he is actually entering her home. And people could stand on top of these battlements and throw things or shoot arrows down on the people coming in.

Coach: Of course, the audience may not get exactly what you mean, but knowing the meaning helps you, the actor. It gives you the confidence to speak the line the way the author meant it.

Some actors abhor research. They prefer to work with "natural talent." But if you do the research, then turn to your natural talent, you will be better than if you haven't done the research. In your research, you're looking for the meaning of the word before it was used by Shakespeare in a play. To know what Shakespeare probably means, it doesn't do much good to assume the modern meaning. Find out what the word meant before the year 1600.

Many professional actors do their research, figuring out all text problems and meanings, before rehearsals begin and before getting on their feet. This is an exceptionally good practice. I hope you will all do the same.

Bride: "Pall." It's an interesting word and it was first used in *Macbeth*.

Coach: So Shakespeare probably invented it. But take the line in the sentence—

Bride: "And pall thee in the dunnest smoke of hell."

Coach: And the audience today hears—"Paul"—who's Paul? Or I might hear "impalled," as in a mispronounced "impaled."

Bride: And the word actually means "concealed," or "cloaked."

Coach: So how do you get the audience to hear that meaning?

Bride: I'll try putting it in quotes. *(She does.)* This is a good example of Shakespeare going on without you.

Coach: And you've still got "dunnest." What do we think when we hear that?

Ryan: I hear darkest. Or "done-est," the most done part of hell. *(Laughter.)*

Coach: You can only get it so clear, or your effort becomes terribly overacted. But knowing the difficulty of these two words makes you as the actor slow down and try to make the audience hear what you mean.

Bride: How do we do it?

Maggie: We can exaggerate the meaning.

Coach: To a point, right. But the audience is not going to understand everything you say. They will understand your intent, if you understand it. And we shouldn't expect otherwise. Just look at yourselves: You're actors, and you still don't know what the language is saying until you look up words—then you still have to choose meanings, then you still have to say them in such a way that the listener hears "something." The audience is hearing the word as it goes by—and another line is coming at them. Sometimes all they get is an impression, but often that's enough. They get an idea of your meaning, then an easier line comes along and they get it all, and appreciate your skills.

Emily: Won't imagery help here? You've got the image in your mind, so that will affect your reading, even if the audience doesn't know what your image is.

Coach: Right. And we'll get to imagery very soon. If you rush through the line, it won't mean a thing. You will immediately lose the audience. If you "handle" the line, and "handle" each word, the audience will stay with you.

Alicia: If Shakespeare invented the word, the audience at the time didn't know what it meant either.

Coach: Wonderful observation. So they too had to understand what the actor was saying by the way he handled the word. Just like you have to do today.

Alicia: The actors also had to guess, unless the author was right there.

Coach: And they didn't rehearse much, so they had to choose a meaning quickly for all words. So everyone is clear why we're using the *OED*? Why you have to go to the library? Or pay the fee and use the *OED* online? *(All are clear.)* So let's take a break.

Alex: It's so much faster online. You go right to the word and don't have to page through a dozen similar words to find the one you want.

Bride: I belong to a regional library that is a member of *OED* online. That's great, because I can access it with my library card number.

Coach: *(After the break.)* Now I want to take a little time on structure of speeches. We'll start with a sonnet. What I'm passing out to you are analyses of each of your sonnets. Scholars have been interpreting the sonnets and writing books about them for nearly three hundred years. You'll find a few dozen of these books in most libraries. I'm giving you copies of the views of the two scholars identified in chapter 9 of our book, Stephen Booth (*Shakespeare's Sonnets*, 1977) and John Kerrigan (*William Shakespeare: The Sonnets and A Lover's Complaint*, 1986), and you need to find one more—because you want three interpretations plus your own. You might check Helen Vendler's *The Art of Shakespeare's Sonnets* (1997).

Next, I want you to check your monologue against the *First Folio* to see how your version differs from the original. Here is a copy of the original *Folio* and here is a modern-type version of that *Folio*. *(I show them copies of the original First Folio of 1623 and Neil Freeman's modern-print Applause First Folio Editions of 2000. The copies are left on a table so that the actors can check their monologues.)* Let me show you something in the original—here's *Romeo and Juliet* in the way it came to the printer. See how the *s*'s were printed like *f*'s? They used a *u* for a *v*. Notice the few stage directions—exit, enter, etc. And notice the various words that are capitalized. It's slow reading, but enjoyable. Freeman's modern-type version is easier to read. See how that works. Check the same speech in each of the books. When you do this, you will see how editors over the years have changed words and often created new punctuation. You may prefer the original.

Let's move on. Go to the section on structure on page 50. Most sonnets will have what structure?

Emily: 4, 4, 4, 2.

Coach: That might give you a hint that Shakespeare's longer speeches also have a structure. But look at the sonnet on the next page. We're going to read through it and determine how the structure works. Then you do that with your sonnet. Does anyone know this sonnet?

(Nobody does, so I start the reading and we discuss every two lines. We discuss the 4, 4, 4, 2 structure of Sonnet 57 and the meaning of each line.)

Notice how the thought was set up in lines 1 and 2, and then the thought is explained in lines 3 and 4. Then the writer starts to explore the thought and that continues through line 12. He then summarizes the problem that was set up in line 2. That structure is pretty close to the structure of many monologues.

Look at the King's speech on the next page. Somebody read through it slowly. *(Alex does.)* Notice the setup—"I have this need for you so I sent for you." The reason is that "Hamlet is acting strangely." "What could have caused this? So what I need from you two boyhood friends is to stay awhile and draw out what's wrong with him. It must be something we don't know about; if we know, we can fix it."

But actually, the King wants to know if Hamlet's problem is in any way related to suspicion of the King himself. You can play subtext here, but it's already in the idea of the speech. And if you add too much subtext, you give away the intent to Rosencrantz and Guildenstern. So you can usually ask these questions: What is the speech about, what is the setup idea, how is the idea developed, what is the conclusion? Is that clear to everyone? *(It is.)* Okay, read the first four lines of some of your monologues.

(Various actors do this and we determine what the setup is for each speech. In many, it is immediately very clear.) In performance you must be very certain that the audience understands the setup, or you do the entire speech to a passive audience.

Now let's look on page 53 at the breaks in the rhythm, or trochees. The speech is from *Henry VI,* part 2. Who wants to read through it? *(Alicia does.)* Notice how the meter is broken in lines 5, 6, and 7. All three begin with a trochee. Everybody see that? *(They do.)* Let's read it. *(Everyone does.)*

Notice the Clarence speech—line 2. There's a break in the meter in line 2, the third foot, "shed." It's also the active verb for the line, so that's a hint for you. And in *The Comedy of Errors* speech, line 2 is broken and the responses both begin with a trochee. Usually we don't stress pronouns. This is a place where they would be stressed. Questions? *(There are none.)*

With a trochee, you usually take a caesura before it. You have to set up the word that breaks the rhythm. So now it's time to work out the structure of your monologue, and your sonnet. Have this done for next time. And read chapter 8, on antithesis.

Alex: On to an-ti-thesis.

Coach: Check the *OED.* See you next time.

CHAPTER 20

Session Ten

In this session: • Antithesis • Next assignment

Coach: Today we're going to start on antithesis. Add antithesis to your monologue for next time. On your copy, circle all antithetical words, phrases, or ideas and draw lines connecting them. It's your job as an actor to work out your analysis, which includes antithesis. If you rely entirely on your director to do this for you, your performance may be damaged. You could luck out and have a director who requires you to do this analysis, but likely you won't. So you must take the time to find your own antithesis. I've found this works better if you work in small groups, like three or four actors getting together and checking each other's material. Three brains are better than one when it comes to finding antithesis. We spend time finding the antithesis for this reason: If you read the verse without allowing the listener to clearly hear the antithesis, your reading becomes generalized. And what did Stanislavski—?
Bride: " 'In general' is the enemy of art."
Coach: Right. Of course, it's more than just finding it; then we have to play it. If you don't dig out and play the antithesis, your work will not be as specific as it can be if you stress the antithesis. I have some examples here. Look on page 57 at Romeo's speech to Benvolio. This is the classic example used in most books. Let's read through it first, then we'll go back and take it line by line. *(Maggie and Bride read the speech, and then I explain what is happening in the play at this point.)*

We're going to look for words and ideas that are opposites, that can play one against the other. Back on the first page of the chapter is Webster's definition of antithesis: "The placing of a sentence or one of its parts against another to which it is opposed to form a balanced contrast of ideas." One idea against another. Sometimes antithesis is illustrated by a line from a famous American, Thomas Paine. What is it?

Kristin: Give me liberty or give me death.

Coach: So you play liberty against death. You stress each equally. One idea against the other. Antithesis can also be a complete sentence against another complete sentence, or one group of sentences against another group, or even the first half of a speech against the second half. So without looking at the answers, take the first two lines and identify what is antithetical.

Jerrod reads the first two lines and we work out the antithesis. He then reads the lines again and stresses the antithesis, one idea against another. This takes a number of tries because he doesn't want to be specific. He only wants to stress part of each antithesis. Finally he gets it and we move on to the other lines, the actors taking turns finding the antithesis, then reading the lines until the antithesis is clear. We also pause to check scansion, to insert caesuras, and to define words. We review the answers that are already in the book.

Coach: Good. Now, let's each read the speech and use all the antitheses. *(Reactions.)* It's fun—try it! *(All read the speech, listening to each other play the antithesis. They hear when another actor misses one of the antithetical ideas.)* Be sure to circle your antithetical words and draw a line connecting them. When you memorize, memorize these ideas as well and you will be very close to reading the line correctly. Of course, all lines don't contain antithesis. If you don't find any, don't worry about it. But find what is there.

Look at the speech from *Henry V*, page 58. Who would like to read through it? Nice and slowly, just let us hear the ideas. *(Bridgett reads the speech.)* Let's interpret what he's saying.

We discuss the speech and its inherent meanings. I clarify what the "opposed numbers" are at Agincourt and discuss the background to Henry V achieving the crown. We look through Henry's list of tributes that he offers to gain God's support for the battle today. Then the actors take turns reading one line at a time and finding the antitheses. After doing this, each actor reads the entire speech and we listen to how each handles the antithesis.

Coach: Good. Let's take a break, then we'll continue.

There are a few teaching technique that have worked especially well for me when coaching an actor to handle verse. As each actor reads a speech like Henry's, the others are required to follow along. By doing this, they begin to hear when an antithesis is not stressed. Hearing this helps them when it's their turn to read the speech. The readings, then, improve as more actors read. This technique also works on the phrasing and breathing exercises—and we find ourselves breathing along with the actor who is speaking!—and in marking scansion—i.e., putting difficult lines on the board to work out together. Also, whenever one actor is presenting a monologue, all other actors can be assigned to listen for different specific skills (e.g., scansion, phrasing, breathing, feminine endings, elision, antithesis, trochees, etc.), and each gives notes on what he hears or doesn't hear. The technique keeps all actors involved and improving, even when it appears that only one is working.

Coach: *(After the break.)* Antithesis is not always black and white, although it often is. Let's move on to the speech from *Twelfth Night*—Olivia on page 59. Who would like to read it? Nice and slowly. And now everyone start listening for the antithesis right away—even if you're the person reading—like a cold reading at an audition.

Kristin reads the speech. She plays a number of the antithetical words, but misses some. We define meanings of words in the speech, then each actor takes a line or two and works out the antithesis. We discuss how the antithesis in this speech differs from the one in Henry V, *and we find all of it.*

Coach: One of you suggested that there should be an antithesis to "pride," but can't find one. "Prejudice" should be there, right? Okay, bad joke. Do you all know *Pride and Prejudice*? Have you all seen the BBC six-part version? Absolutely fabulous; I have it if anyone would like to borrow it.

Now let's look at Margaret on page 60. Just glancing at it, notice the antithesis. Here it's pretty much black and white. Who wants to read? Good. Everyone look for the antithesis as she cold-reads the speech. *(Bride reads as all others watch for antithesis.)* Look at all the antithesis in this speech. Shakespeare is filled with it, and if you don't find it and play it, you simply pass over the meaning of the line. How is the audience supposed to get it?

We talk through the antithesis in the speech and then move on. Different actors read the other speeches presented in the book and everyone helps to find the antithesis. These speeches include Petruchio, Richard II (which everyone wants to read, so all take a turn with it), Bolingbroke, and Phebe.

Coach: Wonderful. Now take your own monologues and work with the first four lines. Take your time and see what you can find. *(All work on this for fifteen minutes or so.)* Everyone please read your first four lines so we can clearly hear the antithesis. Remember, all lines don't have antithesis. You don't want to force it. *(The actors take turns and read aloud their first four lines, adding antithetical ideas to what they had read at the last session. Not all have antithesis in their first four lines.)*

That will do it for today. For next time, add antithesis to your entire monologue, and don't forget your sonnet. *(Groans.)* And don't forget, you're in this workshop by choice. You were not forced to be here.

Alex: No, I was forced. *(All laugh.)* Because I wanted to get better at this, I didn't have a choice. So I was forced.

Amber: Then so was I.

Coach: Well, I wasn't. I'm doing it because I enjoy it. Hope you're enjoying it, too. See you next time and we'll run all of the monologues, complete with antithesis.

CHAPTER 21

Session Eleven

In this session: • *Running the monologues* • *Checking word definitions*
• *Transitions* • *Breaking the attitude habit* • *Next assignment*

Coach: Today we'll run our monologues and see how your application of skills is coming along. As you know, this usually takes the complete session. So we all want to stay involved, even when we're not the one speaking. Everybody take one skill to listen for—scansion, which we'll break into two parts; stresses and irregular feet, like trochees and feminine endings; phrasing and caesuras; breathing; end-of-line-support; antithesis, word meanings that seem unclear; and speech structure. Each of you take one skill to listen for. *(They do.)* Do we have an order for the presentations? *(The actors work out an order.)* The person going first has no skill yet, but takes the skill of the person who follows next. Everyone have his or her texts? *(Everyone finds the texts of the monologues.)* Okay, let's do them, and everyone establish your breathing before you begin. Relax and breathe.

The actors run their monologues in this order: Kristin, doing Isabella in Measure for Measure, *shows good growth; Emily's Viola from* Twelfth Night *is coming very nicely; Amber does Kate from* The Taming of the Shrew *and is growing effectively; Bridgett offers Julia from* The Two Gentlemen of Verona *with only small growth; Bride's* Lady Macbeth *is satisfactory and nearly complete; Jerrod's* Othello *shows only small growth; Alex, offering Prince Hal from* Henry IV, Part 1, *has solid growth; and Maggie's Helena from* A Midsummer Night's Dream *is very successful. Alicia and Ryan are absent and have missed this opportunity. The actors listening give their notes and I check on a few word definitions. We discover a little laziness. But most have looked up their words.*

Coach: Some of you, as we noted, are really handling the skills well and are ready to move on. You still have imagery to add, but you can already start working on a delivery of the speech that allows the skills to be automatic—in other words, not obvious. Start working on being real, which is hard to do when you're concentrating on skills. But it's time to start moving on. Remember always that these skills are for the actor's preparation for rehearsal. They are for learning what the language is doing. Once you have that, forget the skills, so to speak, and start concentrating on being natural. If you know how to handle the line, which is where the skills come in, you can then trust yourself to use them automatically, and concentrate on being real in the given situation. Now we're getting to interpretation and character, which is where we want to go.

Regarding the notes in general: Those of you taking the time to breathe deeply are displaying wonderful, rich voices. You know how much I like you to breathe through your mouth, and breathe deeply. There are many coaches, voice teachers, and singing coaches who want you to breathe entirely through your nose. You can fill your lungs much faster if you breathe through the mouth, and some days your nose is plugged and you still have to breathe, and you may very well have a performance that day.

Those who are phrasing correctly are never rushing, which is very good. Most of us are having transition problems, probably because we haven't worked much on that, so remind me to get to it. What do I mean by "transition"?
Emily: Ideas are changing, so you have to do something different.
Coach: Keep going—you're on the right track.
Alex: Like in a sonnet, if the first four lines are a setup, but the fifth line changes the idea, we have to do something vocally to help the audience hear the change.
Coach: Good. And notice in these speeches how transitions occur after every few lines. At those moments, you have to help me hear the change. We'll work on that.

I'm concerned that some of you don't really know your plays. Maybe you've only read an act or two. Well, you're wasting your time. It's hard to memorize lines when you don't understand what you're saying. And if you stumble over the lines, it's impossible to phrase correctly. You must know how your speech fits into the action of the entire play—what is gained by the speech, and what is lost if the speech is cut. You absolutely have to know what you're saying. Next time I'll ask a few questions about each play.

Those who insist on adding an attitude to the speech—an early character choice like anger or irony, etc.—will soon be falling behind if they don't break that habit. Don't you want to enter rehearsals with an open mind and see what the other actors are giving you before you make those kinds of decisions? I think so.

Good work today. Next time, chapter 9, analysis. "Something wicked this way comes." See you then.

CHAPTER 22

Session Twelve

In this session: • Listening to ourselves • Questions about the plays
• Summary list of skills • Short lines • Text analysis • Checking scholarly sources
• "Natural talent" • Next assignment

Coach: Now we'll listen to ourselves. Today let's run through the monologues without comment, and I'll record them. Then we'll listen and let you point out the problems. *(They all do their monologues, and then we play them back. The actors point out what they have missed, and any other problems that are obvious on the recording.)*

Alex: I hate listening to myself.

Coach: But what did you hear?

Amber: Bad voice, not breathing right.

Bridgett: Overemphasizing the end-of-line support. I was kicking the box too hard.

Alicia: Rushing. I wasn't phrasing correctly. I understand better, now that I've heard myself.

Bride: Is my voice that high?

Maggie: Not all the time—not when you breathe more consistently.

Bridgett: It's embarrassing to stumble over a word—it really shows up.

Coach: Like we said earlier, this material will expose you more quickly than realism. It's more like singing a solo and forgetting the lyrics. We'll record again in a couple of weeks to see if you think you've improved. Now, please turn to page 64 of your book. Here's the line that introduces the chapter: "By the pricking of my thumbs, / something wicked this way comes." Who speaks that line?

Bride: One of the witches in *Macbeth*.

Coach: Right. I used it here because the "something wicked" is how many actors, especially young ones, feel about analysis. Present company excepted, of course.

Alex: Of course. *(Echo of that around the studio.)*

Coach: But first, I promised to ask a few questions about each play. *(Groans, but I ask three or four questions about each play to the actor who has the monologue from that play. They answer pretty well, so we move on.)*

Here is a summary list of all the skills and techniques we're learning. *(We review all the skills studied to date.)* The first three are clear—but number four, short or shared lines, we haven't talked about very much. What do you think?

Bridgett: Is that when another actor finishes your line with her line?

Coach: That would be a shared line—two different speeches are connected on their last and first words, respectively, half of the line from one speaker and half from the next. What about short lines?

Bride: I have one line that's only three feet. I think I'm supposed to do something to finish it out.

Coach: Most directors believe that is what "short or shared lines" require—finishing the short line with an action. At any rate, you've got to take the pause to keep the rhythm going. We've now worked on all of the skills on the list except imagery. "Text analysis" means all of these things, but it also means the specific analysis of a Shakespearean speech or sonnet. Without getting into character, we'll do a little text analysis to prepare us for imagery.

I've selected one of the sonnets as an example, number 15. To understand the possibilities of what the ideas expressed in the sonnet might mean, I've used two sources—two scholars who have analyzed the sonnet. I've already given you two analyses of your sonnets and asked you to find a third. Here we'll work with the same two. Look on page 66. I used two editions of the sonnet—Pelican and HarperCollins, and the scholars are Kerrigan and Booth. Now I'll show you why. Let's read through this sonnet nice and easy.

(Bride reads it. We pause after each idea to discuss what our first impression of the idea might be without looking ahead to see what others think. The actors come to love the sonnet, as I already do.)

Now, first we check the footnotes in the text—in our case, two texts. Notice that only one editor elects to define "holds in perfection," and the other editor elects to define "stage." Notice that all the way through, sometimes both editors define a word or phrase and sometimes they choose different ideas to define. For that reason, you're better off using more than one edition. *(We check all footnotes in both editions.)* Let's go now to the two scholars. Notice that Kerrigan elects to define lines 3 and 4 individually, but Booth puts lines 1 through 4 together.

Here's a beautiful example of how analysis helps the actor with imagery. Notice how Kerrigan defines one of the words in line 4. *(They study it.)*

Bride: He defines what the Elizabethans meant by "influence." The "stars" pour down an ethereal fluid that they call "influence."

Amber: So the stars are affecting us by pouring this fluid into us—into our ear?

Coach: I don't know about the ear, but that's probably a good assumption. Do you notice that if you as the actor are aware of Shakespeare's use of this word, it affects your imagery for that phrase?

Bride: You can really see something. "Influence" as we think of it today would be hard to find an image for.

Coach: Right. See how the actor can use this? Let's go through everything these two scholars contribute to the sonnet, which will sound all too scholarly for an actor. But there are wonderful things to discover. You don't need to pay attention to all of their analysis, as much is very scholarly—English literature—and it won't help you for performance. But if you just go through it, you'll have the discoveries—like "influence"—that you can use, and you wouldn't otherwise have these thoughts to work with.

We find many useful ideas—like "cheered" and "height" and "wear their brave state"—perhaps like some older ladies wear little fox collars on coats, and to them it is high fashion. "Height," when used to mean "later in age" or "at the peak of one's skills," becomes antithetical to "rich in youth." The actors gain a deep appreciation for the sonnet but seem strained.

Coach: It doesn't really take long to review some scholarly ideas about Shakespeare's words. Some very smart people have spent years of their lives working out these ideas, and they can help you as an actor. They will give you something you didn't have before you did this.

Do this analysis with your sonnets—but also do it with your monologues. You're already looking up the words, and that's a big part of it. It's your job as an actor to know exactly what you're saying.

Alicia: I think that's why some actors of Shakespeare, like Kenneth Branagh, seem so good. You believe they know exactly what they're saying.

Kristin: Even if you don't.

Bride: And it doesn't matter, because they know and you just accept.

Coach: Now you see why so many actors seem poor at Shakespeare. We could name many. It's hard work to get under this language, to have a complete feel for what it's doing. And who wants to work that hard?

Maggie: We like to use "natural talent."

Coach: And then you're never quite sure that you're right. So the acting seems tentative. Most of what I see in amateur Shakespeare productions has that, and sometimes even professional productions suffer from it. So how does an actor take that next step? Well, look at what we just did. If you were to perform this sonnet and only look at the footnotes, ignoring the other information that's available to you, you would never realize the discoveries we just discussed. You would never know what "influence" meant when used with "stars." Or "height" as perhaps an actor's career, or "wearing your finery," or your love becoming disfigured. If your love becomes disfigured, what does that do to you emotionally? You'll never get that from the sonnet just by reading the footnotes and relying on your "natural talent."

Any comments? Do you understand why I ask you to do this analysis? *(They do.)* Don't rely only on your natural talent. That's like a superior athlete who goes drinking every night and plays at seventy percent of his ability. Where does that take you? To a short career and depression, probably.

Next time we're going to run the monologues to see what new information you might have discovered, then move on to imagery. So complete the analysis of your monologue. See you then.

CHAPTER 23

Session Thirteen

In this session: • Running the monologues • Applying structure and
text analysis • Next assignment

Coach: Today let's run all of the monologues without much comment, but with an observation of how structure and analysis of the speeches have been applied, and how new information might have improved the speech. I'll record so you can hear what you do. This will take the entire session. Next time we'll move on to imagery.

The actors run their monologues twice. After the first time we point out very briefly how each has applied the new skills. We record the second time through, then listen to the monologues and give more extensive notes. Each actor listens to his or her own usage of the skills. The monologues are getting quite strong—only two are lagging behind.

It has been my experience that in a group of ten or twelve experienced actors, or student-actors, about six will truly learn the material, three will learn it but immediately forget it, and the others will never learn it satisfactorily and will "fall behind." Sometimes those who can't learn it simply haven't the ear to hear the skills in use, but I'm afraid that more often the problem is laziness or indifference. The latter attitude seems to stem from the belief that an actor's "natural" talent is sufficient.

In community workshops, I've taught these skills to people of all ages— including children as young as seven or eight—who have no experienced ear for dialogue but can rapidly learn the material and read it beautifully. When an experienced actor cannot or will not learn the material, his or her Shakespeare remains ponderous and unclear—and terribly boring.

Coach: Great growth today, as you can hear. I love what some of you have discovered and are able to use. That will really help you make the language your own when you get to character choices. Next time we'll apply imagery and you'll be amazed at what happens. See you then.

CHAPTER 24

Session Fourteen

In this session: • Imagery • Imagery exercise • Next assignment

Coach: Today we're working on imagery. Each of you will have an opportunity to do the imagery exercise. We do the exercise individually, so I will lead each of you through it. You can see this will take some time. But I don't think you will find it wasted, even when you're listening to others. I want your ear to start hearing what I'm hearing. Let's create an order, and we'll go as far as we can today, then continue next time. You need a clean copy of your monologue to give to your reader. Others can follow along on their copies, or just sit back and listen for what I'm listening for. Who's first?

(Emily joins me in the playing area, where I have set up one chair. Everyone else gathers around on chairs or on the floor. I'm on the floor. This exercise is written out on page 72.)

This exercise allows you to take the next step toward making the material your own. You want to control the language. Here's what we do. Emily will lie on her back on the floor and relax, arms at her sides. Amber, her reader, will sit in the chair near her. But before we use the reader, Emily will go through her monologue nice and easy so we can hear how she's doing it now. Then we'll do the exercise and hear it again. So go ahead. *(Standing, Emily reads through her monologue.)*

That was pretty clear, wasn't it? Not bad. Now lie down and be comfortable. Arms at your sides. Amber will read Emily's monologue to her slowly. As you lie there and listen to your monologue, whenever you hear anything that might generate an image, just raise your hand a little bit. The reader will pause and wait. Get the image clearly, very clearly, in your mind, and when you have secured it clearly, lower your hand and the reader will continue. At the next image, raise the hand again, etc. Do not rush. Do not think we are being bored. Don't lower your hand to signal the reader to continue until you have the image clearly, because later you will be asked to bring it back. The reader must go slowly, watch you carefully, and not try to influence you by pausing on her own if she senses an image. She doesn't pause unless you raise your hand. Everybody understand? Then let's do it.

(Amber begins reading Emily's monologue very slowly, pausing whenever she sees Emily's hand lift up, and continuing when the hand goes down. We go through the monologue this way. In fifteen lines, she finds eight or nine strong images.)

Now, stand up and go through the speech. Let your complete concentration and focus be on this: Make us, the listeners, see the same images you see. Make us see them. Don't be in a hurry. *(Emily stands and does the speech. Awesome things happen.)* For each thought, Emily has found a clarity that we never heard before, and we've heard this speech at least ten times. The ends of her phrases are strong, because she needs the emphasis to make her points. She takes her time and helps us to see what she sees, she doesn't worry about boring us, and she never rushes. And she has great commitment to the words, all of the individual words. Because she is working hard to make us see what she sees, she gains complete control of the language. The language becomes a means to an end. And that's what your character will want.

Isn't that amazing? You can't just do this by notes. Once you start trying to make us see what you see, you take amazing control of the speech. This time we saw what before we only heard you talking about. How did it feel doing it?

Emily: The images were like a slide show, popping off the back wall.

Coach: Did that damage your concentration in any way?

Emily: I already knew what I was saying, but by doing this I walked into that world. It became mine.

Coach: That's one reason why I leave this exercise for the end. I want you confident, feeling good and sounding good, then I want you to add this. You must be completely in control of your material first, and then, by actually seeing what you're saying, you gain an entirely new level of control. But remember, as with all exercises, this is a rehearsal technique. Use it when you're developing your role. Use it to help you gain complete control of the language. Then forget it. What you've put into your mind will be useful to you later, but you can't force it to happen in performance. Some of it will happen automatically, some of it will never happen. That doesn't matter. Having learned that image, you will gain control over that passage, image or not.

I love this exercise, and what it does for actors. It works every time. And notice that you can't both rush and do the imagery. And that's a great plus. Who's next?

(*We continue the exercise with Kristin, Alex, Jerrod, and Bride. Each stands to do his or her speech, and then lies down and does the imagery exercise. They then stand and do the speech again. We listen to the difference. The other actors will get their chances next time.*)

We're out of time. Great work today. See you next time.

CHAPTER 25

Session Fifteen

In this session: • *Imagery exercises* • *Next assignment*

Coach: We'll begin today with more of the imagery exercises. Let's give everyone who hasn't done the exercise a chance to try it. Remember exactly how it works. The actor first speaks the monologue. Then she lies on the floor and listens for the images, raising her hand when she hears one. She captures the image thoroughly, then lowers her hand. The reader continues until the speech is completed. The actor then stands and speaks the monologue again, working to help us see the images she sees. We listen to the changes that happen in the monologue after the images are added. So let's begin. *(The next two actors, Alicia and Amber, do the imagery exercise.)*

Does anyone think this exercise is a gimmick, or artificial?

Alex: I may not see exactly what she sees, but I'm captivated.

Emily: I like the tempo—the actor working to find the image.

Amber: I understood so many things in the monologues that I barely even heard before. So the actor must be helping the audience understand the speech, because I certainly understood more.

Coach: Yes. This is no gimmick. But a problem with this exercise is that it takes so long. If you're crunched for time, it's almost impossible to do this as a group, or to have an entire cast try it. If you have a three-month rehearsal period and actors who know the play well, you can spend two days on this and reap the benefits—for, as you can see, there are huge benefits. And this is another reason why you need a long rehearsal period to do this kind of theatre. Anything less and you are right away putting limits on what you're going to achieve. Of course, finances often dictate the rehearsal period. It's hard to do these exercises on your own, but if the director, or another actor, teaches everyone the exercise, maybe they can practice it in small groups.

Amber: One thing I did was force myself not to continue with the speech until the image had resolved itself. That forced me to slow down. It really worked for me.

Alicia: It also helps to remove attitude. I'm having that problem, but I see that concentrating on the images removes attitude.

Coach: Good. Break time.

Coach: *(After the break.)* The imagery exercise is a discovery exercise. You work to discover what else is in a speech—what else after you have completed your analysis. After imagery, the speech is pretty much yours, and you are in a position to hear any direction and let your character try anything without stumbling over the language. We're about ready to start talking character. But let's finish up. Who's next? *(The next actor, Maggie, works the imagery exercise. We discuss all of the discoveries we hear.)*

Something else you may have noticed. When you're concentrating on using the images, you stop trying to "perform" the monologue. Other exercises have also helped with that, and this one certainly contributes.

Alicia: I felt weird doing this exercise. It was like I actually went someplace else.

Coach: You're all doing very well on this exercise. Any questions? See you next time, when we'll finish up imagery and move on to "moving the language forward."

CHAPTER 26

Session Sixteen

In this session: • Imagery exercise • Falling behind • Actor questions
• Finding the images in text • Intentions and actions • Active and
passive choices • Next assignment

Coach: While we conclude the imagery exercise, let's add a new dimension. While the next actor is listening for images, and raising her hand and holding it to firmly grasp the image, everyone else lie on their back and also listen for the images. Let's see if you see images similar to what Bridgett sees, and how that affects your concentration as a listener. This is just for fun. I have no idea what it might lead to. I've never tried this before. But every time I do this Shakespeare workshop, I like to try one or two new things to find new exercises. Okay, let's do the last one. *(The next actor, Bridgett, does the imagery exercise, with everyone else working along with her. We discuss the changes in the monologue after she has found the images. Then we discuss the involvement of the other actors.)*

Emily: Probably what I saw wasn't what she saw. We can't really know what she sees.

Amber: The listener will probably never have the exact same image as the actor.

Alex: It doesn't matter. We see some of what the actor is seeing and we know she is seeing something. We don't see the world she's in.

Coach: How much do you want to get into that world?

Emily: I don't know. It's so much easier lying down than when you stand up.

Coach: Isn't that the point of rehearsal? To find what you can get out of the material, including the other characters, then work on making it all believable?

Bride: To me, the second time she did the monologue I wanted to know what she was seeing, which made me concentrate on every word. The first time it was all more general.

Coach: What about when you're still reading a line incorrectly? I heard three or four in that last speech. What's that telling us?

Bridgett: I haven't worked enough on it. I will before next time.

Coach: You're assuming that we can follow you, but that doesn't put you in command of the language.

Bridgett: I can tell I'm doing that.

Coach: What about the rest of you? Did you get anything from listening for her images?

Alex: It's interesting in itself, but it just sort of informs me that she's going to find an image at that spot.

Amber: I kind of like to be surprised by her images, and when I'm already connected to the image it seemed to take something away.

Coach: That surprises me, but no doubt that is what you experienced. For me, when I see and hear professional actors perform one of the plays I know really well, I'm always delighted when they handle an idea or an image or a character in a different but honest way.

Amber: I don't think that's the same as lying here and listening specifically for images.

Bride: But if I were directing this play, it would be amazing to do the imagery exercise with the entire play. I would see what all the actors would be looking for, and might be able to help them.

Coach: You're right, of course. Oh, well, it was worth a try. So what do these images have to do with directing Shakespeare?

Bride: From a directing point of view, I liked hearing the concentration, even though the tempo was very slow. That can be fixed later.

Coach: Yes. We don't ever want to force tempo—except perhaps in farce. The tempo will happen, and you can encourage the actor to think faster. He will automatically pick it up.

Amber: Good images are helpful for staging purposes—like pictures. I might not use them, but they are there to consider.

Coach: This is kind of tacky, but it's also funny. I have a basic rule for directing Shakespeare and keeping the action moving—and it's a sexual analogy. It's, don't stop, don't stop, don't stop! Let's take ten!

Coach: *(After the break.)* A couple of you are having problems. You continue to rush, and you don't seem to concentrate. Can you tell us what the problem is—what you're feeling when you do your monologue?

Bridgett: I guess this isn't my gig.

Coach: What do you mean?

Bridgett: Doing Shakespeare. I don't think I can be any good at it.

Coach: Is doing Shakespeare any harder than anything else?

Bridgett: There are more words to learn and deal with.

Maggie: You really have to prepare to do it. In another play I'm working on, we had it memorized in two days. The words were so simple, and there was no structure, in the sense that you mean it—oh, I know there was structure, but it seemed so much easier.

Alicia: You can't be lazy and expect to do this material. Like you said, it exposes you.

Alex: There's something good, though. The structure, especially in the verse, makes it very easy to memorize—at least for me. And the breaking it down, the analysis, gives me a confidence I don't always have with other plays.

Kristin: When you do it well it seems so real.

Coach: Which is the actor's job, right? Make it real for the audience. So the idea of preparation is probably very important.

Jerrod: I sometimes feel overwhelmed.

Coach: How can you get past that?

Jerrod: I have to be willing to put a lot more hours into it.

Coach: That's probably true. Now that you've all seen the kinds of skills it takes just to read this language—read it so that others can understand both you and the language—it does appear that the larger the role you get in a Shakespearean play, the more hours it will take to prepare. If you're not interested in doing that, or haven't the time, best to stick to the smaller roles and do them well.

Let's all sit around the table. *(We do.)* Please turn to the imagery chapter of the book, page 70 and the next page. Shakespeare's characters need images to express themselves. We don't write this way anymore. Some authors use images, but it doesn't seem that the characters need those images; they could as easily make their point in another way. Perhaps in some Tennessee Williams we can find some of Shakespeare's type of imagery. But look at Juliet's speech—a thirteen-year-old girl—and she uses nine images in seven lines. *(We read through the "Gallop apace" speech and discuss the images.)*

And look at Chorus describe the King's departure in the *Henry V* speech. Look at the images in those few lines. You can all see those images—the ships, the sails, the boys climbing the rigging, the prow of the ship breaking the waves, etc. Now, that can all be very lovely—and passive. How do you make it active? Imagery will temp you to be sentimental or reflective. Reflective would be natural, and it would probably be passive, wouldn't it? And what about lyricism? But you can't play lyricism on top of lyricism. The language may be lyrical already, so you have to find something else. If you don't, it's as boring as watching an actor play a villain by using only the villainous characteristics—villainy on top of villainy. But if the character is already a villain, you don't need to play that. If you do, you're completely one-dimensional.

If the passage is lyrical, that quality has to be there automatically, and you have to be playing something far more active. I wonder what that could be?
Maggie: Your action.
Coach: Yes, now we have to return to playing our action. You have to drive the language, not lay back on it. And you drive it to reach your intention. Sentimentality, reflection, and surface attitudes like villainy are almost always in the way of driving your language to get to your objective, unless you elect to use one of them for a specific reason. Let's take the first four lines of a monologue and read them as you have been reading them, then we'll check for clarity of intention. *(Amber reads her first lines.)*

> Kate: Such duty as the subject owes the prince,
> Even such a woman oweth to her husband;
> And when she is froward, peevish, sullen, sour,
> And not obedient to his honest will,
> What is she but a foul contending rebel
> And graceless traitor to her loving lord?

Coach: That's very lovely and very passive. What is your intention? *(She struggles to explain it.)* What do you really want?

I am so often surprised when reaching this point of the workshop. Defining intention and playing the action are at the core of realistic actor training, along with finding the motivations and using the subtext. These actors have all had considerable actor training and many are very active in productions. Because of their experience, I always assume the actors can state intentions and define and play actions, and usually discover that they can't articulate their intentions at all.

Amber: She's playing the game, going along with what her husband wants her to do.
Coach: Intentions aren't reflective or sentimental ideas—intentions are active pursuits, achieved through actions. What is the real action in this speech?
Amber: To please her husband.
Coach: That's a long-term intention, but it's not an action. What's a physical action you need to achieve here?
Amber: Berate these two women.
Coach: That's an action. And what do you hope to achieve by berating them?
Amber: I keep going back to pleasing the husband.
Coach: Sentimentality. Don't you want these two women to respond to exactly what you tell them to do? Wouldn't that be the first step in winning

your husband's approval? He's waiting for you to bring out the other two wives, which you've done. Now he wants you to teach them what's what.

Amber: She wants to achieve a good marriage.

Coach: Yes, so what are your actions to get to that objective?

Amber: To get these two women to do what I tell them to do.

Coach: How will you measure that?

Amber: They either do or they don't.

Coach: So what is your intention?

Amber: To make these women do exactly what I want.

Coach: And if they don't, you're going to pull out their hair! So what is your action?

Amber: To make them do it!

Coach: So let's go through the speech without you giving those women a choice. You need to be firm, right? And don't dawdle, because that lets them walk away. You can't allow them to walk away. If you do that, you're not being active. You have to kick their butts if they don't do what you want—they must not dare to walk away. *(Amber reads the lines again.)*

You're *suggesting* that they do what you want. You're not insistent. And you're not using some of the wonderful words—like "foul," and "graceless," and "traitor." And the other two men are standing by your husband with their hands out, ready to win the "one hundred crowns" bet. You can't "suggest" or drag it out. *(She reads the lines again, this time with more insistence and more quickly, not allowing the other two women to ignore her. It's much improved because Amber is playing her simple action of making the women do what she wants them to do.)*

As soon as you can define your intention and play the actions that get you to it, you immediately gain strength and believability. But actors have such trouble defining their intentions and isolating their actions. Amber, you've got it now, and I look forward to hearing the entire speech.

Amber: Well, I feel more secure with the speech, and I understand the intention and actions thing, but I'm unclear about sentimentality. What makes it sentimental?

Coach: In the lines above, suggesting rather than insisting is sentimental. The sentimental is based on an attitude and emotion, rather than an action. It's the "nice" approach to an action, "nice" at all costs. But it's rarely active. It's reflective—and it's the assumption that what you want is clear, even without you going after it. Let's take the line "I am ashamed that women are so simple / To offer war where they should kneel for peace." If you read the line based on an emotion—for example, nostalgic—it would be a very "nice" line, but that would not support your intention and your action is sentimental, rather than active. Does that make sense? *(They say it does.)* Now, let's do the speech again, and this time add two people to play the wives. *(Kristin and Emily become the wives.)* The wives should ignore you if you allow them to. And you should handle them in whatever way you need, including physically, to achieve your goals. *(We try this various times, and the struggle with the other two women helps Amber clarify her actions. She also develops much more physical strength—which she needs to control the indifferent women—and a stronger walk. She also uses her height to her advantage.)*

This, again, is a rehearsal exercise. In performance you may or may not physically handle the two wives—that's to be determined in rehearsal. But using the wives here has helped Amber define her action, and play it. Now she could play the action with various intensities, depending on choices in rehearsal.

Remember, achieving your intention is measured in the other person. You win or lose based on what they do *when you've completed your action.* If the two women do what Kate wants, then she's achieved her intention. If they don't, she hasn't.

Let's read a few lines and illustrate different pits we can fall into if we're not playing our actions. Somebody read four lines very sentimentally. *(Alex reads Prince Hal sentimentally and we get a lot of laughs.)* Now reflectively. *(Bride reads Lady Macbeth reflectively and we all pretend to fall asleep.)* We could keep going, but you can see how easy it is to resort to attitudes, and when you do that, the language just dies. Play your actions!

Bride: Hard!

Coach: Yes. But you're all capable.

(We then work with the intentions of Emily's Viola speech and Bride's Lady Macbeth. I try to give thirty to forty minutes to clarifying intentions in each speech. We'll get to the others next time.) Remember, rehearse this material out loud, not to yourself. It needs the vocal energy. So now, at this point in your work, you know the speeches, so forget about learning lines and all the other skills, which will come automatically, and start concentrating on your intention. Drive your words to reach your intention. Look at some examples on video. Now that you know what to look for, watch some really fine actors handle the language, and a character, and watch how the character needs the language to reach the intention.

We're into character, right? You've got the language—you know what it's doing—so who is it that is saying these words, and why does he or she need them? That's your character. Now that you have the language, your character won't stumble over it—which would ruin your character and immediately make her phony.

I'm anxious to start running the monologues and discussing the characters who speak them. But first, we'll do the intention work that we did today with all of the other speeches. We'll want to know your exact intention—why you're saying these specific words. And I'll be asking you to read the speeches with different intentions, even though they might be totally wrong, so you can feel how the language serves you and is never in your way. These words will allow you to play an action and to reach a goal, regardless of what the goal is. I'll prove that to you.

We'll define all intentions next time—be prepared with yours—and then record the monologues with your intentions played, then again with a new intention given to you. The words will get you there, as you'll hear. See you next time.

CHAPTER 27

Session Seventeen

In this session: • *Character* • *The actor's job* • *Being specific*
• *Defining character intentions* • *More enhancing verbs* • *Active intentions*
• *Using the skills subconsciously* • *More listening to ourselves*
• *Becoming natural* • *Next assignment*

Coach: Today the actors we didn't get to last time will state their character's intentions in the respective speeches, and we'll work on applying those intentions. Later, we'll work on character to the extent that we have time remaining in the workshop. For more extensive work on character and scene study, you'll need to enroll in another workshop, one that has that focus. Here, in summary, we learned the skills required to speak the language convincingly, to speak it confidently, and to know what we're saying. With that ammunition, our characters can move and speak and relate to other characters without the burden of language block, or language fear. What do you think is the greater obstacle to good Shakespeare performance, fear of the language or unwillingness to learn how to handle it?

Kristin: A weeks few ago I would have said fear, because that's what I had.

Alicia: Me, too. But after a few sessions I lost my fear and realized how much work it was going to be to learn how to speak it. So I think you start with fear as an obstacle, but later that changes.

Coach: I think that's an accurate observation, and is probably applicable to most actors who study this material. Do you trust yourselves to use the skills and handle the language to the point that you don't need to think about it? Because if you do, you're ready to develop your character.

Amber: I trust myself right now. I don't know about next year. And what if you have a director who doesn't require the actors to—well, for example—support the end-of-the-verse lines? Everything will be very sluggish, and what can the actors to do about it?

Coach: Not an enviable situation, is it? But remember, learning your language and developing your character is an actor's responsibility. Doing the homework is your job. In the situation you mention, you might have to get some actors together outside of rehearsal and work on the language, listening to and helping each other.

Bride: I feel that way too, but what do I do if I'm working with an actor who just paraphrases and generalizes, yet thinks he's doing it right?

Coach: I can't really answer that, because it would depend on the situation. But would the problem be any different if, instead of a heightened-text play, you were doing a realistic play? If the other actor is paraphrasing and generalizing, you still have the same problem: how to get him to be "specific." In heightened-text plays, there are certainly a few more steps involved to reach "specific," but the goal is the same.

Always remember that when you speak the words you've memorized, you communicate your character's intention to the other actors. Don't let *your* intentions be general, reflective, or not measurable. For example, "To make her understand how I feel" is not a good intention, because "understand" is not measurable. And there's something else it's not—it's not an action. State your intention *as an action* that will affect another character—or maybe just the audience, if you have a soliloquy. If your fellow actors are paraphrasing and generalizing, remember that intentions are *measured in the other characters*, not in the speaker.

Another example: Let's say my intention is "to make you realize that I don't like the way you're talking to me." As an actor, you work with "make you realize"—but it's vague; it gives you so little to work with. And if the person does "realize" what you mean, how will we, the audience, know that? However, using the same intention, if you make it, "to belittle him for talking to me that way," now you have something to play. "To belittle" is active and playable. If you communicate that action, and the other character backs away or crawls under a table or something, we can then see that you've achieved your intention; you have a *reaction*! So, your success is measured in the other character. Notice how we enhanced the verb to make the action more effective.

I hope that helps you some. I'd have to be working with the actor to give more precise suggestions. Maybe give him a copy of the book! Let's do some more work on intentions.

We work for a long time on finding ways to make the intentions active and measurable. There is much agony and searching. Eventually, the actors restate the intentions. They have become much more active. Here is one choice for each:

Jerrod's Othello: Demean Desdemona for doing what you think she's done.
Kristin's Isabella: Appeal to Claudio's love, then reject him.

Alicia's Lady Margaret: Intimidate, scorn, and divorce him.

Bridgett's Julia: Strive to bring Proteus back—by reassembling those pieces of the letter on which both names are written.

Alex's Prince Hal: Command your rightful place.

Maggie's Helena: Embarrass Hermia, and entreat her to illustrate her skills in wooing Demetrius.

Bride's Lady Macbeth: Conjure the strength and method to do the deed.

Amber's Kate: Provoke the women to do what you need them to do.

Emily's Viola: Stroke Olivia's ego.

Coach: You might elect to use other intentions, of course—whatever works for you. But these examples are active choices. Be sure yours is active. When playing your intentions, once they're active, forget this is verse. Just go after your goal. The verse won't get in the way, because you know how to use it. Forget all of that—just go out and achieve your goal. Don't allow me as the audience to ignore you. So don't suggest, be specific. Demand that I pay attention to you. If you can state the urgency that causes you to speak, that will help you considerably. The stakes for your character must be clear in your mind.

We agree on at least one intention for each speech and practice the urgency of speaking to achieve our intention. We run some of the monologues, working to play the intention in a direct and honest way. This is tedious and takes a lot of time, but in the end the monologues are more specific and honest. Everyone agrees that improvement has been made.

Amber: I don't know how to play my intention and antithesis at the same time.

Coach: Forget antithesis! You already know how to play it. If you've done your analysis, and you have, it will happen automatically. Remember, forget the skills. Throw them away now! All of that work and money was for nothing! *(Laughs.)*

Kristin: Verse was always foreign to me, but we really have to be confident with it—have the language down solid, isn't that it, before we can play our intention?

Coach: I understand what you mean, but, no, you actually could start right out playing some intention. What do you think the result would be? Would it be successful? For example, if I had asked each of you to come to this workshop with a monologue already memorized, which you all would have done to some degree, and the very first session I asked you to perform the monologue with a specific intention, what would happen?

Emily: I see. You could create and play an intention, but who would listen or understand? The language would be a muddle and would get in your character's way.

Coach: Sure would. Yet we often see that. It's a lot easier to go straight to intention and character and skip learning the skills.

Maggie: So the only difference between heightened text, like Shakespeare, and realism is in the difficulty of the language?

Coach: That's pretty much it. I'm reminded of that line from the film *A League of Their Own* when Geena Davis' character quits the baseball team and says, "It just got too hard." And the Tom Hanks character says, "It's supposed to be hard. If it wasn't hard, everyone would do it. The hard is what makes it great!" In other words, when you master that which is "hard," the result is on a much higher level than when you master "easy." In our case, the result is acting a role by speaking incredibly powerful language, all blended together into a work of art—something of beauty. The actor's art blending with the playwright's—but neither cheating the other. (*We finish running the monologues, working the same issues. Most improve, and we take a break.*)

Coach: (*After the break.*) Let's tape the speeches now, then listen to them so that you can hear what intention you're using, and see if the audience can hear it. (*We record all the monologues, listening to each played back. This takes a great deal of time, but the actors clearly hear what they've accomplished.*)

This language is so rich, there is so much for the actor to work with, if you only know where to look for it! Well, now you all have a pretty good idea of what it is and where to look. Of course, doing it is something else.

Remember that for most monologues, you need to find ways to do more with important words, words that allow you to be specific about what you mean. Find those, use them; don't be timid with them. You each have a number of those words in your chosen monologues; here's one from each: In *Henry IV*, "scour" comes to mind—what a great word; in *Othello*, "steeped"; in *Henry VI, part 3*, "shame"; in *Macbeth*, "chastise"; *A Midsummer Night's Dream*, "sway"; *The Taming of the Shrew*, "ashamed"; *Measure for Measure*, "reprieve"; *The Two Gentlemen of Verona*, "wounded"; *Twelfth Night*, "hallo."

Those are just examples. You each have many wonderful active words. And also remember to look for transition moments and use your voice to best advantage.

Bride: What do you mean?

Coach: In some speeches, the passion, intensity, even the tempo increase as you progress. You "climb the ladder" when, for example, you go from gentle to intense. Use that shift to your advantage. You voice can indicate these transitions, which, in turn, helps the audience hear and understand the sequence of ideas.

Just remember to work on simply being real, not "performing." When actors begin on Shakespeare, they sometimes believe they have to "perform" their character, which is almost always a bad choice. It's natural that all of the monologues are a little wooden at the moment, which is caused by our specific work on skills—so try to forget the skills and work to make your speaking completely natural. Trust yourself that the skills you've learned will make the language understandable and you won't trip over it. And making the character real and honest is now your job. So those are your assignments. Plus, next time I'll be asking you questions about your character and his or her place in the play. We've got two more sessions to see how many of these things we can accomplish. Then we'll bring in some friends to see you do the monologues. See you next time.

CHAPTER 28

Session Eighteen

In this session: • *Knowing your character* • *Character questions*
• *More listening to ourselves* • *Physicalization* • *Next assignment*

Coach: Today I'm going to ask you questions about your characters. These are the questions for each of you. Do you think this character could be you? Could you do what this character does? In other words, do you need to do anything other than be yourself in the situation? Who is your character and what does she believe? What does your character actually do? Why does she *do* what she does?

Can you see your character's position? What are the stakes for her? Do you understand how her background allows her to do what she does? Does your character state what she wants, or does she suggest? Who are you speaking to? What is her intention—why are you bothering to say these words? How does she propose to reach her goal?

Okay, who would like to answer the questions first? *(Nobody volunteers.)* Alicia, how about you and Queen Margaret? *(Alicia takes the chair across from me.)*
Coach: What's the matter?
Alicia: I'm scared.
Coach: There's nothing to be scared of. I promise there is no torture in this. Do you have clearly in your head the place and reason for this character in the play?
Alicia: Yes, I think so.
Coach: Could this character be you, had you lived at that time?
Alicia: Perhaps. She's strong and quite vocal. If that's me. I guess it is.
Coach: To play this role, do you need to do anything but be yourself in the situation?

Alicia: Not really.

Coach: Now that you know what she's saying, do you know who she is?

Alicia: She's extremely loyal, she wishes she had more power, she thinks her husband is a coward.

Coach: Why does she think that? He's a king.

Alicia: He maintains that he was forced into his weak position, but she doesn't believe that.

Coach: Can you see his position at all?

Alicia: No, not really. I see only my position.

Coach: Is she a mother?

Alicia: She's a mother and a monarch.

Coach: So *her* power is being usurped as well. How strong can you be?

Alicia: She can be very strong, to the point of leading the army. And she's going to divorce him. Researching the words, this is the first time "divorce" is used in English—in her line. It's also the *OED*'s example.

Coach: Then it's probably one of the words Shakespeare invented. Does she hold back—that is, does she suggest things or demand them?

Alicia: I think she looks down on him. She doesn't need to suggest.

Coach: Who are you speaking to?

Alicia: She's speaking to her husband, the king.

Coach: And what is her intention? Why does she bother to say these words?

Alicia: She wants her son reinstated—but she has more problems than just that.

Coach: Okay, so what is she trying to do, just in this speech?

Alicia: She's demanding that he take responsibility for what he's done, and that he stop blaming it on other people.

Coach: How would he take that responsibility? What do you actually want him to do?

Alicia: Own up to what he's done?

Coach: How would he do that?

Alicia: Stop blaming other people.

Coach: How would he do that? Remember, your intention is measured in the other character. Being successful with your intention depends on what your fellow actor does when you finish. What might he do?

Alicia: I want him to be ashamed of what he's done, to take some action—

Coach: But that's a long-term goal. What about right this minute? *(Long pause.)* You see what I'm after, right? I want you to be really clear about what you're trying to achieve with these immediate words.

Alicia: After this speech, she just leaves the room.

Coach: So what is your immediate intention?

Alicia: To shame him.

Coach: Into what?

Alicia: Into reinstating his son. But you say that's too far away.

Coach: So what about right now?

Alicia: I guess he could reinstate his son right now—he's the king. He could write an order right now.

Coach: Good, that's an achievable intention. You're going to get that written order. And when you don't get it, you divorce him. Are you going after him directly, or are you going to suggest this intention?

Alicia: I think I'll try it various ways.

Coach: "Shame" is a pretty strong verb.

Alicia: Maybe I'll go directly after him.

Coach: I think you're pretty clear about your character. Now you simply decide the way you want to play her. Shall we give it a try? If you'll get the hair out of your face ...

Alicia: I know! I have it pinned, it just won't stay. *(Maggie brings her more pins and we get the hair out of her face.)*

Alicia does the monologue, and we work with the speech and do it three times. Then I give her a completely new intention, one that is totally wrong for the situation. I tell her, "Convince him that you really don't want to divorce him, that he should come to you in gratitude when you finish speaking." She does the speech with that goal. She uses her words to reach her goal, even though the goal is a poor choice for the character. We illustrate that once you know the language and the character, you can play it any way that's asked of you. By working off of the other characters in the play, you will find the way you actually want to play your character.

Coach: Everyone, remember to express your intention with an active verb—one that clearly allows you to act it, not think about it, like Alicia's "shame." What do you want the other character to do once you have finished speaking? Remember, success in reaching your intention is measured in what the other person does. So what do you want him to do—right this minute, not long-term? I want you to be really clear about what you want to happen *right now*, as you finish speaking.

And please don't allow your hair to hang in your face. Don't let your acting be about hair—we see enough of that every day.

I ask these questions, or similar questions, of each actor, and after they complete the discussion, answering as best they can, they stand up and do their monologue, which I record. We replay each monologue, and all of the actors listen and comment. This takes a lot of time but is very much worth it. After we have heard the monologues played back, I make some blocking suggestions that they will try next time.

We also talk about physicalization for many of the characters. Everyone participates in these discussions.

I then give each actor a specific assignment that is based on the weakest skill we heard, or didn't hear, in the monologue. In this type of discussion about character background and choices, which we do sitting face to face, I again discover that most of the actors cannot state their intention with an active verb. Some cannot say what response they want from the character they are speaking to. They do answer most of the other questions.

Coach: We all noticed how weak we were in stating our intentions with active verbs. For some very good information on this skill, see William Ball's book, *A Sense of Direction.* You should all own it. He has a superb chapter on verbs and enhancing first choices of verbs into verbs an actor can really play. Are there questions or comments?

Alicia: Why didn't you ask those questions about our characters a long time ago?

Coach: Because then you would be concentrating on character traits and not on learning the language skills. And your wonderful work on learning the character would be wasted because nobody would understand what you were saying.

Alex: I have to admit that I like feeling confident with the language. When we started, I didn't feel that confidence at all.

Coach: Next time, we'll offer our monologues and just see what we've accomplished. And I want you to give me your sonnets with the complete analysis so that I can see you analyze something other than one monologue. See you next time.

Session Nineteen

In this session: • Achieving your intention • Loving your words
• Adding a monologue partner • Blocking suggestions • Actor reactions to partners
• Rhetorical questions • Prepare for performance

Coach: Thanks for all the sonnets that are stacked up here. I'll go through your analyses and return them to you next time. Today we're going to do our monologues and enjoy it, by God! That's like "Try to relax," isn't it? But seriously, I want you to work on shaking it loose, on not letting nerves make you tight, on not evaluating yourself while you work. Think only about achieving your intention by using Shakespeare's words. We could change the words, couldn't we? We could rewrite the speech so that the character would speak only realism, and then everyone would have an easier job of it. But that misses the point, doesn't it?

These are magnificent words, and you've learned how to speak them. Now it's time for the character to speak them. I encourage you to find an appreciation for the opportunity to speak them. You probably won't get many Shakespeare productions in your careers, but that shouldn't stop you from loving the words. You probably won't play Emily Dickinson either, unless you do *The Belle of Amherst*, but that shouldn't stop you from loving her words.

Play with your words, use them, don't let them use you. Take any chances and any liberties you feel like—treat this like a rehearsal and experiment without fear. Who's first?

Maggie does the first monologue, then I add a second actor, giving Helena a Hermia to talk to—rather than, for example, focusing on a spot on the back wall. Before proceeding, we add second actors to all of the monologues except the Lady Macbeth soliloquy; in this case, we decide the audience can be the listener—as Shakespeare probably intended. Partners added include a Desdemona for Othello, a brother for Isabella, an Olivia for Viola, a king for Prince Hal, a Hermia for Helena, a friend and confidant for Julia (and actors to play the wind and blow about the torn pieces of the letter), two wives for Katherine, and a king for Margaret. Using a partner, Maggie now does her monologue again, and it becomes more specific and takes on more solid emotional involvement. Everyone sees the value of the partner.

Coach: I always like to add partners so that you can connect with someone and work off his reactions. And you people playing the partner, don't stand like a stick—you can react and you can move, even if seated, by turning, etc. Do what the words require you to do. Of course, in most auditions, but not all, you just get up and do your piece or read from the script. But some directors will pair you up, when the union allows it, and now you see that that can add to or detract from your work. Partners can sometimes upstage. But for workshop rehearsing I like using the partner. Of course, when we expand the monologue to the scene, a second or third character is already there.

(We run the other monologues and discuss each one, preparing to run them again. I make more blocking suggestions for the second run.)

Notice some common notes: Finding and using important and useful words is still incomplete for some of you; if you're stiff, you know it; if you can't stop judging yourself while acting, you know it. Tell yourself to shut up—let the character talk.

Kristin: When I'm the partner, I hear things I didn't hear before—when I was just sitting out here and listening.

Coach: Yes, you're more involved, aren't you? And you want to speak. When there is time, I enjoy allowing the partner to speak—say anything you like that's an honest response to what the speaker has said. It rattles the speaker, but it also makes him hear and not be rhetorical. The speaker can't help but see how the listener responds, and must respond in turn, using only the set words. It's a frustrating but fun exercise. It's especially good if someone is becoming extremely rhetorical. What do I mean by that?

Amber: He doesn't expect a response?

Coach: Yes. A rhetorical question is posed but is not meant to get a response. Not much for duet acting scenes, is it? But you can break the habit by allowing the partner to respond. The speaker gets a response, whether or not he wants one.

Maybe we'll have time to try one exercise where the partner is allowed to speak. There are so many things we need time for!

Bride: I like the monologues better when there's a partner. People seem to be connecting rather than just presenting. Not that they were "performing" in the negative sense, but with a partner we don't seem to be talking to the air or, like you said, some spot on the back wall, or even speaking to an imagined listener. I was taught in acting classes to do that.

Amber: What do I do when my voice goes back up and I can't keep it down?

Coach: Short of practice, practice, practice? More voice work with a good leader. It also might help you to get your voice established where you want it before you walk onstage. Stay in the wings and establish your voice. Something else that is often useful: Select a few checkpoints in your work, like a line of only one word, or a special word or line. Train yourself to speak that word or line at a certain pitch, one that pulls you down in case you've gone up. A barometer, so to speak—a checkpoint. Good work today. Next time, our last, we'll have some friends in to hear you.

CHAPTER 30

Session Twenty: The Final Session

In this session: • Performance • Summary
• Actor comments about the workshop

Coach: Thanks to our guests for stopping by to hear our Shakespeare. There's been some hard work, and much of it has really paid off. Let's begin.

I introduce each monologue as the actor comes forward. The audience is very appreciative of the work and responds enthusiastically. All monologues are recorded so that the actors can hear their final product. The growth since the first session is amazing. After the guests have departed, we try to sum up.

Coach: Now that you can make the language work, I encourage all of you to find some good scene workshops, environments where you can really concentrate on character development and character relationships. We were able to do a little of that, but it wasn't the intent of this workshop. Our job was to bring the language under control and make it clear. Depending on where you live, and will live, I hope you can find a character-study workshop. Doing that, while not forgetting how to discover the language, is the next step in your evolution as a Shakespearean actor.

When you hear about a professional production of one of these plays, go see it. I've often driven a thousand miles to see a good production, and have rarely regretted it. I go to the Shakespeare festivals in the United States and in Canada, and to the shows in New York and London. I don't ever seem to get too much of it! Perhaps some of you will develop that same enthusiasm.

Comments or reactions? Perhaps each of you would tell us one thing the workshop meant to you, or something you got out of it that might help you in your career. Would you do that?

Speak for yourselves; my wit is at an end.
LOVE'S LABOR'S LOST, V, ii

Alicia: One of the things I learned that is easily transferable to other aspects of acting is the kick-the-box activity. Also, keeping breath support throughout the line is so important to all acting, yet it is amazing how many actors don't do it. I also thought that Shakespeare had subtext, but Shakespeare doesn't have subtext because the lines tell you what the character is feeling. Adding a subtext that conflicts with what the lines are saying is distracting.

Amber: By developing a better feeling for scansion, I learned how to elide words and which words to stress in both verse and prose. I also have specific areas of growth to work on, long after this workshop is over.

Bridgett: I made lots of discoveries that will help me in my acting career, like supporting ends of lines and kicking the box to help me with falling inflections. I learned a lot about myself. Conquering my mental block of "Oh, crap, it's Shakespeare" really made me realize my strengths and weaknesses as an actor. I know that if I want to do Shakespeare, I have a long way to go. But at least I know where to start.

Emily: Many of the exercises used for Shakespeare's text can be used in contemporary texts as well, and really aid in both understanding the playwright's intent as well as creating believability for both actor and director. I have and will continue to make use of these exercises and skills, particularly breathing and kicking the box. While they are helpful for the actor, I found all of these skills and exercises especially helpful as a director.

Bride: Aside from the skills, really putting myself in the world of Shakespeare—knowing the meaning of the language and what life was like at the time—helps me feel connected to the character. I understand and love Shakespeare. Like you, I hate bad Shakespeare. It makes me want to set fire to the stage!

Alex: Discovering the tricks of Shakespeare made me realize I didn't need to push and "try too hard" to be real. Once I realized I could act Shakespeare realistically, it gave me more confidence with realistic contemporary works as well.

Maggie: Learning the skills it takes to understand and perform Shakespeare made me realize what you must do for any script. Whether it is contemporary or heightened language, the skills I learned for Shakespeare finally showed me how important each step is for any script and character. Now I am able to take a script and confidently break it down. When I look at my character's dialogue, I now find important words that help me understand the character. Phrasing, playing important words, and remembering to kick the box makes every thought and action of the character necessary. Instead of picking up a script and trying to immediately "act," I now fully analyze and take all the steps needed. Doing this will eventually create the character on its own. It isn't until you have broken down the script and the words of your character that you can begin to make your own choices to bring that character to life.

Jerrod: After taking a Shakespeare workshop, one thing that really helped me was the application of these skills to modern plays. Working on modern scripts will be a lot easier for me now.

Coach: Thanks for your comments, and for being such good sports for my recording of the workshop. And so we end it. And there will be no mouthing of words, I pray you.

Here is the end of the charge.
MUCH ADO ABOUT NOTHING, III, iii

_____

PART THREE

For Secondary Schools and Community Theatres: Reading Shakespeare Aloud

I have studied eight or nine wise words to speak to you,

MUCH ADO ABOUT NOTHING, III, ii

CHAPTER 31

Reading Shakespeare Aloud

IN THIS CHAPTER, selected material from part 1 is condensed for second-ary English and drama teachers, and students who may not have time to study the complete book. High school students could begin their Shakespeare studies with this chapter. Shakespeare reading groups and persons who simply enjoy reading the plays and poems could also begin here. When more detailed instruction is needed, refer to part 1.

Worksheets are included. These may be enlarged and reproduced so that each reader or student has a copy. Combined with the worksheets, a teacher might use this chapter as an outline for a unit of instruction on Shakespeare. Selected scenes and monologues suitable for student practice are listed.

While studying specific skills, examples of film and video performances as noted in part 5 may be helpful. For the student who wants additional study, many useful works are included in the bibliography.

What is the end of study, let me know?
LOVE'S LABOR'S LOST, I, i

PREPARATION

Many people do not realize that Shakespeare is meant to be read or spoken aloud. Not only is the work better aloud, it is ten times better! By learning only a few reading (and acting) skills, anyone can read and enjoy the plays, sonnets, and poems.

Most Shakespearean studies concentrate on one of these:
- "Meaning" of the thoughts, metaphors, or imagery
- The historical significance of specific events as they relate to the plays
- Analysis of characters—why do they do this or that?

These types of studies are important and will help you as an actor or reader. They are especially helpful when acting or reading a "realistic" play, which means a play with language written like modern speech. On the other hand, with a Shakespearean play, that research and background won't help you in the same way.

Background knowledge is useful only *after* you've taken a preliminary step not usually necessary with a realistic play. With Shakespeare, or any play written in "heightened" language—which is language composed with a specific rhythmic pattern—you must first learn *what* the language is doing and read it according to its rhythm and meter. If you don't first learn the skills required to speak the language, information from other studies won't do you one bit of good, because the listener will have no idea what you are saying.

You may already believe that Shakespeare is too difficult to understand. Perhaps you have heard it read aloud, or read it aloud yourself, and concluded that it makes no sense. If that is the case, you are simply reading without applying the speaking skills required to clarify the language, or you are hearing someone else read who is not using the skills. Of course, once you've learned the skills, any background information can and should be used to make your reading or acting as complete and truthful as possible. But first you must know and use the speaking skills.

Here is a helpful analogy: You want to play a song on the piano. You bang away at the keys, but don't know which ones to hit. How many listeners will recognize the song? With Shakespeare, the words are the notes. Hit the right notes, and the listener will know what you mean.

FOUR SIMPLE SKILLS

The key to reading Shakespeare aloud is knowing which words to emphasize. Selecting these words is really quite simple, and the following easy-to-learn skills will get you started. If this information is completely new to you, don't feel alone. Most people, including many actors, haven't a clue how to do this. But if you use these four skills and read the verse aloud, it will make sense:
- Support the final word in each line
- Emphasize the stressed words or syllables
- Separate the thoughts (phrasing)
- Breathe only at punctuation points

Follow these simple guidelines and discover that Shakespeare is, indeed, better—a lot better—than it might have first seemed. It is, in fact, remarkably beautiful.

SIMPLE BREATHING WARMUP

When working on Shakespeare (or any dramatic text), it's helpful to be relaxed and breathing properly. You want your breathing to be deep and fill the lungs. To experience that feeling, lie on your back on the floor, arms at your sides, knees raised, and breathe deeply in through your nose, out through your mouth. As your lungs fill, you will feel your lower back press into the floor. Establish a slow breath in/breath out rhythm. Notice how easy it is to concentrate. Allow your focus to become concentrated. Now memorize what your muscles are doing to fill your lungs with air. When you sit or stand up, try to keep that muscle group working and your breathing deep.

Now you're ready to read this language. (And here is an added benefit: If you read some of the lines while lying on your back and breathing correctly, you will notice how nicely your voice lowers in pitch and fills out in resonance.)

FIRST SKILL: SUPPORT THE FINAL WORD IN EACH LINE

The end of the blank verse line is usually more important than the beginning or middle. (Blank verse is explained in the next section.) When reading Shakespeare aloud, support the end of the line—including both the final phrase and final word—and notice the sudden clarity. This speaking style is dramatically opposed to the modern tendency to allow lines to fade away, like songs without endings.

For example, here is Portia speaking to Shylock in the courtroom scene of *The Merchant of Venice*.

Portia: The quality of mercy is not strained,   (IV, i)

Read the line aloud, and let the second phrase ("is not strained") fall away so that you can barely hear it. When read that way, the line seems to be about something called "mercy" and something else we aren't quite sure about.

Now read the line aloud a second time, and support the second phrase ("is not strained") with equal or more power than you give the first phrase ("The quality of mercy"), and be certain to emphasize the final word "strained." What is the line about? Now it's about a quality called "mercy," which is not obtained by "straining" at it. Now the line makes sense.

Romeo has this response to Friar Laurence's counseling:

Romeo: Thou canst not speak of that thou dost not feel.   (III, iii)

Read the line aloud and let the final word "feel" drop away so you can barely hear it. What is the line about? Romeo is telling the Friar he can't speak. Now read the line aloud again and support the word "feel." What is the line about? Romeo may be telling the Friar, who is presumed celibate, that he has never known the love of a woman, so how can he counsel? Now the line is rich with possibilities.

Try this very effective exercise. Select a few lines of verse—there are examples in Skill Worksheet #1, beginning on page 188—then place a cardboard box on the floor in front of you. Be sure that each line you select consists of ten syllables. We'll work on eleven- and twelve-syllable lines in the next section.

As you read the lines, kick the box on the final syllable of each ten-syllable line. Kicking the box puts energy into your reading, allows your entire body to become involved, and forces you to support the end of the line. Kick on exactly the final syllable. Using Romeo's line, don't kick on "not," and don't kick after "feel." Kick on the *f* of "feel." On Portia's line, kick on the *s* of "strained." Practice this skill with other lines, and you'll soon discover that supporting the final word through use of the diaphragm becomes second nature. You will notice that people listen to you.

Refer to Skill Worksheet #1 for other practice lines and speeches. Check the index for more detailed study of this skill.

SECOND SKILL: EMPHASIZE THE STRESSED WORDS OR SYLLABLES

To make your reading even more understandable, add this second skill. Blank verse—which is a form of writing the English language in ten-syllable lines, not necessarily rhyming—has a specific rhythm, which identifies the important words.

Each pair of syllables creates one "foot." So the blank verse line has five "feet." Each foot has a soft stress and a hard stress. Think of your own foot: The heel is soft, and the ball is hard. When you walk, the rhythm is soft/hard, soft/hard, soft/hard, and so on. Try it and speak the rhythm aloud. In blank verse, this rhythm becomes dee dum, dee dum, dee dum, dee dum, dee dum—five feet, five soft stresses, five hard stresses, one blank verse line. This type of line is called iambic pentameter.*

Most scholars and stage directors agree that blank verse is the closest written expression of English speech. Without realizing it, you speak blank verse all the time. For example, "What would you like to do this afternoon?" and "Let's go to town and buy an ice cream cone" are two lines of blank verse! For your own enjoyment, converse for awhile in blank verse, and write some original lines.

*See *iamb* and *iambic pentameter* in the Glossary of Terms.

Breaking a blank verse line into feet and marking the stresses is called scanning the line, or scansion. Here is Romeo gazing at Juliet's balcony:

But soft! What light through yonder window breaks?   (ii, ii)

Break the line into five feet, two syllables per foot:

But soft! / What light / through yon / der win / dow breaks?

Now mark the stresses, ∪ for soft, / for hard:

$$\overset{\cup}{\text{But}}\ \overset{/}{\text{soft!}}\ /\ \overset{\cup}{\text{What}}\ \overset{/}{\text{light}}\ /\ \overset{\cup}{\text{through}}\ \overset{/}{\text{yon}}\ /\ \overset{\cup}{\text{der}}\ \overset{/}{\text{win}}\ /\ \overset{\cup}{\text{dow}}\ \overset{/}{\text{breaks?}}$$

When you read the line aloud, stress the hard syllables: "soft," "light," "yon," "win," "breaks." With your hand, beat out these stressed words or syllables on the table or chair, while you read the line aloud three or four times. Then forget scansion and read the line naturally.

Notice that you still give a slight emphasis to the stressed words. Your goal is to achieve naturalness and honesty, while stressing the correct words. By *not* achieving this goal, you unintentionally disguise the meaning of the line. To prove this point, read the line aloud and emphasize the soft syllables: "But," What," "through," "der," "dow." Notice the problem? That is what happens if you emphasize the wrong word or words.

Shakespeare's language is written in this *regular* "dee dum, dee dum" rhythm, with effects achieved by use of *irregular* lines. For example, a word to be stressed might be placed in the unstressed position, or an eleventh syllable—a "dee" without a "dum"—might be added. Here's an example of breaking the rhythm in the opening speech of *Romeo and Juliet*.

Chorus:	Two households, both alike in dignity,	(1)
	In fair Verona, where we lay our scene,	(2)
	From ancient grudge, break to new mutiny,	(3)
	Where civil blood makes civil hands unclean.	(Pro) (4)

Lines 1, 2, and 4 are regular blank verse lines; but notice line 3. First, separate the line into feet:

From an / cient grudge, / break to / new mut / iny.

In the third foot, the verb "break" (in the non-stressed position) is more important than the preposition "to" (in the stressed position). The stress in that foot is inverted, and you must read it accordingly. This type of foot is called a trochaic foot, or trochee, rather than an iambic foot.

Read the line aloud twice, first emphasizing "to," then emphasizing "break." How do you know when a word breaks the rhythm? Scan the line, and with a little practice, your common sense will tell you.

For example, in the fourth foot of the same line, you could argue that "new" also breaks the rhythm and is as important as "mut." That's a good argument, because it points out that an earlier mutiny is starting over again. Read it aloud twice, once each way, then choose the way which seems right to you.

You might also argue that, in line 1, "Two" is as important as "house." That's a reader choice, but could be a good one, because it clarifies the number of families involved in the fray. Lines often have three or more stresses back-to-back (there are even lines with ten stressed syllables), as this line has "Two," "house," and "holds," all of which you could choose to stress.

In each case, scan the line to decide if and where the rhythm breaks, then speak accordingly. If you decided to stress "Two," "holds," and "new," the lines would scan like this:

$$/ \quad / \quad / \quad / \quad \cup / \quad \cup / \quad \cup /$$
Two house / holds, both / a like / in dig / ni ty

$$\cup / \quad \cup / \cup \quad / \quad \cup / \quad \cup \quad /$$
In fair / Ver o / na, where / we lay / our scene,

$$\cup \quad / \quad \cup \quad / \quad / \cup \quad / \quad / \quad \cup /$$
From an / cient grudge, / break to / new mut / i ny,

$$\cup \quad / \cup \quad / \quad \cup \quad / \cup \quad / \quad \cup \quad /$$
Where civ / il blood / makes civ / il hands / un clean.

The next example, the most famous line in Shakespeare, illustrates an added syllable—a "dee" without a "dum"—as Hamlet contemplates action.

To be, or not to be—that is the question: (III, i)

The line scans like this:

$$\cup / \quad \cup / \quad \cup / \quad \cup / \quad \cup \quad / \quad (\cup)$$
To be, / or not / to be— / that is / the ques / tion.

This line has eleven syllables and calls for a soft or unstressed ending. This "feminine" ending, used throughout Shakespeare, allows a line to end without a stressed syllable. You kick the box on "ques-"—not on "-tion." Let "-tion" just be there, giving the line a soft ending.

When scanning a blank verse line, if you don't count ten syllables and five feet, you may be looking at a feminine ending. But another possibility is to change the eleven-syllable line to ten by eliding two syllables or words into one. For example, "I will" becomes "I'll" and is spoken as one syllable.

For another example, in the following eleven-syllable line, Shakespeare has already elided a two-syllable word into one syllable, but the reader must elide another word, as "man" is stressed and would not make a feminine ending.

Hamlet: Horatio, thou art e'en as just a man.   (III, ii)

Note "even" is already elided to "e'en" and pronounced as one syllable. The reader must elide "Horatio" to "Horat'o," pronounced as three syllables. Now the line can be spoken in ten syllables with correct rhythm.

$$\breve{} / \quad \breve{} / \quad \breve{} / \quad \breve{} / \quad \breve{} /$$

Hor a / t'o, thou / art e'en / as just / a man.

In the previous line, "question" is not spoken with emphasis on the second syllable; it can be a feminine-ending line. But "man" is a stressed word, so you must find an elision somewhere in the line to compress it to ten syllables. Often feminine-ending words end in "-ing," "-en," and "-tion."

See Skill Worksheet #2 on page 190 for more examples of elision and for practice lines and speeches. If you want more study of this skill, check the index.

THIRD SKILL: SEPARATE THE THOUGHTS

You now have two skills for reading Shakespeare: (1) supporting the end of the line and (2) scanning to emphasize the stressed words and rhythm changes. There's a third skill, phrasing, which is no more difficult than the first two. All blank verse lines can be divided into phrases. When you read aloud, separate the phrases slightly. Each phrase is a thought; if you run the thoughts together the listener gets lost.

Many phrases are separated by punctuation marks. When there is no punctuation, separate each phrase with a slight pause. This pause is called a caesura (si-zhoor´-ə), meaning a "sense pause." This is not a "breath" pause; it's much shorter. It is just a slight pause that allows the ear to hear an emphasis placed on the phrase or word you just said or are about to say.

If you use the caesura (marked //) to practice separating phrases, then forget the pauses and speak naturally, you will notice that, even when speaking rapidly, the phrases have been embedded in your mind as individual thoughts, and you will automatically handle each separately. In this next example, Brutus's answer to Cassius, after hearing the suggestion that Caesar has grown too strong, is broken into phrases by inserting caesuras. Where a phrase is already identified by punctuation, a caesura is not inserted.

Brutus:	What you have said //	(1)
	I will consider; what you have to say //	(2)
	I will with patience hear; and find a time //	(3)
	Both meet to hear and answer // such high things.	(4)
	Till then, my noble friend, chew upon this:	(5)
	Brutus had rather be a villager //	(6)
	Than to repute himself a son of Rome //	(7)
	Under these hard conditions // as this time	(8)
	Is like to lay upon us.	(I, ii) (9)

Work on the speech, separating the thoughts as marked (some readers and actors prefer to circle the phrases rather than to use caesura marks), then forget the marks, and read the speech naturally.

You should discover that you give individuality to each thought, regardless of how quickly you speak. (The final line is called a "short line," meaning that either a pause sufficient to complete the ten-syllable rhythm is intended, or the line is finished by the next speaker. In this case, Cassius will finish the line with "I am glad," to make ten syllables.)

At this point you might create an exercise designed to focus the reader's attention on separation of phrases. *Read aloud from punctuation point to punctuation point* (which are also your breathing points), and force yourself to stop at each point. Give the reader something to do at each point. For example, read lines 1 and 2, up to the word "consider." (Note that the line contains two phrases, as do other lines that follow, but only walk and breathe at punctuation points.) Then walk silently to another spot in the room before reading the next line, which ends on "hear." Then walk silently to another spot in the room, and so forth. Moving between the punctuation points causes you to consider what you *have* said and what you *will* say as separate thoughts. After reading the speech with the thoughts separated, forget the moving, and read the speech naturally.

Separating phrases separates individual thoughts. You must also watch for shorter phrases within longer ones. For example, "Under these hard conditions" is a shorter phrase within the longer one, which includes all of lines 6–9. You may want to expand the exercise to move on these inside phrases as well. Once the phrases are separated, it will be easy to discover different interpretations for the individual thoughts and then to select the reading you like.

Refer to Skill Worksheet #3 on page 194 for additional phrasing exercises. If you want more study of the phrasing skill, refer to the index.

FOURTH SKILL: BREATHE ONLY AT PUNCTUATION POINTS

Added to the three skills you've now learned—kicking the box, scanning the line, and phrasing— remember to breathe at the right places. When reading Shakespeare, random breathing can destroy the sense of the line, because the misplaced pause for a breath fractures the thought.

A reliable guide is this: Breathe at the punctuation points. Don't breathe at the end of a phrase (as in Brutus's lines 1, 2, 3, 6, 7, and 8) unless the phrase ends with a punctuation mark (as in the middle of lines 3, 4, 5, and 9). The speech appears in worksheets #3 and #5 on pages 194 and 203.

Verse lines are often *enjambed*, which means the thought in the line continues to the next line without pause or punctuation. Shakespeare's lines are more often than not enjambed. Brutus's speech above has end-of-line punctuation (and breathing points) only on lines 4 and 5. The other lines require breathing at the punctuation points *within* the lines. In Macbeth's speech below, all lines are enjambed except 1, 2, and 4. Line 10 is enjambed into 11, because it continues "He chid the sisters/When first they put the name of King upon me."

In this example, Macbeth, having killed the king, now contemplates killing his friend, Banquo.

Macbeth:	To be thus is nothing, but to be safely thus—	(1)
	Our fears in Banquo stick deep,	(2)
	And in his royalty of nature reigns that	(3)
	Which would be feared. 'Tis much he dares;	(4)
	And to that dauntless temper of his mind	(5)
	He hath a wisdom that doth guide his valour	(6)
	To act in safety. There is none but he	(7)
	Whose being I do fear; and under him	(8)
	My genius is rebuked, as it is said	(9)
	Mark Antony's was by Caesar.	(III, i) (10)

This speech contains typical Shakespearean punctuation. The breathing points are the punctuation marks. Circle them, and then read the speech aloud, breathing at each mark. You will find that it is quite easy to speak from one breathing point to the next. The longest stretch is two and one-half lines. (In the previous Brutus speech, the longest stretch is three and one-half lines.)

Don't breathe after "Banquo" in line 2 (the end of a thought), but after "deep," and take the pause needed to finish the rhythm of this short line. Don't breathe after "that" in line 3 (the end of the verse line on paper), but try it once to discover the problem for yourself. Likewise, try breathing after "mind," "valour," "he," "him," and "said." Your common sense and good ear will tell you that the choice is wrong.

You might want to practice an exercise to focus your attention on breathing correctly. This works effectively: At each punctuation point, whether you have spoken one word or four lines, exhale all unused breath, then fill your lungs with a deep breath before speaking the next line. Do this at each punctuation point. Do not hurry, or you may sense dizziness. Concentrate on making yourself take the time to breathe deeply and fill the lungs before continuing. Try not to take little gasping breaths that fill only one-third of your lung capacity. After doing the exercise, read the speech naturally, and notice that you automatically breathe more deeply at the appropriate points. Reserve breath gives you power; running out of breath signals weakness.

In Skill Worksheet #4 on page 198 are a few more good speeches for breathing practice. For more advanced study, check the index.

A CONCLUDING NOTE

When reading Shakespeare, it's natural to want to "act it out." Readers will often "enhance" the language with sounds, gasps, crying, whispering, pauses for effect, sighs, and "ahs." Such enhancements tend to destroy the rhythm. When the rhythm is lost, the thoughts—and the audience—are also lost.

Overpowering blank verse with emotion because "my character would do this" simply doesn't work. Your reading becomes indulgent, because you've lost *what* is being said in favor of *how* it is being said. Generally this direction works: If you want to cry, cry after the line, not during the line. We must hear the words first, then we can experience your sorrow without the irritation caused by a muffled line.

The emotions needed by the character are already written into the verse. All you have to do is speak the lines honestly by using your newly-acquired reading/acting skills. These four skills are all you need to begin enjoying Shakespeare. Have fun!

I have some private schooling for you both.
A MIDSUMMER NIGHT'S DREAM, I, i

MORE ADVANCED STUDY

When reading Shakespeare aloud, the language will make sense if you use the four skills you've just learned. The meaning of most lines will be clear. There is, of course, more to learn. For advanced training, here are a few more skills. Refer to the index for more study of each.

Learn to handle antithesis, which is placing one word or thought against an opposite word or thought—like "To be" (one thought) "or not to be" (an opposite thought). Shakespeare is full of antithesis, and you will read better if you can identify the antithetical thoughts and play them. For more information and some exercises, see Skill Worksheet #5 on page 203.

Practice using elision. Lines often have eleven or twelve syllables. Sometimes they are feminine-ending lines, but sometimes words or pairs of words must be elided, or condensed together, so the rhythm will work. Some examples are included in Skill Worksheet #6 on page 206 and the Glossary of Terms.

Learn about the structure of speeches. The pattern is usually (1) introduction of an idea, (2) development, and (3) conclusion or summary.

Identify the imagery. Unlike modern playwrights, Shakespeare's language is rich in images and metaphors—like Romeo's "...Juliet is the sun" or Juliet's "Gallop apace you fiery-footed steeds."

Learn to analyze the text. Study what others before you have discovered about the meaning of specific words, ideas, and references. Write out a speech or sonnet in your own words.

Learn the acting skill of saying what you think when you think it. This skill is unlike the acting approach that allows you to think about the thought, *then* speak the subtext. See part 1, chapter 6 for work on this skill and also on playing your action to achieve your objective.

Many of the basic skills learned for acting realistic texts can be applied to Shakespeare, especially the skills of playing your action to achieve your objective and staying in the moment. Listen to what the other character is saying, and respond honestly to that, don't plan ahead. For more training, see part 4 and the bibliography of books available on acting Shakespeare. If you become interested in this greatest of all writers, consulting some of these works will be both exciting and rewarding. Enjoy the Bard!

USEFUL IDEAS TO REMEMBER:

CHAPTER 32

Worksheets

NOTE:

These worksheets may be enlarged and reproduced without author permission. Answers are included following the exercises for each skill.

SKILL WORKSHEET I

SUPPORT THE FINAL WORD OF EACH LINE ("KICK THE BOX")

A. Here are the two examples used in the chapter:

Portia: The quality of mercy is not strained;   (*MV,* IV, i)

Romeo: Thou canst not speak of that thou dost not feel.   (*Rom,* III, iii)

B. Here are other speeches with which to practice. The first three examples are from *Julius Caesar.*

1. Portia speaks to Brutus after the conspirators have left. Kick the box on the last syllable of each line. However, one line has a feminine ending, so kick on the tenth syllable of that line, and there is a trochaic foot in one line.

Portia: You have some sick offense within your mind,
Which by the right and virtue of my place
I ought to know of; and upon my knees
I charm you, by my once-commended beauty,
By all your vows of love, and that great vow
Which did incorporate and make us one,   (II, i)

2. Calphurnia speaks to Caesar. Kick on the final syllable of each line. However, one line has a feminine ending, so kick on the tenth syllable of that line. Also, in one line, a one-syllable word must be spoken as two syllables to keep the rhythm, and there is a trochaic foot in one line.

Calphurnia: Caesar, I never stood on ceremonies,
Yet now they fright me. There is one within,
Besides the things that we have heard and seen,
Recounts most horrid sights seen by the watch.
A lioness hath whelped in the streets,
And graves have yawned and yielded up their dead.   (II, ii)

3. Here is Mark Antony alone with Caesar's body. Again, kick on the final syllable of each line. However, once again, one line has a feminine ending, so kick on the tenth syllable of the line. Also, in two different lines, a one-syllable word must be spoken as two syllables to keep the rhythm.

Antony: O, pardon me, thou bleeding piece of earth,
That I am meek and gentle with these butchers!
Thou art the ruin of the noblest man
That ever lived in the tide of times.   (III, i)

4. Here is an example from *Romeo and Juliet*. The Nurse is speaking to Lady Capulet about Juliet's age.

Nurse: Even or odd, of all days in the year,
                Come Lammas Eve at night shall she be fourteen.
                Susan and she (God rest all Christian souls!)
                Were of an age. Well, Susan is with God;
                She was too good for me. But, as I said,
                On Lammas Eve at night shall she be fourteen;
                That shall she, marry; I remember it well.   (I, iii)

In this speech, kick on the tenth and final syllable of each line. However, two of the lines have feminine endings, so in these lines, kick on the tenth syllable. Also, in one line, you must practice *elision* (combining two words into one—e.g., "I will" into "I'll,"—or removing a vowel from a word to shorten it, as "int'rest" for "interest"). This is done so that you can read the line with fewer syllables and make the rhythm work. There are more examples of elision in Skill Worksheet #6.

Practice the kick box exercise with any verse lines of Shakespeare. Be sure to check for feminine endings and elision to keep the rhythm, then kick on the tenth syllable.

TIPS AND ANSWERS FOR SKILL WORKSHEET I

B. 1. You were correct if you selected "beauty" for the feminine ending and kicked on the first syllable of the word.

2. Selecting "ceremonies" as the feminine ending and "whelped" to be spoken with two syllables ("whelp'ed") would be correct. The fourth foot of line four is a trochee, as "seen" breaks the rhythm.

3. "Butchers" is the feminine ending. Both "ruin" and "lived" must be spoken with two syllables: "ru-in" and "liv'ed."

4. In this speech, each "fourteen" is a feminine ending. Elide the *e* from the final syllable of "remember" and combine with "it" to get "re mem b'rit," eliding from four to three syllables. Now you can keep the rhythm. The line would scan:

$$\overset{\cup}{\text{That}} \overset{/}{\text{shall}} / \overset{\cup}{\text{she}} \overset{/}{\text{mar}} / \overset{\cup}{\text{ry;}} \overset{/}{\text{I}} / \overset{\cup}{\text{re}} \overset{/}{\text{mem}} / \overset{\cup}{\text{b'rit}} \overset{/}{\text{well.}}$$

SKILL WORKSHEET 2

SCANSION: EMPHASIZE STRESSED WORDS OR SYLLABLES

A. Here are the three examples used in the chapter. For practice, mark the scansion of these lines as you worked it out on page 180. Circle words that break the rhythm.

Romeo: But soft! What light through yonder window breaks? (*Rom*, ii, ii)

Chorus: Two households, both alike in dignity,
              In fair Verona, where we lay our scene,
              From ancient grudge, break to new mutiny,
              Where civil blood makes civil hands unclean.   (*Rom*, Pro)

Hamlet: To be, or not to be—that is the question.   (*Ham*, iii, i)

B. Here are three practice speeches. Mark the scansion of these lines. Most are regular blank verse lines of ten syllables, two syllables per foot.

    1. The first is Helena to her companions in *A Midsummer Night's Dream*:

Helena: O Spite! O hell! I see you all are bent
              To set against me for your merriment.
              If you were civil and knew courtesy,
              You would not do me thus much injury.   (iii, ii)

    2. Here is Juliet to the Friar in *Romeo and Juliet*. One line has a trochaic foot and another foot could be a spondee (both syllables stressed):

Juliet: Conceit, more rich in matter than in words,
             Brags of his substance, not of ornament.
             They are but beggars that can count their worth;
             But my true love is grown to such excess
             I cannot sum up sum of half my wealth.   (ii, vi)

    3. In the same play, Mercutio to Romeo, three words break the rhythm:

Mercutio: O, then I see Queen Mab hath been with you.
               She is the fairies' midwife, and she comes
               In shape no bigger than an agate stone
               .On the forefinger of an alderman.   (i, iv)

C. The next two examples require more thought. Mark the feet, the stressed words, and any words that break the rhythm.

1. Puck to the Fairies in *A Midsummer Night's Dream*:

Puck: The King doth keep his revels here tonight.
   Take heed the Queen come not within his sight.
   For Oberon is passing fell and wrath,
   Because that she, as her attendant, hath
   A lovely boy, stolen from an Indian King.   (ii, i)

In one line, there are twelve syllables without a feminine ending, so you must elide two. See if you can do it. One word breaks the rhythm.

2. Here is Antonio's opening speech in *The Merchant of Venice*. One line has an irregular rhythm:

Antonio: In sooth I know not why I am so sad.
    It worries me, you say it worries you;
    But how I caught it, found it, or came by it,
    What stuff 'tis made of, whereof it is born,
    I am to learn;
    And such a want-wit sadness makes of me
    That I have much ado to know myself. (i, i)

One elision is necessary. One word might be emphasized to break the rhythm. One line is a "short line." See if you can figure out how to read it.

D. Take any of Shakespeare's verse lines and practice marking the feet, then the stressed syllables, the feminine endings, the words that break the rhythm, and any words that must be elided to keep the rhythm.

TIPS AND ANSWERS FOR SKILL WORKSHEET 2

B. 1. All are regular lines. Each two syllables makes one foot for five feet per line.

O spite! / O hell! / I see / you all / are bent

To set / a gainst / me for / your mer / ri ment.

If you / were civ / il and / knew cour / te sy,

You would / not do / me thus / much in / ju ry.

2. Most are regular lines, two syllables per foot, five feet, but notice that "Brags" and "true" break the rhythm.

> Con ceit, / more rich / in mat / ter than / in words,
>
> Brags of / his sub / stance, not / of orn / a ment.
>
> They are / but beg / gars that / can count / their worth;
>
> But my / true love / is grown / to such / ex cess
>
> I can / not sum / up sum / of half / my wealth.

"Brags" is an action verb, more important than "of." Line 4 can also be read as a regular line, with "true" unstressed. But doesn't it work better if you stress it? You might also choose to stress "But."

3. All are regular lines, five feet. Notice that "O," "Queen," and "fore" break the rhythm.

> O, then / I see / Queen Mab / hath been / with you.
>
> She is / the fair / ies' mid / wife, and / she comes
>
> In shape / no big / ger than / an ag / ate stone
>
> On the / fore fin / ger of / an al / der man,

C. 1.

> The King / doth keep / his rev / els here / to night.
>
> Take heed / the Queen / come not / with in / his sight.
>
> For O / ber on / is pass / ing fell / and wrath,
>
> Be cause / that she, / as her / at tend / ant, hath
>
> A love / ly boy, / stol'n from / an In / d'an King;

To make a ten-syllable line of the final line, elide "stolen" (which also breaks the rhythm) to one syllable (stol'n) and "Indian" to two syllables ("Ind'an"). Now the rhythm works.

2. In line 3, elide "by it" to "by't." Line 5 is a "short line" that calls for a pause of three feet (dee dum dee dum dee dum) to complete the rhythm before you read line 6. (Short lines may also be completed by the next speaker, but that isn't the case here.) In line 3, "came" may break the rhythm, if you choose that reading.

In sooth / I know / not why / I am / so sad.

It wor / ries me, / you say / it wor / ries you;

But how / I caught / it found / it or / came by't,

What stuff / 'tis made / of, where / of it / is born,

I am / to learn; / (dee dum) / (dee dum) / (dee dum)

And such / a want- / wit sad / ness makes / of me

That I / have much / a do / to know / my self.

SKILL WORKSHEET 3

PHRASING: SEPARATE THE THOUGHTS

A. Once readers learn to phrase, they will not rush the language. Many phrases are identified by the punctuation marks. Others must be discovered. Watch for where the thought changes.

Here is the example that was worked out on page 183, as Brutus answers Cassius. For practice, circle the phrases or mark them by use of the caesura (*//*).

Brutus:	What you have said	(1)
	I will consider; what you have to say	(2)
	I will with patience hear; and find a time	(3)
	Both meet to hear and answer such high things.	(4)
	Till then, my noble friend, chew upon this:	(5)
	Brutus had rather be a villager	(6)
	Than to repute himself a son of Rome	(7)
	Under these hard conditions as this time	(8)
	Is like to lay upon us.	(*JC*, 1, ii) (9)

B. Read the following speeches and mark all phrases. You might also do the complete scansion.

1. The first is Richard III's opening monologue. Richard is not yet king, but covets the throne. Blocking his way are his two brothers: the present King Edward IV, who has two sons of his own, and Clarence. Yet, with the House of York returned to the throne through war, Richard is closer to his goal than he has ever been.

Richard:	Now is the winter of our discontent
	Made glorious summer by this son of York;
	And all the clouds that lowered upon our house
	In the deep bosom of the ocean buried.	(*RIII*, 1, i)

Here is the speech broken into phrases by use of the caesura (*//*), with shorter phrases or breaks within the phrases marked with one /. Too many phrases would be wrong for performance, of course, but can be very right for reading and rehearsal, as the phrases force the reader to separate the thoughts. (Scansion is shown in the Tips and Answers.)

> Now / is the winter // of our / discontent //
> Made / glorious summer // by this / son of York;
> And / all the clouds // that lowered / upon our house //
> In the deep bosom // of the ocean / buried.

Note that the first phrase, "Now is the winter," contains two thoughts, not one: "Now" and "is the winter." When practicing phrasing, consider various possibilities for each thought. For example, "Now" could mean right now at this moment, now as a period of time, now after something else has passed, now as opposed to later, and so on. The phrase "is the winter" could mean winter of the year, the latter part of life, a coldness, a desolate time, the opposite of summer, and so on. Once you have considered the many possibilities for each thought, select one and try it. Then try others until you are satisfied with the reading. What you are doing is determining the possibilities within the language *before* you decide *how* to read the line and *before* you make character decisions. This approach will help you make strong choices.

2. These are Capulet's orders to Tybalt, who has recognized Romeo in disguise at the Capulet party and wants to challenge him.

Capulet: Content thee, gentle cuz, let him alone.
           'A bears him like a portly gentleman,
           And, to say truth, Verona brags of him
           To be a virtuous and well-governed youth.
           I would not for the wealth of all this town
           Here in my house do him disparagement.
           It is my will, the which if you respect,
           Show a fair presence and put off these frowns,
           An ill-beseeming semblance for a feast.   (*Rom*, I, iv)

3. In this speech, Romeo asks the Apothecary for poison.

Romeo: Come hither, man. I see that thou art poor.
           Hold, there is forty ducats. Let me have
           A dram of poison, such soon-speeding gear
           As will disperse itself through all the veins
           That the life-weary taker may fall dead,
           And that the trunk may be discharged of breath
           As violently as hasty powder fired
           Doth hurry from the fatal cannon's womb.   (*Rom*, v, i)

4. Here is Brutus (the commander) to Cassius (one of his generals) in the battle that follows the murder of Caesar in *Julius Caesar:*

Brutus: Remember March; the ides of March remember.
           Did not great Julius bleed for justice sake?
           What villain touched his body that did stab
           And not for justice? What, shall one of us,

That struck the foremost man of all this world
But for supporting robbers—shall we now
Contaminate our fingers with base bribes,
And sell the mighty space of our large honors
For so much trash as may be grasped thus? (IV, iii)

5. In one of Hamlet's soliloquies, study the four lines without punctuation, and circle the many phrases within them.

Hamlet: To be, or not to be—that is the question:
Whether 'tis nobler in the mind to suffer
The slings and arrows of outrageous fortune
Or to take arms against a sea of troubles
And by opposing end them.   (*Ham*, III, i)

6. In this final example, mark the phrases as Theseus asks for a play to be performed in *A Midsummer Night's Dream*.

Theseus: Come now, what masques, what dances shall we have,
To wear away this long age of three hours
Between our after-supper and bedtime?
Where is our usual manager of mirth?
What revels are in hand? Is there no play
To ease the anguish of a torturing hour?   (V, i)

For additional study of phrasing, refer to the index and the appropriate chapters in the main text.

TIPS AND ANSWERS FOR SKILL WORKSHEET 3

B.1.

Now is / the win / ter of / our dis / con tent

Made glo / ri'us sum / mer by / this son / of York;
(Elide "glorious" to "glori'us," pronounced as two syllables.)

And all / the clouds / that lower'd / u pon / our house
(Elide "lowered" to "lower'd," spoken as one syllable.)

In the / deep bo / som of / the o / cean bur / ied.
(A feminine ending.)

2. Phrase endings not identified by punctuation: after "him," line 3; "virtuous," line 4; "not" and "town," line 5; "house," line 6; "presence," line 7; and "semblance," line 8. For scansion, in line 4, elide "virtuous" to "virt'ous." All lines except 8 are regular. "Show" breaks the rhythm.

3. Phrase endings are "gear," line 3; "itself" and "veins," line 4; "taker," line 5; "trunk" and "breath," line 6; "fired," line 7. "Hold" and "life" break the rhythm. For scansion, line 7 has twelve syllables. Elide "violently" to "vi'lently" and "fired" to "fir'd," or let it have a feminine ending. All others are regular lines.

4. Phrase endings are "bleed," line 2; "body," line 3; "man" and "world," line 5; "fingers," line 7; "space" and "honors," line 8; and "trash," line 9. In line 8, "large" breaks the rhythm. For scansion, the second "remember" has a feminine ending, "Julius" is read as two syllables, and "grasped" is pronounced "grasp'ed." All other lines are regular.

5. Phrase endings include "mind," line 2; "arrows" and "fortune," line 3; "arms" and "troubles," line 4; and "opposing," line 5. Lines 1–4 have feminine endings. Some actors like to break the rhythm with "that" in line 1. In line 4, "Or" breaks the rhythm.

6. Phrase endings are "age" and "hours," line 2; "play," line 5; and "anguish," line 6. "Come" and "age" break the rhythm. Elide "usual" to "us'al" and "torturing" to "tort'ring."

SKILL WORKSHEET 4

BREATHE ONLY AT THE PUNCTUATION MARKS

A. This is the example that was used in the text on page 184. Circle the breathing places (the punctuation marks), separate the phrases, and mark the stressed words. Underline those words that break the rhythm. Read the speech aloud, breathing only at the correct places.

Because of the Witches' prophesy that Banquo's children will be heirs to the throne, Macbeth, now King, contemplates killing Banquo.

Macbeth:	To be thus is nothing, but to be safely thus—	
	Our fears in Banquo stick deep,	
	And in his royalty of nature reigns that	
	Which would be feared. 'Tis much he dares;	
	And to that dauntless temper of his mind	
	He hath a wisdom that doth guide his valour	
	To act in safety. There is none but he	
	Whose being I do fear; and under him	
	My genius is rebuked, as it is said	
	Mark Antony's was by Caesar.	(*Mac*, III, i)

B. Here are practice speeches. Circle the breathing places. Then practice reading the speeches aloud, breathing only at the correct places. Don't forget to identify the phrases, mark the stresses, and underline words that break the rhythm. Work out any necessary elisions.

1. Helena, frustrated because both Lysander and Demetrius profess love to her, speaks of Hermia in *A Midsummer Night's Dream*:

Helena:	Lo, she is one of this confederacy.	
	Now I perceive they have conjoined all three	
	To fashion this false sport in spite of me.	(III, ii)

2. The imprisoned King Richard II, overthrown by Bolingbroke and sensing his death, begins his famous monologue like this:

Richard:	I have been studying how I may compare	
	This prison where I live unto the world;	
	And, for because the world is populous,	
	And here is not a creature but myself,	
	I cannot do it. Yet I'll hammer it out.	(*RII*, v, i)

3. Prince Escalus condemns the riotous families after the act I brawl in *Romeo and Juliet:*

Prince: What, ho! You men, you beasts,
    That quench the fire of your pernicious rage
    With purple fountains issuing from your veins!
    On pain of torture, from those bloody hands
    Throw your mistemp'red weapons to the ground
    And hear the sentence of your moved prince.   (I, i)

4. Here are Juliet's words as she paces and waits for the Nurse to bring news of Romeo.

Juliet: Give me my Romeo; and, when he shall die,
   Take him and cut him out in little stars,
   And he will make the face of heaven so fine
   That all the world will be in love with night
   And pay no worship to the garish sun.   (III, ii)

5. Brutus chastises Cassius for stealing from the poor to support his army in *Julius Caesar*. In this speech, practice speaking four lines on one breath.

Brutus: I did send to you
   For certain sums of gold, which you denied me;
   For I can raise no money by vile means.
   By heaven, I had rather coin my heart
   And drop my blood for drachmas than to wring
   From the hard hands of peasants their vile trash
   By any indirection.   (IV, iii)

TIPS AND ANSWERS FOR SKILL WORKSHEET 4

A. While this speech is a good breathing exercise, it is difficult to scan. You may or may not wish to work on the scansion. If you are leading a class through these exercises, you might assign it to some exceptional students and let them enjoy working it out.

  T'be thus / is noth / ing, but / t'be safe / ly thus—
   (You must elide each "to be" if you want ten syllables, although the first and fourth feet can be anapests, and the line reads effectively as twelve syllables.)
  Our fears / in Ban / quo (silent beat) / <u>stick</u> deep (dee dum)
   (A short line with a silent beat. A caesura would precede "stick," which breaks the rhythm.)
  And in / his roy / al ty /of nat're (an extra syllable) / <u>reigns</u> that
   (It does not hurt this line to have three syllables in the fourth foot. "Reigns" breaks the rhythm. A caesura precedes "reigns.")

Which would / be feared. / 'Tis much / he dares; / (dee dum)
   (Another short line.)
And to / that daunt / less tem / per of / his mind
He hath / a wis / dom that / doth guide / his val /our
   (A feminine ending.)
To act / in safe / ty. There / is none / but he
Whose be / ing I / do fear; / and un / der him
My gen' / us is / re buked, / as it / is said
   (Elide "genius" to "gen'us.")
Mark Ant / 'ny's was / by Caesar. (an extra syllable) / He chid /
the sis / ters
*(Elide "Antony's" to "Ant'ny's" The third foot has an extra syllable
which does not hurt the line. The complete line has a feminine
ending).*

Macbeth continues the line with "He chid the sisters" for a feminine
ending. Phrase endings include "nature," line 3; "mind," line 5; "valour,"
line 6; "he," line 7; and "him," line 8.

B. 1. Lines 2 and 3 should be read with one breath. Scansion is like this:

Lo, she / is one / of this / con fed / 'ra cy.
   ("Lo" breaks the rhythm; elide "confederacy" to "confed'racy.")

Now I / per ceive / they have / con joined / all three
   (Some actors would emphasize both "all" and "three.")

To fash / ion this / false sport / in spite / of me.
   ("False" can break the rhythm.)

Phrase endings include "there," line 2, and "sport," line 3.
   2. The first two lines should be read with one breath. Scansion is like
this:

I have / been stud / y'ng how / I may / com pare
   ("Studying" is elided to two syllables.)

This pris / on where / I live / un to / the world;

And, for / be cause / the world / is pop / u lous,

And here / is not / a crea / ture but / my self,

Ĭ can / nŏt do / ĭt. Yet / Ĭ'll ham / mĕr't óut.
(Elide "hammer it" to "ham mer't.")

Phrase endings include "studying" and "compare," line 1, and "live," line 2.

3. The previous line begins and completes the short line that opens this selection.

Wĭll they / nŏt hear? / Whăt ho! / Yŏu men, / yŏu beasts,

Thăt quench / thĕ fire / ŏf your / pĕr ni / cĭous rage

Wĭth pur / plĕ foun / tăins is / sŭ'ng from / yŏur veins!
(Elide "issuing" to "issu'ng.")

Ŏn pain / ŏf tor / tŭre, from / thŏse blood / ў hands

Thrŏw your / mĭs temp / 'red weap / ŏns to / thĕ ground
("Mistemp'red is already elided by the author.)

Ănd hear / thĕ sen / tĕnce of / yŏur mov / 'ed prince.
("Moved must be pronounced "mov'ed.")

Phrase endings include "fire" and "rage," line 2; "fountains," line 3; "hands," line 4; "ground," line 5; and "sentence," line 6.

4. The scansion is regular, except as indicated.

Give me / my Rom / 'yo; and, / when he / shăll die,
(Here "Romeo" is spoken as two syllables, pronounced "Rom'yo.")

Take him / ănd cut / him out / ĭn lit / tlĕ stars,

Ănd he / wĭll make / thĕ face / ŏf heav'n / sŏ fine
(Elide "heaven" to one syllable, "heav'n.")

Thăt all / thĕ world / wĭll be / ĭn love / wĭth night

Ănd pay / nŏ wor / shĭp to / thĕ gar / ĭsh sun.

Phrase endings include "fine," line 3; "night," line 4; and "worship," line 5.

5. The scansion is regular, except as noted.

Which I / re spect / not. I / did send / to you
(The end of the previous line begins this line.)

For cer / tain sums / of gold, / which you / de nied / me;
(Feminine ending.)

For I / can raise / no mon / ey by / vile means.

By heav / en, I / had rath / er coin / my heart

And drop / my blood / for drach / mas than / to wring

From the / hard hands / of peas / ants their / vile trash

By an / y in / di rec / tion. I / did send
(The line that follows completes the thought.)

Phrase endings include "you," line 1; "money," line 3; "heart," line 4; "drachmas," line 5; and "peasants," line 6.

MORE ADVANCED STUDY: SKILL WORKSHEET 5

ANTITHESIS

According to Webster, "Antithesis is the placing of a sentence or one of its parts against another to which it is opposed to form a balanced contrast of ideas" (e.g., "Give me liberty or give me death"). Shakespeare frequently uses antithetical words, phrases, or thoughts, and you will be a better reader (or actor) of the language if you can identify them and allow the listener to hear them. For a more extended explanation of antithesis, see chapter 8.

Playing one antithetical word, phrase, or thought against another can be as simple as this example: "Rather than go to town, let's stay on the farm." When reading the line, play "go" against "stay," and "town" against "farm." Then, simultaneously play the entire first phrase, "Rather than go to town," against the second phrase, "let's stay on the farm," which is antithetical to it in thought. Read the line aloud a few times, and practice giving emphasis to the antithetical ideas.

A. Here are examples of antithesis in a Shakespearean speech.
  1. First, Brutus to Cassius in *Julius Caesar*:

Brutus:	What you have said	(1)
	I will consider; what you have to say	(2)
	I will with patience hear; and find a time	(3)
	Both meet to hear and answer such high things.	(4)
	Till then, my noble friend, chew upon this:	(5)
	Brutus had rather be a villager	(6)
	Than to repute himself a son of Rome	(7)
	Under these hard conditions as this time	(8)
	Is like to lay upon us.	(i, ii) (9)

Dig out the antithetical words, phrases, and thoughts in this speech, so you can play them against each other.

Now read the entire speech, and play the antithetical words or thoughts against each other. Notice how everything becomes clearer.

  2. In this next example, Romeo talks of love with his cousin, Benvolio, then notices that a street fight has taken place.

Benvolio:	Alas, that love, so gentle in his view,	(1)
	Should be so tyrannous and rough in proof!	(2)
Romeo:	Alas, that love, whose view is muffled still,	(3)
	Should without eyes see pathways to his will!	(4)
	Where shall we dine? O me! What fray was here?	(5)

Yet tell me not, for I have heard it all.   (6)
Here's much to do with hate, but more with love: (7)
Why, then, O brawling love! O loving hate!   (8)
O any thing, of nothing first create!   (9)
O heavy lightness! serious vanity!   (10)
Mis-shapen chaos of well-seeming forms!   (11)
Feather of lead, bright smoke, cold fire, sick health!   (12)
Still-waking sleep, that is not what it is!   (13)
This love feel I, that feel no love in this.   (14)
Dost thou not laugh?   (15)

Benvolio: No, cuz, I rather weep.   (*Rom*, I, i) (16)

Find the antithetical words, phrases or thoughts. Now read the speech aloud and play all the antithetical possibilities.

3. In *Richard II*, after having King Richard murdered, Bolingbroke, who will become the new king, condemns the killer, Exton.

Bolingbroke: They love not poison that do poison need,
              Nor do I thee. Though I did wish him dead,
              I hate the murderer, love him murdered.
              The guilt of conscience take thou for thy labor,
              But neither my good word nor princely favor.
              With Cain go wander through the shade of night,
              And never show thy head by day nor light.   (v, vi)

Dig out the antithesis in this speech. Note the elision of "murderer" to "murd'rer" and the three syllables for "mur-der-'ed." (For line 6, I have used the *Folio*. The Pelican edition prefers "through shades of night.")

If you wish to work on the skill of digging out antithesis in more detail, use the complete book from which this worksheet is taken, and practice the many other examples to be found there.

ANSWERS AND TIPS FOR SKILL WORKSHEET 5

A. 1. Lines 1/2: "have said" is antithetical to "have to say"

Line 4: "hear" and "answer" are antithetical

Lines 3/4/5: "find a time/Both meet to hear and answer" (lines 3/4) is antithetical to "Till then... chew upon this" (line 5)

Lines 6/7: "a villager" and "son of Rome" are antithetical, as are "be" and "repute"

2. Line 1/2: "gentle in his view" and "tyrannous and rough in proof" are antithetical

Line 4: "without eyes" and "see pathways"

Line 6: "tell me not" and "have heard it all"

Line 7: "hate" and "love"

Line 8: "brawling" and "loving," "love" and "hate"

Line 9: "any thing" and "nothing"

Line 10: "heavy" and "lightness," "serious" and "vanity"

Line 11: "Mis-shapen chaos" and "well-meaning forms"

Line 12: All four phrases

Line 13: "still-waking" and "sleep," "is not" and "is"

Line 14: "love" and "no love"

Lines 15/16: "laugh" and "weep"

Also, the thought in line 13—"That's not what it [love] is" is antithetical to the type of "love" expressed in lines 7–12.

3. Line 1: The first phrase is antithetical to the second phrase—one might not love killing, but will do it anyway.

Line 2/3: "wish him dead" and "hate the murderer"—he had to die, but how could you kill such a fine king?

Line 3: "hate" and "love," "murderer" and "murdered"

Lines 4/5: "guilt of conscience" and "good word nor princely favor"—your reward for killing him is not my praise nor money, but guilt.

Lines 6/7: "wander" and "show"—wander around, never show up here "shade of night" and "day nor light"—your existence is forever changed from light to darkness.

SKILL WORKSHEET 6

ELISION

Put simply, elision means either to shorten a word by omitting a vowel—as "int'rest" for "interest" or "virt'ous" for "virtuous"—or to combine two words into one by eliding a letter or letters—as "I'd" for "I had" or "I've" for "I have." Elision is used to shorten words, when necessary, so that fewer syllables are spoken to achieve the ten-syllable rhythm.

A. 1. Here are some examples.

Brutus: I had rather be a dog and bay the moon,   (*JC*, IV, iii)

The line has eleven syllables, and the rhythm is lost if you read the first foot "I had." Therefore, you elide "I had" to "I'd," and the first foot becomes "I'd rath." And the line scans like this:

$$\smile \,/ \quad \smile \,/ \quad \smile \,/ \quad \smile \,/ \quad \smile \,/$$
I'd rath / er be / a dog / and bay / the moon,

In an eleven or twelve-syllable line, before eliding, you must decide if the final syllable is a feminine ending. If it is not, then find the word or words to elide.

2. Here's another example of an eleven-syllable line.

Helena: Wherefore was I to this keen mockery born?   (*MND*, II, ii)

"Born" is obviously not a soft-ending word; it requires stress. Therefore, something has to be elided. Try eliding "mockery" (which has three syllables) to "mock'ry" (which has only two), and the rhythm works.

3. However, note this example from *The Merchant of Venice:*

Portia: The quality of mercy is not strained;
It droppeth as the gentle rain from heaven
Upon the place beneath.   (IV, i)

In line 2, there are eleven syllables. But the "en" in "heaven" can be a feminine ending (the word is pronounced with stress on the first syllable), so the rhythm works without elision. You would not want to stress "en," as that would make the word sound very strange. Try it and see.

B. The next three examples are from *Twelfth Night.* Try this eleven-syllable line, and decide whether to elide one word or to have a feminine ending.

1.

Captain: A virtuous maid, the daughter of a count.   (I, ii)

2. Here is an eleven-syllable line of the Duke. Choose between elision or a feminine ending.

Duke: I have unclasped
            To thee the book even of my secret soul.   (I, iv)

3. And here is Antonio's line to Sebastian—eleven syllables, same choice:

Antonio: To-morrow, sir; best first go see your lodging.   (III, iii)

(A hint: feminine endings are often "tion," "en," or "ing.")

For additional work, obtain the complete book from which this worksheet is taken, and begin on part one. If you become interested in the study of Shakespeare, you will find advanced work exciting and stimulating. It will turn on your brain and challenge your talent. Enjoy!

TIPS AND ANSWERS FOR SKILL WORKSHEET 6

B. 1. You must elide "virtuous" to "virt'ous," as "count" would not be a feminine ending.

2. You must elide "even" to "e'en," pronounced as one syllable and stressed.

3. The "ing" on "lodging" is not stressed, so it can be a feminine ending. Try saying "lodging" by stressing the "ing." That's probably not what you want!

CHAPTER 33

Scenes and Monologues

But when they ask you what it means, say you this;

HAMLET, IV, V

REFER TO YOUR complete collection of Shakespeare. While any edition will do, some are more helpful than others. In this book, line notations are taken from *The Pelican Shakespeare,* edited by Alfred Harbage (Viking Penguin, 1977). In other editions, lineation and punctuation may differ. The punctuation in the Pelican edition is especially good. Check the scenes and monologues listed in this chapter for the rehearsal material. All of these will work with students. After selection, consider the following study or rehearsal procedures.

Copy the scene. Then have the students type it themselves, double spaced, and check it for spelling and punctuation accuracy. Have the students read the entire play aloud and know how this scene (or monologue) fits into the overall action.

This study can be done in small groups comprised of those students who are working on scenes or monologues from the same play. In a class of twenty, you might use scenes and monologues from four plays; so each reading/study group consists of five students.

First, have the students look up any word that may have had a different meaning in the year 1600. Write the meaning in the rehearsal script. The OED is the definitive source for this task.

Next, work out the scansion. Mark stressed syllables, mark feminine endings or elide as necessary, and underline words that break the rhythm. Circle all phrases and breathing points, and look up all words. If you have time to uncover the antithesis, do that; it will add immeasurably to your success. Only now are you ready to begin rehearsing the scene.

Scenes of two or three minutes in length (five minutes maximum) are enough for young actors—about forty to fifty lines, or twenty to twenty-five lines for each actor. To get fifty lines "right" is a challenging task, and allowing students to work on more than twenty-five lines each simply means that many more hours of rehearsal per scene are required. For monologues, twelve to fifteen lines are sufficient.

If you intend to present the scenes as an "evening of Shakespeare" or similar performance, short scenes and one-minute monologues work very well. For monologues, it's often helpful to use a second, nonspeaking actor standing downstage, giving the speaker someone to address. For soliloquies, the single actor can use the entire class as the audience. When performing, you might have someone other than the actors introduce the scenes, but have the actors introduce their own monologues.

The majority of scenes and monologues listed below are taken from the most "popular" eight plays, from which you probably select your curriculum. A few selections from other plays are also listed. Roles written for men can often be played by women.

SCENES AND MONOLOGUES FROM THE EIGHT MOST POPULAR PLAYS

As You Like It
Scenes
- I, iii, lines 1–36, for two women (Celia and Rosalind), in prose. To continue, add one man (the Duke) for lines 37–85, for a section in verse. After the Duke exits, Celia and Rosalind have a verse scene from lines 86–134, which, in itself, makes a short scene.
- III, ii, lines 157–240, for two women (Celia and Rosalind), in prose.
- III, v, lines 1–137, for one man and two women (Silvius, Phebe and Rosalind—cut Celia and Corin), in verse. After Rosalind exits at line 79, there is a two-person verse scene between Phebe and Silvius.
- IV, iii, lines 76–181, for one man and two women (Oliver, who has most of the dialogue, Celia and Rosalind), mixes prose and verse.
Monologues
- II, vii, lines 139–166, for a man (Jaques), in verse.
- III, v, lines 35–63, for a woman (Rosalind), in verse.
- III, v, lines 108–134, for a woman (Phebe), in verse.
- Epilogue, a woman (Rosalind), in prose.

Hamlet
Scenes
- I, iii, lines 1–136, for two men and one woman (Laertes, Ophelia and Polonius), in verse.

- III, i, lines 88–161, for one man and one woman (Hamlet and Ophelia), mixed prose and verse.

Monologues
- I, iii, lines 10–44, for a man (Laertes), in verse.
- II, iii, lines 1–18, for a man (King), in verse.
- All acts, Hamlet's soliloquies, for men or women, in verse.

Henry V

Monologues
- Each act, Chorus soliloquies, for men or women, in verse.
- I, ii, lines 260–298, for a man (King), in verse.
- III, i, lines 1–34, for a man (King) in verse.
- IV, i, lines 216–270 (some cutting recommended), for a man (King), in verse.
- IV, i, lines 275–292, for a man (King), in verse.
- IV, ii, lines 15–37, for a man (Constable), in verse.
- IV, iii, lines 18–67, for a man (King), in verse.

Julius Caesar

Scenes
- I, ii, lines 25–177 (some cutting possible), for two men (Cassius and Brutus), in verse.
- II, i, lines 229–308, for one man and one woman (Portia and Brutus), in verse.
- IV, iii, lines 36–123, for two men (Brutus and Cassius), in verse. By cutting lines 124–143 and adding Lucius, the scene can continue with lines 144–162.

Monologues
- II, i, lines 10–34, for a man (Brutus), in verse.
- II, ii, lines 13–26, for one woman (Calphurnia), in verse.
- III, i, lines 254–275, for one man (Antony), in verse.

Macbeth

Scenes
- I, v, lines 1–70, and I, vii, lines 1–82, for one man and one woman (Macbeth and Lady Macbeth), in verse. Separate scenes or combine for one longer scene.
- II, ii, lines 1–73, for one man and one woman (Macbeth and Lady Macbeth) plus knocking sounds, in verse.
- III, i, lines 1–43, for two men (Macbeth and Banquo), in verse. Can continue as a scene for three men and a servant (Macbeth and Two Murderers and the servant), lines 44–144.

Monologues
- I, v, lines 36–52, for a woman (Lady Macbeth), in verse.
- I, vii, lines 1–28, for a man (Macbeth), in verse.
- III, i, lines 1–10, for a man (Banquo), in verse.

A Midsummer Night's Dream

Scenes
- II, i, lines 1–59, for one man and one woman (Puck and Fairy), in verse.
- II, i, lines 188–244, for one man and one woman (Demetrius and Helena), in verse.

Monologues
- I, i, lines 181–193, for a woman (Helena), in verse.
- I, i, lines 226–251, for a woman (Helena), in verse.
- II, i, lines 248–267, for a man (Oberon), in verse.
- III, ii, lines 6–34, for a man or a woman (Puck), in verse.
- III, ii, lines 145–161, for a woman (Helena), in verse.
- III, ii, lines 192–219, for a woman (Helena), in verse.
- III, ii, lines 254–277, for a man (Oberon), in verse.

Romeo and Juliet

Scenes
- I, i, lines 158–236 (cut as necessary), for two men (Romeo and Benvolio), in verse.
- II, ii, lines 1–138 or lines 139–190, or combine the two scenes, for one man and one woman (Romeo and Juliet), plus the off-stage voice of the Nurse and an off-stage noise, in verse.
- II, iii, lines 31–94, for two men (Friar and Romeo), in verse.
- II, iv, lines 152–202 or through line 204 if another character added, for one woman and one or two men (Nurse, Romeo and Peter), mixed prose and verse.
- II, v, lines 1–77, for two women (Juliet and the Nurse), in verse.
- III, ii, lines 1–143, for two women (Juliet and the Nurse), in verse.
- III, iii, lines 1–175 (cut some lines from the longer speeches), for two men and one woman (Friar, Romeo and Nurse), in verse.
- III, v, lines 65–126, for two women (Juliet and Lady Capulet), in verse. By adding the Nurse and Capulet, the scene continues with lines 127–205; this is followed by a Juliet and Nurse scene, lines 206–244.

Monologues
- I, i, lines 79–101, for a man (Prince), in verse.
- I, iii, lines 17–48 (some cutting recommended), for a woman (Nurse), in verse.

- I, iii, lines 79–94, for a woman (Lady Capulet), in verse.
- I, iv, lines 53–94, for a man (Mercutio), in verse.
- II, i, lines 1–23, for a man (Romeo), in verse.
- III, ii, lines 1–34, for a woman (Juliet), in verse.
- III, ii, lines 97–127, for a woman (Juliet), in verse.

Twelfth Night

Scenes
- I, v, lines 133–297, for three women and one man (Malvolio, Olivia, Viola and Maria—Viola and Olivia have most of the lines), mixed prose and verse. Can begin at line 208 with Viola and Olivia; need a Malvolio for two lines.
- II, iv, lines 78–123, for one man and one woman (Viola [disguised as a man, Cesario] and the Duke), in verse.
- III, i, lines 91–176, for two women (Olivia and Viola), in verse.

Monologues
- II, ii, lines 16–40, for a woman (Viola), in verse.
- IV, iii, lines 1–21, for a man (Sebastian), in verse.
- V, i, lines 66–84, for a man (Antonio), in verse.

OTHER SELECTED SCENES AND MONOLOGUES

The Comedy of Errors

Scenes
- III, ii, lines 1–71, for one man and one woman (Antipholus of Syracuse and Luciana), in verse.
- IV, ii, lines 1–66, for two women and one man (Adriana, Luciana, Dromio of Syracuse), in verse.

Monologue
- V, i, lines 136–160, for one woman (Adriana), in verse.

The Taming of the Shrew

Scene
- II, i, lines 168–182, for one man and one woman (Petruchio and Kate), in verse.

Monologues
- IV, ii, lines 175–198, for a man (Petruchio), in verse.
- V, ii, lines 141–184, for a woman (Kate), in verse.

The Two Gentlemen of Verona

Scenes
- I, ii, lines 1–140, for two women (Julia and Lucetta), in verse.

- II, vii, lines 1–90, for two women (Julia and Lucetta), in verse.

Monologues
- II, iv, lines 189–211, for a man (Proteus), in verse.
- II, vi, lines 1–43, for man (Proteus), in verse.
- IV, iii, lines 11–36, for a woman (Silvia), in verse.

Love's Labor's Lost

Monologues
- III, i, lines 162–194, for a man (Berowne), in verse.
- V, ii, lines 89 –118, for a man (Boyet), in verse.
- V, ii, lines 779–802 for a woman (Princess), in verse.

The Merchant of Venice

Scene
- I, iii, lines 1–177 (or any section), for three men (Shylock, Bassanio and Antonio), in verse.

Monologue
- IV, i, lines 182–203, for a woman (Portia), in verse.

Much Ado About Nothing

Scenes
- III, i, lines 1–136, for four women (Hero, Beatrice, Ursula, and Margaret [one line]), in verse.
- IV, i, lines 253–328, for one man and one woman (Beatrice and Benedict), in prose.

All's Well That Ends Well

Scene
- I, iii, lines 130–249, for two women (Countess and Helena), in verse.

King Henry VI, Part 1

Monologue
- I, ii, lines 72–92, for a woman (Pucelle [Joan of Arc]), in verse.

King Henry VI, Part 2

Monologues
- I, i, lines 212–257, for a man (York), in verse.
- III, i, lines 4–41, for a woman (Queen Margaret), in verse.

King Henry VI, Part 3

Monologues
- II, v, lines 1–52, for a man (King), in verse.

- III, ii, lines 124–195 (with some cutting), for a man (Richard, Duke of Gloucester), in verse.

Richard III
Scene
- I, ii, lines 1–263 (use sections), for one man and one woman (Richard and Lady Anne) plus a few guards, in verse.
Monologues
- I, ii, lines 1–41, for a man (Richard), in verse.
- V, iii, lines 238–261, for a man (Richard), in verse.

King Henry IV, Part 1
Scene
- II, iii, lines 33–113, for one man and one woman (Hotspur and Lady Percy), in verse.
Monologue
- III, ii, lines 129–159, for a man (Prince Hal), in verse.

King Henry IV, Part 2
Monologue
- II, iii, lines 9–45, for a woman (Lady Percy), in verse.

Othello
Scenes
- III, iii, lines 93–257, for two men (Othello and Iago), in verse.
- IV, iii, lines 9–103 (with cutting), for two women; (Desdemona and Emilia), in verse.
Monologues
- I, iii, lines 377–398, for a man (Iago), in verse.
- II, i, lines 280–306, for a man (Iago), in verse.

King Lear
Monologues
- I, ii, lines 1–22, for a man (Edmund), in verse.
- II, iii, lines 1–21, for a man (Edgar), in verse.

Timon of Athens
Monologue
- IV, i, lines 1–41, for a man (Timon), in verse.

The Winter's Tale

Scene
- II, ii, lines 1–167, for one man and two women (Jailer, Emilia and Paulina), in verse.

Monologue
- III, ii, lines 90–115, for a woman (Hermione), in verse.

The Tempest

Scenes
- I, ii, lines 189–305, for one man and a second character who can be either a man or a woman (Prospero and Ariel), in verse.
- II, ii, lines 1–182, for three men (Caliban, Trinculo, and Stephano), mostly prose.
- III, i, lines 1–91, for one man and one woman (Miranda and Ferdinand), in verse.

Our revels now are ended.

THE TEMPEST, IV, i

PART FOUR

For Professional Actors and Coaches: The One=Day Brush Up

I long to know the truth hereof at large.

THE COMEDY OF ERRORS, IV, iv

CHAPTER 34

The Morning Session

Prepare thy battle early in the morning.
RICHARD III, V, iii

You are a realistic actor. An opportunity arises to play Shakespeare, Molière, or another "classical" writer. You must read for the role. What do you do? How do you prepare this audition?

Here let us breathe
And haply institute a course of learning.
THE TAMING OF THE SHREW, I, i

EARLY CHARACTER CHOICES

Before beginning on the skills, here are some procedures to keep in mind. Try not to think about the character you plan to read. Shocking advice, I suppose. You want to dig out the subtext and the character choices and play those. But if you can wait on those choices, it will pay off handsomely.

Forcing a preconceived character, action, or method of "How one is supposed to play Shakespeare" on Shakespeare's language is one of the worst mistakes you can make. Forcing means you begin rehearsal knowing *how* you want to play the character *before* you have thoroughly mastered *what* the text is saying.

On the other hand, it is not forcing to have studied the text, perhaps seen a few productions of the play, and determined how you might play a specific role if given the opportunity. But be patient and, for the moment, forget "character." There are more important things to do first. We'll get to "character" later on.

Here are some of those "more important things":

- *When playing realism,* your job as an actor is to find your action and play it. Use a strong and clear voice, and play your action. "Play your action" refers to the things you do to achieve your objective.
- *When playing Shakespeare,* do the same thing. All you need to add are a few skills to handle the language. If playing realism is like walking, then playing Shakespeare is like dancing. You simply need to add a few "moves" to a process you already know and find the correct rhythm.

But it is also true that if you play Shakespeare without mastering these skills, your work will be as uninteresting and painful to the audience and your fellow actors as the ill-trained dancer is to the beholder and the partner.

This thought may be helpful: If you can hear the tune of a Beethoven sonata in your mind and you desire to pass this pleasure to the audience through the piano, your fingers must have the skills to play the notes. In playing Shakespeare, the skills you are about to learn are the composer's directions to you, like musical notations, and your voice is the instrument.

The four skills outlined below are as easy to learn as baseball and can be used at various levels of training and success. But to not use them is like playing baseball with your glove on the wrong hand. Not only does this blunder cause you to be a poor fielder, it also forces you to throw with the wrong arm. In both cases, you have crippled your own ability and won't be effective.

> *Little joy have I*
> *To breathe this news; yet what I say is true.*
> RICHARD II, III, iv

Among other benefits, these skills will enable you to allow Shakespeare's language to be understood and heard clearly by the audience (or the director at your audition). Most American directors haven't spent much time analyzing Shakespeare's language. The directing jobs are elsewhere—for example, modern realistic plays, musicals, video, film—in a ratio of about 300:1. There is nothing that you, the actor, can do about this. When auditioning with Shakespeare, remember that casting agents and producers have even less background than directors, so let their lack of preparation motivate you to be vocally strong and very clear.

> *Or—not to crack the wind of the poor phrase.*
> HAMLET, I, iii

Regarding your voice, say what you mean, and say it loud and clear. Try to use your best voice—not some selected "character" voice. If saying what you mean involves subtext, use it. But don't indulge or rely on subtext when speaking Shakespeare, as problems (discussed in detail in part 1) will surely arise. And, strong voice or weak voice, don't waver from getting what you want from the person to whom you are speaking.

Another vocal clue: say what you think as you think it, and don't "reflect" on the thought before you speak. Don't think, then talk. Talk and think at the same time. Act on the words, not between the words. If you want to study this skill in more detail, refer to chapter 6 in part 1 of this book.

Above all, avoid asking, "How am I going to play this role?" If you speak clearly what you mean and pursue your intention in whatever way is necessary to achieve it, you will automatically discover a character. Let this discovery come to you through those actions.

Don't impose a character on this language. Rather, know the language, and you will discover the character who uses it. Be brave. Let the language guide you. It will show you "how" to play the role.

In summary, even if you know *how* you want to play a Shakespearean character, it won't help you one bit unless you know *what* the language is doing. Your character will be ineffective if what you are saying is unclear to the listener. At your audition, the director needs to hear if you can handle the language. Can you be understood? Are you believable?

We have to start here.

A double spirit
Of teaching and of learning instantly.
HENRY VI, PART 1, V, ii

FOUR BASIC SKILLS

If you use four basic skills, the director at your audition will listen to you and understand what you are saying. *These skills work, even if you don't understand what you're saying—as, perhaps, at a cold reading.*

The four skills are scansion, phrasing, end support, and breathing.

You might wonder about *analysis of text*, which won't receive much attention in this one-day lesson. But once the phrasing is correct, the actor will be very close to truthful line readings. Analysis also includes playing the antithetical words, phrases, or thoughts, which we will study. Complete chapters on antithesis and analysis are also included in part 1 of this book.

Don't forget word meanings. Take the time to open the dictionary (the *OED* if it's available) and check every word that may have had a different meaning in the year 1600. Write down that meaning.

You might also ask about *subtext*. When you set out to examine the emotional and psychological state of your character, it is difficult to ignore subtext. On the other hand, you can't really explore the character until you are certain what the character is doing. In Shakespeare, that action is discovered more through the text than the subtext. In this one-day lesson, we are concerned with the skills required to discover what the character is actually saying and doing. The actor can decide later what subtext, if any, is needed.

Think of Shakespeare's language this way:

Scan it • Break it up • Kick the box • Breathe!

FIRST NEW SKILL: SCANSION

So pause a while . . .

To begin, select the passage or section that you are preparing for your audition, or sections of the play from which you will be reading. You are probably looking at blank verse. (If, by chance, you are reading a prose section—i.e., the language looks ordinary and without verse form—skip scansion and review the other three skills.) As you proceed, if you want more detailed explanations or examples for any definition or concept, the index will guide you to other sections of the book.

Blank verse is not poetry. It can be poetic, but in itself, it is merely a form of writing the English language. It was first used in the mid-sixteenth century and then perfected by Shakespeare and his contemporaries. It should not cause you any insecurity, because you actually speak blank verse all the time. ("Let's go to town and buy an ice cream cone" is blank verse!) A *regular* blank verse line consists of ten syllables, with a stress placed on every second syllable. The form is called iambic pentameter, with a rhythm that goes "dee dum dee dum dee dum dee dum dee dum."

This concept of "stresses" is valuable for actors, because it guides you to both the important words in the line and the author's intention. Marking the soft and stressed syllables in a blank verse line is called scanning the line, or scansion.

Let's do one. We'll break a line into "feet" of two syllables each for a total of five feet and ten syllables, then mark the stresses.

> Let's go to town and buy an ice cream cone.

Break the line into feet:

> Let's go / to town / and buy / an ice / cream cone.

Now mark the stresses: ∪ for unstressed, / for stressed.

> Let's go / to town / and buy / an ice / cream cone.

Here's a better line from *Romeo and Juliet*:

Romeo: But soft! What light through yonder window breaks?   (II, ii)*

But soft! / What light / through yon / der win / dow breaks?

But soft! / What light / through yon / der win / dow breaks?

When you read the line, place emphasis on the stressed syllables: "soft," "light," "yon," "win," "breaks." With your hand, beat out these stressed words or syllables on the table or chair. Read the line a few times by *beating out* and *over-stressing* the five stressed words or syllables. Then forget the scansion, and read the line naturally.

If you've beat out the rhythm with your hand and emphasized the stressed syllables, you will discover that when you "forget" scansion and read the line more naturally, you automatically give a slight emphasis to the stressed words. You will achieve naturalness and honesty, and do so by stressing the correct words.

For the Shakespearean line to be truthful, it is necessary to play the correct stresses. Let's test this idea by reading a line incorrectly. Here's the opening line from *The Merchant of Venice*:

Antonio: In sooth I know not why I am so sad.   (I, i)

In sooth / I know / not why / I am / so sad.

If we follow the scansion, the stresses are "sooth," "know," "why," "am," "sad." Read the line instead by stressing "In," "I," "not," "I," "so," and see what you get. That's probably not what you want for your audition!

For anything so overdone is from the purpose of playing.

HAMLET, III, ii

So pause awhile ...

Now you need a pencil, not a pen. Put this book down for thirty minutes, and select ten or twelve lines from your audition material. *Mark the scansion.* This will pay off handsomely later.

After marking the scansion on your ten or twelve lines, read them aloud a few times, hitting the stressed syllables. *Overdo it. Pound it out.*

*All Shakespeare quotations are taken from *The Complete Pelican Shakespeare,* Viking Penguin, 1977.

You can pull back to naturalism later. By overdoing, you discover meaning and "problems." Are there "problems?" Likely there are, so let's find them. For example, is there a stress that seems wrong? Or is there a line that won't scan to ten syllables? No, you're not miscounting, and, yes, trust your common sense. You've found an *irregular* line. Shakespeare obtains much of his effect by *inverting* stresses, which *changes* the rhythm of a line. Instead of "dee dum," a foot might be scanned "dum dee." He will also write *eleven*-syllable lines and, on some occasions, lines of twelve to fourteen syllables. On the following page are examples of these two variations.

So pause awhile . . .

Before continuing, if you need to brush up on the following terms, check the glossary or index for the following items:
- blank verse
- regular blank verse line
- feminine ending
- short or shared line
- rhymed couplet
- caesura
- elision
- iambic pentameter

Now we shall know some answer.
TITUS ANDRONICUS, III, iv

FIRST USUAL PROBLEM: SCANSION IS IRREGULAR

Here is an example from *A Midsummer Night's Dream*. (Refer to pages 18 and 190 for an example from *Romeo and Juliet*.)

Oberon:	There sleeps Titania sometime of the night,
	Lulled in these flowers with dances and delight;
	And there the snake throws her enamelled skin,
	Weed wide enough to wrap a fairy in. (II, i)

Look at line 3. You may have one or more similar lines in your material.

And there / the snake / throws her / enam / elled skin,

Using *regular* scansion, in the third foot of the line, the word "throws" would not be stressed. The line would scan *incorrectly* like this:

And there / the snake / throws her / e nam / elled skin,

For the sense of the line, however, your common sense tells you that the verb "throws" is more important than the pronoun "her." And you are correct. So the third foot in the line is *irregular* and is called a trochee (pronounced tro' kee) or trochaic foot—which has the first syllable stressed and the second unstressed and scans like this:

And there / the snake / throws her / e nam / elled skin,

"Throws" is an action verb, and actors look for words like this. You would not want to leave it unstressed. This is a typical example of how Shakespeare changes the rhythm of the line and how you, as an actor, play "throws." In fact, for added emphasis, take a little sense pause just before you say it. That little pause is called a *caesura*—pronounced si-zhoor´- ə. It is not a breath pause, just a sense pause.

You discover changes in the rhythm by applying scansion and trusting your common sense. When rhythm changes, play it.

So pause awhile ...

Take fifteen minutes, and circle all words in your speech that break the rhythm.

It is not enough to speak, but to speak true.
MUCH ADO ABOUT NOTHING, V, i

SECOND USUAL PROBLEM: TOO MANY SYLLABLES

Here is an example from *Hamlet*:

Hamlet: To be, or not to be—that is the question: (III, i)

To be, / or not / to be—/ that is / the ques / tion:

Here we have eleven syllables, with the eleventh ("tion") hanging on the end by itself. That syllable is called a *feminine ending*. It creates a soft ending, because in a regular blank verse line, the tenth and final syllable is stressed. Shakespeare uses the feminine ending frequently. You may have some feminine endings in the material you are preparing. Just let these lines end without placing stress on the final syllable. Feminine endings are often "tion," "ing," "eth," "er," and "en."

If you count eleven or twelve syllables in a blank verse line and note that the final syllable must be stressed, you cannot use the feminine ending. In this case, use *elision,* and contract two words or syllables into one— "I will" becomes "I'll." In the following line, Shakespeare has already elided a two-syllable words into one syllable to create an eleven-syllable line; but the actor must elide another word, as "man" is stressed and would not make a feminine ending.

Hamlet: Horatio, thou art e'en as just a man.   (III, ii)

Note "even" is already elided to "e'en" and pronounced as one syllable. The reader must elide "Horatio" to "Horat'o," pronounced as three syllables. Now the line can be spoken in ten syllables with correct rhythm.

Hŏr á / t'ŏ, thóu / ărt e'en / ăs júst / ă mán.

So pause awhile ...

That's a brief explanation of scansion. Before moving on to "break it up," be sure that you have clearly scanned the material you are preparing, marked the stresses, and circled all words that break the rhythm.

That matter is answered directly.
JULIUS CAESAR, III, iii

SECOND NEW SKILL: BREAK IT UP

We're talking about phrasing. According to Webster, a "phrase" may be a group of words that create a thought on which the mind can focus momentarily and which can be preceded or followed by a pause.

If you take any Shakespearean speech or sonnet, many of the phrases are separated by punctuation. Because it is easier to mark the phrases than it is to handle them vocally, you probably have some work to do before your audition.

In this example from *King Henry IV, part 1*, many phrases are clearly marked by punctuation. Here the King demands that Prince Hal explain his unprincely behavior. (See page 225 for another example from *Julius Caesar*.)

King:	Lords, give us leave: the Prince of Wales and I	(1)
	Must have some private conference; but be near at hand,	(2)
	For we shall presently have need of you. *(They exit.)*	(3)
	I know not whether God will have it so	(4)
	For some displeasing service I have done;	(5)
	That, in his secret doom, out of my blood	(6)
	He'll breed revengement and a scourge for me;	(7)
	But thou dost in thy passages of life	(8)
	Make me believe that thou art only marked	(9)
	For the hot vengeance and the rod of heaven	(10)
	To punish my misreadings. Tell me else,	(11)
	Could such inordinate and low desires,	(12)
	Such poor, such bare, such lewd, such mean attempts,	(13)
	Such barren pleasures, rude society,	(14)
	As thou art matched withal and grafted to,	(15)
	Accompany the greatness of thy blood	(16)
	And hold their level with thy princely heart?	(III, ii) (17)

In lines 8–11, there are phrases not separated by punctuation, but notice how many are easily identified.

What about phrases that aren't defined by punctuation? Here are lines 4–11 with caesuras (//) inserted to mark the phrases. (Some actors prefer to circle phrases.)

King:	I know not whether God will have it so //	(4)
	For some displeasing service // I have done;	(5)
	That, in his secret doom, out of my blood //	(6)
	He'll breed revengement // and a scourge for me;	(7)
	But thou dost // in thy passages of life //	(8)
	Make me believe // that thou art only marked //	(9)
	For the hot vengeance // and the rod of heaven //	(10)
	To punish my misreadings. Tell me else, *(etc.)*	(11)

Why bother to mark the phrases? Your goal is to know the phrasing of the line so that you can (1) separate the thoughts, (2) play one phrase against another, (3) allow a thought to continue to the next line, as needed, and (4) identify your breathing spots, just like singing.

The caesuras are inserted only to mark the phrasing for rehearsal purposes. Once your phrasing is clear, remove most of the pauses, and speak from breathing point to breathing point. You don't want to impose pauses similar to those in realistic dialogue on the rhythm of blank verse. That technique simply makes your acting indulgent. Use non-breathing-point pauses only when they are absolutely necessary for clarity.

So pause awhile ...

Take fifteen minutes, and circle or mark the phrases in your material. You should already have looked up all words, marked the scansion and circled the words that break the rhythm. Pause here before you continue to "antithesis."

END MORNING SESSION: LUNCH TIME

You have deserved
High commendation, true applause, and love.

AS YOU LIKE IT, I, ii

USEFUL IDEAS TO REMEMBER:

CHAPTER 35

The Afternoon Session

Thus did he answer me, yet said
I might know more hereafter.

CYMBELINE, IV, ii

———

As YOU PROBABLY know, placing one idea against another is called *antithesis.* Shakespeare uses antithetical words, phrases, or thoughts in nearly every speech. Having the skill to discover and play antithesis is a key to handling Shakespeare's language. For the actor, antithetical words, phrases, or thoughts provide clear insight into the meaning of Shakespeare's text.

ANTITHESIS

To have my praise for this, perform a part
Thou hast not done before.

CORIOLANUS, III, ii

———

Antithesis is a noun meaning contrast or direct opposite. Placing one antithetical word, phrase, or thought against another can be as simple as this example: "Rather than go to town, let's stay on the farm." When reading the line, play (give equal emphasis to) "go" against "stay" and "town" against "farm." Then, simultaneously play the entire first phrase, "rather than go to town," against the second phrase, "let's stay on the farm," which is antithetical to it in thought. You should immediately hear a new clarity in the sentence.

From Brutus' speech on page 24, let's dig out some antithetical words, phrases, and thoughts so we can play them against each other.

Lines 1/2: "do love me" is antithetical to "would work me to." Read the lines aloud, and play these two phrases against each other.

Lines 3/4: the phrase "How I have thought of this" (in the past) is antithetical to the phrase "shall recount hereafter" (in the future). Read the lines aloud, and play these thoughts against each other.

Lines 6/7: "have said" is antithetical to "have to say."

Lines 8/9: "find a time/Both meet to hear and answer" is antithetical to line 10: "Till then... chew upon this:"

Line 9: "hear" and "answer" are antithetical.

Lines 11/12: "a villager" and "son of Rome" are antithetical, as are "be" and "repute."

In a larger sense, the *thought* in lines 1–the middle of line 3 is antithetical to the *thought* in lines 3½–5½. The first thought is pretty much "I hear and understand what you're saying to me; I've also thought about this and will discuss it later." The next thought is "right now I need more time to think, so stop speaking." The idea of "listening to you" followed by "now I don't want to listen to you" is antithetical. You need to set up the first thought, so that you can play against it when you speak the antithetical thought.

Read the first four lines aloud, playing the antithetical words and phrases we've noted, and then play the entire thought of those four lines against the entire thought of the next three. As an actor, you must discover and play these textual clues to clearly reveal what the character is saying.

Now read the entire speech, and play the antithetical words and thoughts against each other. Notice how everything becomes clearer. Practice this example, and you will discover that you are speaking Brutus's words with confidence and understanding. Notice that your work is *specific* rather than *generalized*.

So pause a while...

Take one hour, and dig out the antithetical words, phrases, and thoughts in your material. It works best to have a small group of actors do this together. When it comes to digging out antithesis, four or five brains are better than one. Assemble a group, make some coffee, and plunge in.

Digging out antithesis is—horrors—part of analysis! Many actors, especially when young, hate analysis. These actors prefer to trust their "natural talent," or the director, to guide them to line meanings; or they prefer to discover meaning through action. They hate to "talk about meaning" and are often concerned that too much text study will kill spontaneity.

That attitude is somewhat understandable. With realistic text, you can often discover what a line means by reading it clearly, listening, and playing your action.

However, when using the "discovery-through-action" approach, you will have more success with realism than with heightened text. The reason is simple: Blank verse has a defined structure. This is not to undervalue modern text—good writers always have a language structure—but to clarify blank verse.

When working with blank verse, before committing to an action, you must be certain what the verse is doing. If you select your action before you recognize the stresses, or before you clearly see the antithetical words and thoughts, or before you know which words break the rhythm, you can rehearse for weeks and never once read the line with its best possibilities. You can play your action and listen intently to everything said to you, but if you don't know what the language is doing, your work will remain unfinished. This failure is not a reflection on talent, but on lack of practice or coaching with blank verse.

We that have good wits have much to answer for.

AS YOU LIKE IT, V, i

When working with blank verse, actors who neglect to mark phrasing, find the antithesis, and analyze what the line is doing often "lock in" on a reading and won't budge from that comfort zone. These actors are usually making "character choices" before completing text analysis. The actor may fall back on the idea that "this is how my character would say it."

These actors will cling to an interpretation until the director forces them to try other approaches. Now the work tends to become artificial. The director is no longer suggesting that the actor try other actions, but is bogged down trying to dislodge rote or emotional indulgence.

Text study must precede character analysis. The defense that "this is how my character would say it" may or may not be supported by what the line is actually doing. The response may simply be the actor's easy way out of uncovering those possibilities.

As with selecting actions, it follows that you need to know everything the language is doing before you select a character. If not, your selection may be entirely out of sync with the author's meaning, and you end up trying to force the language to fit the character choice. On the other hand, if you develop your character after you are certain of the text, you will find that the words are exactly what your character needs to achieve the action.

What if you have a director who forces a character choice on you before you are completely certain what the language is doing? This is a serious problem, usually caused by the actor not doing the necessary prerehearsal homework. To avoid this situation, always complete text analysis before you begin rehearsals. Should there be an emergency where you are thrust into a role that is written in blank verse, get some help, and pull a few all-nighters completing your text analysis. Then determine if the director's choices fit the text in a meaningful way that you can play. If you disagree, at least you now have a solid knowledge of the text to support your view and can perhaps win over the director to another choice.

Regarding accents that may be required for some characters, or may be a director's concept, do your complete text analysis first, then slowly add the accent one word or one line at a time. Keep within your truthful sense of the language, and simply allow it to be pronounced differently.

For a funny, yet moving example of a director forcing a preconceived character on an actor, see Neil Simon's film, *The Goodbye Girl,* in which Richard Dreyfuss is required to play Richard III the director's way.

Of course, you can technically perform an action without knowing what you are saying, i.e., you understand only the general sense of a scene or moment but have not researched thoroughly the possibilities within your own lines. For example, in act IV of *The Merchant of Venice*, Portia is trying to persuade (her action is "to persuade") Shylock not to take his "pound of flesh." Her action is properly connected to the other character, and its effectiveness can only be measured in terms of the other's response.

Portia:	I pray you, let me look upon the bond.
Shylock:	Here 'tis, most reverend Doctor, here it is.
Portia:	Shylock, there's thrice thy money off'red thee.
Shylock:	An oath, an oath! I have an oath in heaven:

(IV, i)

You can speak the lines, play your action, and make it convincing. You can get by without knowing what the choices are for the line "Shylock, there's thrice thy money offer'd thee." *But if you do know what the choices are, something more than "to persuade" happens as you play your action.*

Let's assume that you have marked the scansion, worked out the phrasing, tested the antithetical possibilities, and have concluded that there are at least four possible approaches to this line. What you select, of course, will influence how you eventually decide to play the character:

1. No choice. Just read the line, and let the audience decide what it means.
2. Emphasize the amount of money Shylock will receive by foregoing the bond.
3. Read the bond (the prop), then lose patience with his inflexible position.
4. Confidentially urge him, speaking as a neutral legal authority, to make the more merciful choice.

Selecting number four, for example, guides you to read the line differently (although still "to persuade") than if you had selected number three.

Of course, your final selection in performance is based somewhat on how Shylock hands you the bond and his intent with "Here 'tis, most reverend doctor, here it is." But you now have a range of choices from which you can respond, and you have both a mental and a vocal familiarity with the possibilities. That's the position you want to be in during performance. You don't want to be locked in to a specific reading of the line because it "feels good" or "is how my character would say it."

The audience will know what you're saying when you know *what you're saying. Character choices made after text study allow character and language to work harmoniously. Know clearly what you are saying, then know your action. This knowledge will lead you to character.*

I understand thee, and can speak thy tongue.
ALL'S WELL THAT ENDS WELL, IV, i

Here are more difficult lines, which become clear and easy to speak if you analyze them and handle the phrases according to your discoveries:

Sonnet 27

Weary with toil, I haste me to my bed,	(1)
The dear repose for limbs with travel tired;	(2)
But then begins a journey in my head,	(3)
To work my mind, when body's work's expired:	(4)

Read the lines through once, then let the following discoveries (the analysis) help clarify your reading.

1. In line 1, the first and fourth syllables are stressed, not the second and fourth. The first foot is a trochee.
2. In line 1, antithetical words include "weary" and "haste," and also "toil" and "bed."
3. In line 1, "I haste me to my bed" can be two phrases, if you don't overdo it, and that allows you to make something of "haste."
4. In line 1, support "bed." Don't play the pronouns "my," "me," or "I." *Never stress pronouns, unless by deliberate choice called for by the action.* The pronoun is easily assumed, and to stress it causes another part of the line to lose meaning.
5. Line 2 is a regular line, but use three phrases, so you can be clear on "travel tired."
6. In line 3, "But" turns the thought around, but need not necessarily be stressed; the line can be a regular line.
7. Line 3 is antithetical to line 1.
8. In line 3, "begins a journey" is antithetical to "travel tired."

9. In lines 2/3, "head" is antithetical to "limbs."
10. In line 4, "To work my mind" is antithetical to "when body's work's expired."
11. In line 4, "mind" is antithetical to "body."

Read the lines again, playing the antithesis. Notice the difference. These clues have guided you to Shakespeare's meaning through the blank verse structure. Very little modern realism is structured this way, and that is why, with Shakespeare, you must start with the language and know what it offers. Then, if you are clear about the actions you've discovered through the language, your character will take care of itself. Later, in rehearsal, you can develop your character to the full extent of your ability. You will find, if you haven't already, that Shakespeare's language is so good, it actually helps you to achieve your objective.

Actors with limited skills, complete beginners, "personalities," and inexperienced acting teachers or directors often work "in reverse." When approaching a script, they first decide "how" to play a character, then proceed to make the action and line readings fit the character choice.

This reverse approach can sometimes be successful with modern realistic dialogue, especially on film, but it never works with heightened text. You can't play a "personality" here. You must deal with the language, because the language dominates. With Shakespeare, the "character first" approach will fail every time.

Antithesis is such a key to discovering Shakespeare's text that a complete chapter is devoted to it in part one. After you finish the one-day lesson, if you have time to study one more thing, make it antithesis.

PHRASING EXERCISE

So pause awhile . . .

In this phrasing exercise, the actor speaks the language from thought to thought and must deal with each thought individually, not running them together unless by choice. Take the next hour, and do the exercise with the material you are preparing.

Set two objects apart from each other. The objects can be chalkboards, chairs, books, people, trees, it doesn't matter. The distance can be four feet or much more, as you will discover, but you may want to begin with the objects about six feet apart. Stand by one of the objects. Begin your lines. At each punctuation point, pause and cross to the other object (location), then resume. Breathe as you cross, then speak the next line from the next object, until you come to another punctuation point—pause—cross while breathing—speak, etc. You can go around a room like this, speaking thought to thought, from object to object.

The exercise forces you to recognize how the lines are broken into thoughts and how the thoughts must be separated; allows you to use all the air you wish to use on individual phrases; allows you to breathe in while walking to the next object; allows you to prepare the next line while breathing in and moving; and allows you to speak after you've filled your lungs—which you have plenty of time to do while moving to the next object.

In this exercise, you are forced to deal with each phrase individually and can't rush, because you must stop speaking to move and breathe at each punctuation point. This exercise always works.

The exercise can be simplified and practiced in two parts. First, do the exercise, but don't worry about the breathing. Just concentrate on separating the phrases, which you must do to accomplish the exercise. Once you feel comfortable with the separation of phrases, add the concentration on breathing correctly. With practice, you will find a wonderful rhythm: line and breath out, walk and breathe in, line and breath out, walk and breathe in, etc. Ultimately, you should have your objects only four or five feet apart so that you only take one breath in while walking, and fill your lungs completely each time.

Now take the next hour and review all antithetical words, phrases, or thoughts in your ten or twelve lines of material. Practice playing the ideas against each other. Also, do the phrasing exercise while adding concentration on the antithetical ideas and other scansion discoveries.

You now have the basic skills to act your lines from phrase to phrase, which means from thought to thought, and this is exactly what you want to do.

END AFTERNOON SESSION

Have dinner now, and rest your brain.

When my cue comes, call me and I will answer.
A MIDSUMMER NIGHT'S DREAM, IV, i

CHAPTER 36

The Evening Session

If you be not too much cloyed with fat meat,
our humble author will continue the story.
HENRY IV, PART 2, EPILOGUE

Now that we have scanned the lines, found the antithesis, and separated the phrases, our concentration will be on speaking those phrases so that the listener knows exactly what you are saying. A major clue is the realization that in a phrase or verse line, the final word is often the most important.

THIRD NEW SKILL: KICK THE BOX

"Kick the box" means to support the final syllable of the verse line. When you support the final syllable or word, you allow the thought expressed in the line to "continue." The thought doesn't just end, as it does if you ease off on the final word or run out of breath and lose the word.

If you want your Shakespeare to work, you need to develop the skill required to support the final word and thought in each line.

AN ASIDE

Once you have learned this skill, apply it to all text. You may be amazed to discover how frequently the final word or phrase is the most important part of a prose line. Modern writers are not writing blank verse or placing a stress on the tenth syllable of their line, but the idea of supporting the entire second part of the prose line, if not the last word, will almost always work for you. Examples from George Bernard Shaw, Arthur Miller, and Shakespeare are included in chapter 4.

Supporting the last word of the verse line is not easy. Physiologically, our diaphragm doesn't want to work that way. The muscle is "lazy" and prefers relaxation to tension.

During voice training, actors learn to use the diaphragm to support speech. But even after training, many actors forget to "kick the box." They forget for three reasons:

- The effort to read the line "naturally" and truthfully encourages us to fade out at the end.
- We don't practice speaking blank verse on a daily basis.
- Breath support becomes lackadaisical, and rather than support the ends of lines, it is easier to allow them to fade away as they do in our daily speech.

Because our vocal muscles are uncomfortable with a change, any effort to support the ends of lines will seem strange at first and perhaps "overdone." But supporting is correct. If you don't support the end of the verse line, one can project that your Shakespeare will not be clear or truthful. The listener won't quite know what you are saying.

You need great physical energy to speak Shakespeare's verse, and kicking the box helps you to remember to use your body. Energy is a key to your success. Remember, Shakespeare's plays were written to be performed:

- Outdoors
- In broad daylight
- For large audiences
- With much of the audience standing for the entire play
- With people sitting on stage
- Amid concession sales like a baseball game
- With birds flying around
- With the audience probably talking back to the actors

If you try speaking in that setting, you will discover immediately how much vocal energy is required.

THE KICK-BOX EXERCISE

So pause awhile ...

In this example, Romeo is speaking to Friar Laurence:

Romeo: Thou canst not speak of that thou dost not feel.   (III, iii)

Scan the line. Now speak the line in a "natural" way, allowing the final word "feel" to fade away. What is the line about?

Now circle the word "feel." Then place a small cardboard box on the floor and stand by it. Speak the line, and when you get to "feel," kick the box. Don't kick on "not," and don't kick after "feel." Kick right on the *f* of the word.

It may help if you take just a split-second pause (a caesura) before "feel," as this allows you to position yourself (and the word) and to get your leg and balance ready to kick—then kick. Later, forget the pause, which is only for the exercise.

You will notice that the kick does two things—it gets your body physically involved in speaking the language, and it gets you to support the word "feel." The intent here is not to overplay "feel." You don't want to shout it or call great attention to it. You simply support it, as opposed to letting it fade out. Your ear should tell you that the line means different things when you support or don't support "feel."

If you don't support "feel," Romeo seems to be telling the Friar not to "speak of things." That information is in the first half of the line.

If you do support "feel," Romeo may be reminding the Friar that he is celibate and has never felt the love of a woman, therefore how can he advise? That reading gives both actors much more to work with. Try it.

There are other interpretations of this line, but you should see immediately the difference between supporting and not supporting the final word. Not supporting makes the line a "general" comment—supporting makes it "specific." Remember Stanislavski's famous observation: "*In general is the enemy of art.*"

Let's look at two other examples, as one of these may be similar to the material you are preparing. In the first line of *Romeo and Juliet*, the final word has more than one syllable.

Chorus: Two households, both alike in dignity,   (1)

Kick on "ty," not on "dig" or "ni"—because "ty" is the tenth syllable. Again, don't smash it like the box, just support it. If you kick on "dig" (the second syllable of the fourth foot), you will notice that "nity" falls off. Try it.

Remember feminine endings? If the line scans to eleven syllables, you support number ten, not number eleven. With a feminine-ending line, let the last syllable be soft. On "To be, or not to be—that is the question," kick on "ques," and let "tion" be soft.

Here's Portia to Shylock in *The Merchant of Venice* (a line with a feminine ending).

Portia: It droppeth as the gentle rain from heaven   (IV, i)

Kick on "heav" and let "en" be soft.
But here's Shylock to the Duke in the same play:

Shylock: I have possessed your Grace of what I purpose,   (IV, i)

This line has a feminine ending, and you kick on "pur." However, as an actor choice, you might also support "pose" for the added threat implied. Try it both ways.

Trust your common sense. If you find that the last word in a specific line doesn't merit stress, pull back. Don't hit it so hard. Make it real. After you've worked the exercise, forget it—but remember to always kick the box.

Don't take it to the audition with you, and don't take it to a performance. This is a rehearsal exercise designed to help you support the thought all the way through a verse line. It's not academic; the exercise leads to a skill that you will automatically apply to blank verse lines from now on. As with all acting, play the moment, don't try to remember what you rehearsed.

Read these next four lines in a "natural" way, allowing the final words in each line to *fade away* so you can barely hear them.

Sonnet 35

No more be grieved at that which thou hast done:
Roses have thorns, and silver fountains mud;
Clouds and eclipses stain both moon and sun,
And loathsome canker lives in sweetest bud.

Now read the lines again, this time supporting the last words (kicking the box). Notice how the thoughts in the lines continue from line to line when you support the endings. You also allow our ears to enjoy the pleasure of the rhyme!

So pause awhile . . .

Take the next hour, and do this exercise with every line in your material. Practice supporting the final words, then the final phrases. Trust your ear. As with some of the other exercises, this one is most enjoyable if you assemble a small group and take turns reading the lines. Hearing others read your material can be very rewarding.

You've just become a great deal better at reading Shakespeare!

I do believe that these applauses are
For some new honors...
JULIUS CAESAR, I, ii

Now, can you scan it, phrase it, support it, and still breathe? Sure!

REVISITING A FAMILIAR SKILL: BREATHE!

It's absurd for an actor to run out of breath, and doing so can destroy a fine characterization. Even worse, it also destroys the author's line. Tyrone Guthrie liked to say that any well-trained actor could speak seven lines of blank verse on one breath, in a large theatre, with clear diction, and without rushing (*On Acting*, 14). It may take you some time to master that skill, and you won't need it for your audition, but you do need to breathe correctly, even if you can't speak seven lines on one breath.

When do you breathe? It's easy to decide with Shakespeare, but it's harder to discipline yourself to do it. Breathe at the natural stops, which are identified by punctuation marks.

Look at these lines, in which the Friar advises Juliet how to use the sleeping potion. (See page 39 for another example from *Macbeth*.)

Friar:	To-morrow night look that thou lie alone;	(1)
	Let not the nurse lie with thee in thy chamber.	(2).
	Take thou this vial, being then in bed,	(3)
	And this distilling liquor drink thou off;	(4)
	When presently through all thy veins shall run	(5)
	A cold and drowsy humor; for no pulse	(6)
	Shall keep his native progress, but surcease;	(7)
	No warmth, no breath, shall testify thou livest;	(8)
	The roses in thy lips and cheeks shall fade	(9)
	To wanny ashes, thy eyes' windows fall	(10)
	Like death when he shuts up the day of life.	(*Rom*, IV, i) (11)

As clearly as we can tell, this speech has typical Shakespearean punctuation. We must remember that our versions of the plays were taken from actors' scripts, and the punctuation has been "studied and worked" for four hundred years by scholars. Different editions of the plays change the punctuation slightly.

The breathing points are the punctuation marks. Circle them, then read the speech and breathe at each mark. You will find that it is quite easy to speak from one breathing point to the next. The longest stretch is one and one-half lines.

Don't breathe after "run" in line 5 or "pulse" in line 6. But try it once to discover the problem. You will see immediately that the choice is wrong. Your common sense and good ear will tell you.

Don't breathe at the end of a verse line simply because it is the end of the line on paper. Unless there is punctuation, it isn't the end of the phrase or thought. Many verse lines are enjambed, which means the thought in one line continues to another line without separation by punctuation. In the Friar's speech, lines 5, 6, 9, and 10 are enjambed. Breathe at the end of a verse line only if there is punctuation, as in lines 1, 2, 3, 4, 7, 8, and 11.

Read these four lines, which have numerous punctuation points, and breathe at each natural stop (all of the punctuation points). Ariel, a spirit, greets his master, Prospero, who has sent for him in *The Tempest*:

Ariel:	All hail, great master! Grave sir, hail! I come	(1)
	To answer thy best pleasure; be't to fly,	(2)
	To swim, to dive into the fire, to ride	(3)
	On the curled clouds. To thy strong bidding task	(4)
	Ariel and all his quality.	(1, ii) (5)

Did you cheat? Read it a second time, *and make yourself breathe at all punctuation points.* You will find that you don't need that many breaths. You may be able to read the first line breathing only after "master" and the second "hail," cutting two breaths. But don't cut them unless you don't need them. You probably would have used the breaths in the three-thousand seat original Globe Theatre, but won't use them in the audition space, small theatres, or film.

If you breathe after "fly," "swim," and "fire," it may help you create images with each phrase, which would be appropriate for the character.

Trust your judgment. Your goal is to have a reserve of breath power available at all times and to be able to kick the box on the final word of a sentence. If you haven't enough breath left to support the final word, you are not breathing correctly. Inserting more breaths into the lines is not the best solution (although it is one), because these added breaths break up the verse line in an unnatural way, and this will likely leave you gasping and unclear.

| Portia: | The quality of mercy is [*breathe*] not strained; | (*MV*, IV, i) |

If you read the line that way, you are the one who is strained!
On the other hand, the phrasing in most blank verse lines can be separated at least once by inserting a caesura. The caesura, however, is not usually a breathing place.

The quality of mercy // [*caesura sense break*] is not strained;

If you need to insert a breath, do it where the phrasing allows and where it will add emphasis to what you just said or are about to say. But in the above line, you obviously don't need a breath. "Strained" might be emphasized by preceding it with a caesura, but not a breath.

However, try reading the line by pausing to breathe (or emote, or "act") after "quality," "mercy," and "not." If this sounds right to you, postpone your audition for a day. Go back to the top of this "One-Day Brush Up" and start over. You've missed the point!

Your goal is to breathe correctly—to fill your lungs at each breathing point— and to avoid little gasping breaths that fill only one-third of your lung capacity. Take the time to breathe deeply, then speak the line on the exhale. The words ride on the air; just send them out.

> *Yet words do well*
> *When he that speaks them pleases those that hear.*
>
> AS YOU LIKE IT, III, V

Actors accustomed to realistic text often want to "enhance" that text with sounds, gasps, crying, whispering, pauses for effect, sighs, and "ahs." With heightened text, such "enhancements" tend to destroy the rhythm of the language. When the rhythm is lost, usually the antithetical ideas are lost. When the antithetical ideas are lost, the audience listens only passively, because they are not quite certain what you are saying.

For an excellent example of reading heightened text with great heart and commitment, correct breathing, and without breaking the rhythm with unnecessary pauses or character "enhancements," watch Kenneth Branagh speak the Saint Crispin's speech in Act IV of his film, *Henry V.* It's perfection. Other similar examples are listed in part 5.

You can rant and rave with a powerful voice and great energy, but the audience will listen only passively if they don't know exactly what you are saying.

Embellishing the language with emotion for the reason that "my character would do this" will usually not work for you in Shakespeare. Your performance becomes indulgent, because you've lost *what* is being said in favor of *how* it is being said.

Generally this direction works: If you need to cry, cry after the line, not on the line. Reason? We must hear the words first, then we can experience your sorrow without the irritation caused by a muffled line. If you must whisper, do it so that everyone, including the back row, can hear and understand clearly. Again, you risk the irritation caused by the muffled line.

There is more on this subject in part 1 of this book, but for your audition, forget "pregnant pauses" for emotional effect. Keep the language moving, keep the rhythm, and pause to breathe at the correct points.

The emotion, you will discover, is already written into the text. You need only find it and play it honestly.

So pause awhile ...

Here is a good rehearsal exercise. Clearly mark the breathing points in your material. Then read your speech aloud, and use up all of your air on each group of words, from breathing point to breathing point. Make certain that you support the final words, but otherwise empty your lungs between breathing points.

This exercise allows you to discover how much force and power you have available. It also implants in your mind the necessity to breathe. Use all of the air between each breathing point, even if the line has only one word. *Do it now.*

As you practice the exercise, you will begin to notice that taking the breath gives you the split second you need to grasp your next line. As you inhale physically, you also inhale mentally, so to speak, and grab the next line. Then out it comes on the next breath.

If it is your tendency as an actor to break up lines with "embellishments" for emotional effect, this exercise may show you that the only pauses you really need in Shakespeare are the breathing points. Keep the phrases intact, the words moving, and play the antithetical ideas against each other.

You will discover that application of too much emotion to heightened text does nothing but bury the meaning, and the audience stops listening.

Don't get ahead of yourself by thinking ahead. As with all good acting, stay in the moment, listen, and respond. Don't anticipate or indicate. Realize that after you speak a line, your breathing skill allows you to mentally secure your next line, and this skill will help you develop the confidence you need to stay in the moment.

If you have three or four lines with no breathing points, try to conquer them. You will need a deep breath before you start line one and will need to control the release of your air as you speak the lines, or you'll never make it through and surely won't have anything left for the important final word. If you can't yet handle three or four lines, find an appropriate place to insert your breath—but hopefully no more than one. Then begin a walking or jogging program and build up your breath support!

Try this example. In *Henry V*, the Bishop of Canterbury tells the King that if he will attack France, the Church will supply him with the money needed for the war.

> Canterbury: O, let their bodies follow, my dear liege, (1)
> With blood, and sword, and fire to win your right! (2)

In aid whereof we of the spiritualty	(3)
Will raise your highness such a mighty sum	(4)
As never did the clergy at one time	(5)
Bring in to any of your ancestors.	(i, ii) (6)

Read the speech aloud, and see if you can do lines 3 through 6 without a breath. If you can't make it, take a breath after "sum," but notice that the speech flows better without the breath. Note, too, that "spiritualty" must be elided from four to three syllables—spir't'ual ty.

Here are seven lines Chorus speaks before act IV of *Henry V*:

Chorus:	Now entertain conjecture of a time	(1)
	When creeping murmur and the poring dark	(2)
	Fills the wide vessel of the universe.	(3)
	From camp to camp, through the foul womb of night,	(4)
	The hum of either army stilly sounds,	(5)
	That the fixed sentinels almost receive	(6)
	The secret whispers of each other's watch.	(iv) (7)

Read the speech aloud, breathing only at the punctuation points. Support all last words, especially "universe," "sounds," and "watch." Careful—no breath after "dark."

Remember these clues:

- The words ride out on the breath, just send them
- Inhaling gives you a moment to grasp your next line
- Breathe at every opportunity
- If you cut a breathing point, do it intentionally because you don't need it
- Strong breath enables you to speak with power
- Lack of breath signals *weakness.*

What about the common modern habit, especially among film actors, of releasing breath immediately before speaking? This technique is one of many that actors pay good money to learn in various film acting classes. By using it, you lose power and energy, and you probably run out of breath before reaching the end of the spoken line, thus giving you that "fade-away" sound. Whereas some actors and directors believe this approach produces a more "natural" sound, persons who respect language and the actor's gift of voice shun it. You need energy and power to speak well. The idea of allowing the microphone to produce your sound for you kills energy, and that weakens your ability to command the listener—even on film.

So pause awhile ...

Now spend any remaining time reading your material aloud and breathing at the correct places as marked in your text. Apply everything we've discussed.

> *I would applaud thee to the very echo,*
> *That should applaud again.*
>
> MACBETH, V, iii

Always read and work on Shakespeare aloud. This language is meant to be spoken, and much of the sense is discovered through speech. Shakespeare doesn't just "work better" aloud, it works *ten times better!* Therefore, when you work on the lines, use the opportunity to practice breathing and voice skills as well.

CHARACTER

I lied. We never got to "character." Or did we? If you've applied what we've discussed to your material—scansion, phrasing and discovering antithesis, kicking the box, and correct breathing—a character choice has probably emerged all by itself.

If not, develop one. Now you know what the language is doing and what it requires. Apply everything you already know about creating honest and truthful character, and create! Develop the kind of character that would do and say what the language is doing and saying. The character is that person who needs and uses these words. Do your language study before rehearsals begin, then the rehearsal process can be about character and relationships, as it should be.

To explore in more detail how the character you've selected uses your analysis of the language to come alive through the language, here is one more example. Juliet waits impatiently for the Nurse to bring word of Romeo. Her image-rich lines start like this:

Juliet: Gallop apace, you fiery-footed steeds,
           Towards Phoebus' lodging! Such a wagoner
           As Phaeton would whip you to the west
           And bring in cloudy night immediately.   (*Rom*, III, ii)

As the actor playing Juliet, your text analysis of these four lines will tell you many things about the character, including:

- She thinks in images.
- She thinks in classical images ("fiery-footed steeds," "Phoebus' lodging," "wagoner as Phaeton").
- She's had a solid education to know these classical images (she understands that Phoebus is the sun god and his "lodging" is beyond the western horizon, which, when entered, causes night; and Phaeton is his son, with whom the horses of the sun ran away and set fire to the earth, just as the Nurse is bringing "fire" to her).
- She's no "softy" ("whip you").
- She's impatient ("gallop apace," "whip you," "bring... immediately").
- Something is happening too slowly for her (the Nurse is too slow returning).
- She's longing for the night ("bring in cloudy night"), and it's still day ("to the west").
- She thinks of gods controlling her destiny (gods pull the sun across the sky and control day and night—and everything else as well).
- She allows herself to be impatient with these gods, not just with the Nurse.

You can probably find more, but that's the idea of what has come from your text analysis.

The character is the person who needs and uses these words. Juliet's education must be deeply imbedded in her mind, because it is clearly released as her passion for Romeo explodes. Your Juliet will choose what she thinks of Phaeton and the speed with which he runs his out-of-control chariot of the sun, and that choice will be clear in the way you read the words. You can make the choice, because you know exactly what the words mean. Your Juliet will choose how rapidly she wants night to descend, and that choice will be clear in the way you read those words.

As the actor, you know what the words are doing—they are allowing the character to expose her emotional state through her learning—so you choose your way of doing it. The way you play Juliet is your choice. But it is based on knowing exactly what Juliet is saying, not guessing what she is saying, and not trusting to "natural talent" to read Shakespeare's lines.

Your Juliet might elect to make more or less of "immediately." Obviously she could be extremely lustful (one reading), or simply eager (another reading). These are the choices you make that make the character your own. But the author is being served now, and the audience will have every opportunity to hear your choices clearly. You know what you're saying, so the audience will know what you're saying.

We probably all agree that understanding the language will not, by itself, make you a good Shakespearean actor. Moving the words from your brain to the audience's ears still requires all the skill and talent you possess, your trained voice (not a "fall-away" sound), plus your huge energy, and every glimmer of passion that is appropriate for each moment.

The task of acting the play through the character is still up to you, the actor. But when acting Shakespeare, if you complete text study before you begin characterization, you stand the best chance of success.

It takes vivid imagination and great technique to be an actor, plus courage, talent, and drive. Add to your imaginative qualities the skills you just relearned, and be successful with Shakespeare!

And smooth success
Be strewed before your feet!
ANTONY AND CLEOPATRA, I, iii

___

END OF THE PROFESSIONAL ACTOR'S ONE-DAY BRUSH UP

Break a leg!

Well, breathe awhile, then to it again.
HENRY IV, PART I, II, iv

___

Tomorrow to the field.
ALL'S WELL THAT ENDS WELL, III, i

___

PART FIVE

Resources

We may live to have need of such a verse.
TROILUS AND CRESSIDA, IV, iv

CHAPTER 37

More Exercises

Together with the exercises included in the main text (e.g., kick the box), here are a few others. Each addresses a specific problem. When practicing them, many new discoveries will be made.

I have used these exercises for nearly thirty years and can no longer remember where they originated. They are probably combinations of exercises from Stanislavski, Meisner, Berry, Barton, Linklater, Rodenburg, various student and professional actors, and me, and have been sifted, changed, and reinvented while I coached actors and read anything written on the subject of acting, speaking, or analyzing Shakespeare. So acknowledgment is given here to all coaches, directors, teachers, actors, and authors whose influence has helped me to develop these exercises and to pass them along to others without taking personal credit for more than a small share of their effectiveness.

REMEDIES FOR COMMON ACTOR AILMENTS

What to do if:
- *The actor is emphasizing the wrong words.*
  Exercise: Tap out the stresses (chapters 4, 31 and 34).
- *The actor is not phrasing correctly.*
  Exercise: Phrasing exercise (chapters 3, 31 and 35).
- *The actor is not supporting the line through to the end.*
  Exercise: Kick the box (chapters 4, 31 and 36).
- *The actor is not breathing correctly.*
  Exercise: Breathing exercises (chapters 5, 31 and 36).
- *The tempo and rhythm are off, because the actor is playing unnecessary subtext.*

Exercise: Removing subtext (chapters 6 and 35).
* *The actor is not emphasizing the antithetical words, thoughts, and phrases.*
Exercise: Playing the antithesis (chapters 8 and 35).
* *The actor is not properly opening his/her mouth.*
Running and shouting the lines will open the mouth and release the words with energy. Also, singing the lines like an Italian tenor or dramatic soprano to any made-up tune opens the voice and also calls attention to each syllable, because when singing, each syllable gets its own note.
* *The actor is not listening.*
The partner should suddenly whisper the lines. Whispering demands attention. Also, speak the scene in total darkness.
* *The actor is not using the vowel sounds.*
Read the lines speaking *only* the vowels. The actor will discover the wonderful vowel sounds and the opportunities they offer.
* *The actor is rushing, or is locked into rote memorization.*
    1. The actor who is rushing should read the lines for the listening actor to mime. The actor must slow down and clarify each thought, or the mime can't perform.
    2. Use the phrasing exercise from the text, moving on punctuation points.
    3. Perform a physical or mental task while speaking the lines. For example, draw a picture of a specific object on the chalkboard while speaking the lines, or multiply a complex number on the chalkboard while speaking the lines, or arrange the other actors according to last names or height while speaking the lines. When speaking while concentrating on a different task, the actor will find new emphasis for specific words and will automatically slow down.
    4. Two actors sit back-to-back on the floor after having memorized fifteen to twenty lines of a scene. The actor with the opening line says first in her own words what she is going to say via Shakespeare's lines, then speaks the lines. The second actor repeats in his own words what he heard, then states in his own words what he is going to say via Shakespeare's lines, then speaks the lines. This continues until the actors have worked through the scene. Then speak the scene again, but only with Shakespeare's words.
        You can create variations on this exercise, all of which will help actors listen, phrase, discover new ideas, and find tempo. This is an excellent exercise.
* *The actor's voice is high pitched.*
    1. Sit on the floor holding your knees, and rock gently and speak. Feel your voice lower itself in your body. Try to retain that voice when you stand up.
    2. Lie on the floor on your back, and begin speaking your lines. Your voice will slowly lower in pitch. When it is low and strong and supported, stand up without losing that voice. Memorize its placement.
* *The actor has no passion.*
The actor doesn't understand what the character is actually doing. Use analysis to solve that problem first. Then, you might try this technical exercise: Create a resistance. For example, have the actor to whom the first actor is speaking refuse to stand still or to look at the first actor, yet insist that the first actor make eye contact. The irritation that develops will help free the emotions.

You can create variations on this exercise. The idea is to make it difficult for the speaker to communicate.

- *The actors are over-acting.*
  Try placing a "microphone" (a prop will work) within inches of two actors standing very close together and have them read the scene for "television." When they pull back to video/film acting, they begin to listen and discover and stop "performing."

You will find hundreds of other exercises in the various books listed in the bibliography.

CHAPTER 38

Bibliography

Following are selected lists of (1) successful and unsuccessful examples of acting Shakespeare on film and video, (2) books for further study, (3) books on acting Shakespeare, and (4) books on acting realism.

IA. SELECTED VIDEO AND FILM PERFORMANCES

Hamlet

1996—Kenneth Branagh's film of the uncut text. Superb cast and production values, with wonderful performances in the leading roles. Great clarity of plot and character, without loss of language. Verse handled especially well by Branagh (Hamlet), Derek Jacobi (Claudius), Julie Christie (Gertrude), and Nicholas Farrell (Horatio). Marred only by a few whispering scenes and occasional loud background effects that bury the words. Exchanges between Branagh and Jacobi are especially fine to study.

1990—Franco Zeffirelli's film, starring Mel Gibson (Hamlet), who is attractive and usually comfortable with the language (much of which has been cut) and the role. The strong supporting cast of Glenn Close (Gertrude), Alan Bates (Claudius), Paul Scofield (Ghost), Helena Bonham Carter (Ophelia), Ian Holm (Polonius), and Stephen Dillane (Horatio) handle the verse beautifully. Listen especially to Scofield's Ghost speeches.

1990—New York Shakespeare Festival production produced for video by Kimberly Myers, directed by Kevin Kline with Kirk Browning; with Kline (Hamlet), Peter Francis James (Horatio), Robert Murch (Ghost), Brian Murray (King), Dana Ivey (Queen),

Michael Cumpsty (Laertes), Josef Sommer (Polonius), Diane Verona (Ophelia), and Clement Fowler (Player King). The modern dress and very drab production plays like a melodrama, with considerable "over-the-top" acting. The design and acting style may have worked better in the original stage production, but did not translate well to video. Kline's Hamlet is very watery-eyed and often ineffective. Exceptions include the Hamlet/Ophelia confrontation scene, which has a wonderful interpretation, and Hamlet's relaxed, and yet commanding advice to the players.

1948—Laurence Olivier's black-and-white film, starring Olivier (Hamlet), Jean Simmons (Ophelia), Eileen Herlie (Gertrude), Basil Syndey (Claudius), Felix Aylmer (Polonius), Norman Wooland (Horatio), and Stanley Hollaway (First Gravedigger). Effective performance in many ways, and a solid reading of the text. The technique of soliloquies as voice-overs mixed with live dialogue doesn't quite work, and some scenes are melodramatic. Watch especially Aylmer and Hollaway, who offer classic interpretations of their characters.

Henry V

1989—Kenneth Branagh's film, starring Branagh as the King. Superb cast and production. For the American ear, some articulation problems in the first scene (unintelligible whispering) and with Ian Holm's accent for the Welshman, Fluellen. Paul Scofield is brilliant as the French king, as are Emma Thompson as his daughter, Brian Blessed as Exeter, and Derek Jacobi as Chorus. Branagh's St. Crispan's speech is perfection, as is Blessed's charge to the French king.

1944—Laurence Olivier's film, starring Olivier as the King. The acting style may seem a little rhetorical today, but the film still contains some brilliant work. The opening scene is especially useful to students, as it is Olivier's version of what it was like backstage at the Globe during Shakespeare's day.

Romeo and Juliet

1996—Baz Luhrmann's high energy film, set in modern Los Angeles, with Leonardo DiCaprio (Romeo), Claire Danes (Juliet), Dash Mihok (Benvolio), John Leguizamo (Tybalt), Paul Sorvino (Capulet), Brian Dennehy (Montague), and Harold Perrineau, Jr. (Mercutio). An original adaptation that works as the action film it is intended to be. Effects, however, and a restless camera dominate what little language is retained. The older actors do well, but many of the attractive young actors needed much more vocal work and didn't get it. Some excellent examples of reading lines with full stops, a technique (or lack of) that kills the rhythm and the thought within the verse.

1993—The Stratford Festival of Canada created a lovely production starring Megan Porter Follows, Antoni Cimolino, Colm Feore, Barbara Byrne and Bernard Hopkins, and directed by Richard Monette. Video available from Poor Yorick.

1968—Franco Zeffirelli's wonderful film is almost a classic today. Excellent adaptation of a play to film—with very little dialogue left. Fine language coaching of the young actors, Olivia Hussey and Leonard Whiting. Beautiful visual production.

Richard III

1996—Al Pacino's film, *Looking for Richard*, presents scenes from the play, together with improvisation. With Pacino (Richard), Alec Baldwin (Clarence), Kevin Conway (Hastings), Harris Yulin (Edward IV), Penelope Allen (Queen Elizabeth), Kevin Spacey (Buckingham), Winona Ryder (Lady Anne), Estelle Parsons (Queen Margaret), Aidan Quinn (Richmond), and includes comments on Shakespeare from Kevin Kline, Kenneth Branagh, James Earl Jones, Rosemary Harris, Peter Brook, Derek Jacobi, John Gielgud, and Vanessa Redgrave. A successful documentary film containing both comments and acted scenes. Pacino's untrained voice creates a breathy acting style that seems indulgent. This and Baldwin's subtextual style are the direct opposites of Conway and Allen, plus some of the others, who play the heightened text extremely well. Good opportunity to compare acting styles.

1995—Richard Loncraine's film, starring Ian McKellen (Richard), Annette Bening (Elizabeth), Nigel Hawthorne (Clarence), Robert Downey, Jr. (Rivers), Jim Broadbent (Buckingham), Maggie Smith (Duchess of York), John Wood (King Edward), and Kristin Scholl Thomas (Lady Anne). This original and compelling adaptation sets the story in the fascist 1930s. The locale mostly works, and the characters are real. McKellen is outstanding in the title role, having adjusted his performance from the original stage production to film without a hitch. Superb example of character and language in harmony.

1955—Laurence Olivier's film, starring Olivier (Richard), Ralph Richardson (Buckingham), Claire Bloom (Lady Anne), and John Gielgud (Clarence). Olivier changed the soliloquy technique used in his earlier *Hamlet* and now speaks directly into the camera, with marvelous effect and brilliant characterization. A superb accomplishment. Watch especially the soliloquies, and note the superior example of how to hold a thought for forty-one lines in a Shakespearean speech. Olivier does this in his opening soliloquy.

Othello

1996—Oliver Parker's film, starring Laurence Fishburne (Othello), Kenneth Branagh (Iago), and Irene Jacob (Desdemona). Some wonderful acting and directing, but marred by an overdose of breathy whispering, which makes various scenes unintelligible and irritating.

1965—BHE Production from the National Theatre of Great Britain. Stuart Burge's film starring Laurence Olivier (Othello), Frank Finlay (Iago), Maggie Smith (Desdemona), Joyce Redman (Emelia), and Derek Jacobi (Cassio). Originally directed for the stage by John Dexter. Excellent example of an actor (Olivier) developing a voice for a character, and the language is handled beautifully. Smith creates a "mature," but effective Desdemona. Jacobi and Finlay are both excellent.

Macbeth

1978—Thames Television Video Stage taping of Trevor Nunn's 1976 Royal Shakespeare Company production, produced by Nunn, starring Ian McKellen (Macbeth), Judi Dench (Lady Macbeth), John Woodvine (Banquo), Griffith James (Duncan), Roger Rees (Malcolm), and Bob Peck (Macduff). With a "black-and-white" design scheme, the play is presented by only sixteen actors and limited props and sets. Each scene is played against a black background. The camera is always tight, and soliloquies are into the lens. The production values, which probably worked better on stage, become dull on tape—more like a formal reading than a stage production. But the language is handled beautifully.

1976—Roman Polanski's film, starring Jon Finch (Macbeth) and Francesca Annis (Lady Macbeth). An excellent film, with fine acting and beautiful production values. Only the voice-over soliloquies become tiresome.

1948—Orson Welles' eighty-nine–minute film adaptation, with effective black-and-white photography. The soliloquies, all voice-overs, are melodramatic, but Welles is commanding as Macbeth, and Jeanette Nolan's Lady Macbeth is engaging, despite an acting style more suited to the stage. The film was low budget and shot in twenty-three days.

1957—Akira Kurosawa's adaptation of the story for his film, entitled *Throne of Blood*, follows the plot with "Lady Macbeth" given new motivations. Toshiro Mifune and Isuzu Yamada star. Beautiful black-and-white photography. In Japanese with subtitles.

King Lear

1997—BBC/WGBN video of a Royal National Theatre production, directed by Richard Eyre, with Ian Holm (Lear), Michael Bryant (Fool), David Burke (Kent), Barbara Flynn (Goneril), Amanda Redman (Regan), Victoria Hamilton (Cordelia), and Timothy West (Gloucester). Clear and easy-to-follow production, with Holm strong as Lear. The cast is wonderful, and the language is read beautifully.

1984—Michael Elliott's film, starring Laurence Olivier (Lear), Colin Blakely (Kent), Anna Calder-Marshall (Cordelia), Dorothy Tutin (Goneril), Diana Rigg (Regan), and John Hurt (Fool). Wonderful film, with excellent scenes for study, especially between Lear/Fool and Lear/Kent. Olivier's frail, real-life condition helps to creates marvelous empathy for Lear (or Lear/Olivier). The actor's last film.

1971—Grigori Kozintsev's film, with screenplay by Boris Pasternak. Beautifully filmed in black-and-white. Wonderful costume, prop, and setting design, probably the twelfth or thirteenth century (soldiers have cannon, but no muskets), with a revealing look at Lear's retinue, an entourage that would discourage any potential host. Starring Yuri Jarvet (Lear), E. Radzins (Goneril), G. Volcher (Regan), V. Shendrikova (Cordelia), O. Dal (Fool), K. Sebris (Glouster) [sic], and E. Melyandov (Kent). Production has many nice touches, like Cordelia's wedding scene, and follows the original story quite closely. Translated from verse to Russian, then translated back for the subtitles, the language now reads like heightened prose, with very few of the original lines intact.

1970—Royal Shakespeare Company film, directed by Peter Brook, in black-and-white photography, starring Paul Scofield (Lear) and Irene Worth (Goneril). Example of a "heavy" approach to Shakespeare—slow and ponderous; yet some wonderful scenes and characterizations, if you are willing to wait. This production certainly worked better on stage, but did not translate well to film.

1985—Japanese director Akira Kurosawa's film is roughly based on Shakespeare's story of King Lear. Entitled *Ran*, Japanese for "chaos." Magnificent visual and spoken production. In Japanese with English subtitles.

Julius Caesar

1970—Stuart Burge's film, starring John Gielgud (Caesar), Charlton Heston (Antony), Jason Robards (Brutus), and Richard Johnson (Cassius). Gielgud's strong performance of Caesar is overthrown by a few weak ones, notably Robards' subtextual acting style, which kills the verse. Among the Americans, Heston and Robert Vaughn (Casca) fare better.

1953—John Houseman's and Joseph L. Mankiewicz's film, starring Marlon Brando (Antony), James Mason (Brutus), John Gielgud (Cassius), and Louis Calhern (Caesar). Gielgud's Cassius and Mason's Brutus are classics. Brando learned to handle the verse and does not rely entirely on subtext, thus offering an effective performance. However, the acting styles are an exercise in contrast. Worth studying for this interesting variety.

The Taming of the Shrew

1986—Stratford Shakespeare Festival (Canada) video of a live performance, directed by Peter Dews, starring Len Cariou (Petruchio). Superb production, probably the best of this play on tape or film. Cariou's and Sharry Flett's (Kate) wooing scene the best ever. Magnificent handling of the language and marvelous characters throughout. Worth studying everything Cariou does.

1975—Video of an American Conservatory Theatre production, directed by William Ball and starring Marc Singer (Petruchio), Fredi Olster (Kate), and William Paterson (Baptista). Ball elects to shape the play as *Commedia dell'arte,* and the actors are marvelous at playing the *lazzi* in this very lovely production. However, the style begins to dominate the language and the play itself, and one looks forward to the "quiet" moments. The "wooing scene" and Kate's final scene are especially fine, because the actors abandon the "style" and play the language and situation, sans effects. Excellent example of applying a preconceived physicalization to heightened text with mixed results.

1966—Franco Zeffirelli's film, starring Richard Burton and Elizabeth Taylor. Beautiful visual production. Burton strong, if a little old for the role. Excellent example of an American actress, Taylor, in a gutsy effort, successful in many ways, while working with limited vocal power.

A Midsummer Night's Dream

1999—Michael Hoffman's film (director and screenplay), with a cast of American, British, and French actors, including Kevin Kline (Bottom), Rupert Everett (Oberon), Michelle Pfeiffer (Titania), Stanley Tucci (Puck), Calista Flockhart (Helena), Anna Friel (Hermia), Christian Bale (Demetrious), Dominic West (Lysander), Roger Rees (Peter Quince), David Strathairn (Theseus), and Sophie Marceau (Hippolyta). A visually beautiful film (Gabriella Pescucci, costume design, and Luciana Arrighi, production design), with a gorgeous musical score, selected mostly from Italian operas. A serious effort to capture the play on film. Yet the film bogs down in indulgent acting, especially from Pfeiffer and Everett, and uncertainty how to handle the lovers, who are beautiful and capable with the language, but just get boring. Kline, cast against type, takes getting used to as Bottom. But together with Tucci and Rees, he handles Shakespeare's language as it should be spoken, and his dream speech is the highlight

CLUES TO ACTING SHAKESPEARE

of the film. The final-act play offered by the mechanicals almost salvages the film. Worth viewing for both strengths and weaknesses.

1996—RSC video of an Adrian Noble production, with Stella Gonet (Hippolyta/ Titania), Alex Jennings (Theseus/Oberon), Desmond Barrit (Bottom), Barry Lynch (Puck/Philostrate), Monica Doan (Hermia), and Hayden Gwyne (Helena). Workers and fairies also doubled in this colorful modern-dress production. The mechanicals are especially fine, and all the language is beautifully read.

1969—Royal Shakespeare Company film, directed by Peter Hall, with Diana Rigg (Helena), Helen Mirren (Hermia), David Warner (Lysander), Michael Jayston (Demetrius), Ian Richardson (Oberon), Judi Dench (Titania), and Ian Holm (Puck). Excellent examples of language handled to near perfection, while offering honest characters. Clear script without too much cutting.

Twelfth Night
1998—Video of a "Live from Lincoln Center" production, directed by Nicholas Hytner, starring Helen Hunt (Viola), Philip Bosco (Malvolio), Kyra Sedgwick (Olivia), Brian Murray (Sir Toby), Max Wright (Sir Andrew), Paul Rudd (Orsino), and Amy Hill (Maria). Wonderful production, with excellent examples of American actors handling Shakespeare's verse with confidence, a credit to the director's superb sense of language.

1996—BBC film, adapted and directed by Trevor Nunn, starring Ben Kingsley (Feste), Imogen Stubbs (Viola), Helena Bohnam Carter (Olivia), Nigel Hawthorne (Malvolio), Toby Stephens (Orsino), Mel Smith (Sir Toby), and Richard E. Grant (Sir Andrew). Excellent film in all ways. Some fascinating scenes of simultaneous action. Superb cast. Marred only by heavy whispering in places, which kills the dialogue. Probably as good a production of the play on film as will be seen in a long time.

Much Ado About Nothing
1993—Kenneth Branagh's film, starring Branagh (Benedick) and Emma Thompson (Beatrice). Wonderful film, especially the scenes between the two outstanding leads. Marred only by a few American film actors who attempt to force character on the language and struggle with the verse. Worth studying for both examples.

1973—Video of a New York Shakespeare Festival and CBS Television production, brilliantly directed by A. J. Antoon with Nick Havinga. Wonderful and colorful 1900 American design by Tom John and Theoni V. Aldredge, with a sparkling musical score by Peter Link. The American actors handle the language extremely well, led by Kathleen Widdoes (Beatrice), Sam Waterston (Benedick), Glenn Walken (Claudio), April Shawhan (Hero), Douglas Watson (Don Pedro), and Barnard Hughes (Dogberry). May be viewed at the New York Public Library for the Performing Arts.

As You Like It
1986—Stratford Shakespeare Festival (Canada) video of a live performance, directed by John Hirsch. Wonderful taping of a stage production, with a strong cast and first-class production values. The verse is spoken beautifully by Roberta Maxwell (Rosalind), Andrew

Gillies (Orlando), Rosemary Dunsmore (Celia), Nicholas Pennell (Jaques), Lewis Gordon (Touchstone), and most of the others.

All's Well That Ends Well

1978—Video of a New York Shakespeare Festival production, skillfully directed by Wilford Leach with fabulous music by Richard Weinstock. Beautiful production designed by Wilford Leach (sets), Jennifer Tipton (lights), and Carol Oditz (costumes), starring Pamela Reed (Helena), Mark Linn Baker (Bertram), Elizabeth Wilson (Countess), Remak Ramsay (King of France), Frances Conroy (Diana), John Ferraro (Levatch), and Larry Pine (Parolles). Excellent direction that brings out all the humor—the actors occasionally break into song. First class in every way, with American actors correctly handling the verse. May be viewed at the New York Public Library for the Performing Arts.

The Merchant of Venice

2004—SONY pictures released a fine motion picture version of the play starring Al Pacino, Jeremy Irons, Joseph Finnes, and Lynn Collins, and directed by Michael Radford. Beautiful productions values and the language is handled well by everyone. Caution for school use; film shows prostitutes partly nude. On DVD.

1973—John Sichel's video of Jonathan Miller's 1970 National Theatre Company stage production, starring Laurence Olivier (Shylock), Joan Plowright (Portia), Jeremy Brett (Bassanio), and Michael Jayston (Gratiano). The video recaptures the stage production and adds a few more settings. Excellent handling of the verse and wonderful examples of playing subtext without indulging in character or sacrificing the rhythm of the language. Very bold acting, which may seem "large" for film.

1999—Fine RSC production with Anthony Sher and Alexandra Gilbreath, directed by Gregory Doran. Available on DVD from Poor Yorick.

IB. OTHER FILMS AND VIDEOS

2003—PBS showed a BBC four-part, eight-hour, video series on Shakespeare's life and times called *In Search of Shakespeare,* Michael Wood, Host, and based on his book, *Shakespeare.* New York: Perseus, 2003; produced my Maya Vision and BBC, 2003. Excellent to own and for school use. Available from PBS or Poor Yorick.

1984—*Playing Shakespeare.* The Royal Shakespeare Company series of video workshops on the techniques and problems of acting Shakespeare. Host John Barton is accompanied by a dozen actors from the RSC. Excellent examples. A must for all acting programs. Barton's text of the same title is a transcription of the workshops.

1999—*The Working Shakespeare Video Library.* Applause Books' workshop series, produced by Glenn Young, hosted by Jeremy Irons, and taught by Cicely Berry and Andrew Wade. A six-video series similar to John Barton's *Playing Shakespeare,* but more current and featuring a combination of American and British actors, including Claire Danes, Blythe Danner, Lindsay Duncan, Samuel L. Jackson, Victor Garber,

Helen Hunt, Robert Sean Leonard, Toby Stephens, Diane Venora, and Emily Watson. Wonderful demonstrations of the techniques of handling Shakespeare's language.

1999—*Shakespeare in Love*. Miramax Film, directed by John Madden, written by Tom Stoppard and Mark Norman, with Joseph Fiennes, Gwyneth Paltrow, Colin Firth, Geoffrey Rush, Ben Affleck, Judi Dench, and Rupert Everett. Exquisite film, set in sixteenth century England. Madden and his writers create a fictional, and comic, background for the young Shakespeare to create *Romeo and Juliet*. Verse from the play and the non-stage language are handled beautifully by this company of mostly RSC actors. First class in every way.

1982—*Acting Shakespeare: Ian McKellen on Broadway*. CBS Broadcast Center Video of McKellen's one-man show, taped live. Stage production directed by Sean Mathias, produced by Andrew Susskind, directed for television by Kirk Browning. McKellen talks about Shakespeare and performs a dozen or so monologues quite successfully. One of the world's best Shakespearean actors, McKellen is especially good at blending language with character. For actors new to Shakespeare, he offers an informative section on character (Macbeth) and verse analysis, then performs it.

1991—*Prospero's Books*. A Miramax Film. Peter Greenaway's version of *The Tempest*, with John Gielgud speaking most of the dialogue for all characters. Beautifully designed production, with engaging special effects. However, unless you are very familiar with the source, much of this story will be confusing. The narrative approach, with visuals inserted, becomes tedious and creates a split focus. Quite erotic.

1966—*Chimes at Midnight (Falstaff)*. An International and Société des Films Sirius, Harry Saltzman film, conceived and directed by Orson Welles, with Welles (Falstaff), John Gielgud, Norman Rodway, Margaret Rutherford, Jeanne Moreau, and Keith Baxter, narrated by Ralph Richardson. A lovely collection of the Falstaff scenes from (mostly) *Henry IV* (both parts), with Welles a remarkable Sir John. Beautifully acted, wonderful scenes to study.

1992—*Shakespeare: the Animated Tales*. Random House Home Video adapted six of the plays to thirty-minute animation treatment for the child audience. Primarily animated characters with narration. Tapes are available for *Hamlet, Macbeth, A Midsummer Night's Dream, Romeo and Juliet, The Tempest,* and *Twelfth Night*.

Productions of all of Shakespeare's plays were taped for the BBC Shakespeare Series between 1979 and 1984 and are available in most libraries. Quality is mixed, but overall, the series is a remarkable achievement, valued by everyone who enjoys the plays.

In 1989, shortly before the end of its theatrical existence, the English Shakespeare Company, with Michael Pennington as artistic director, taped live performances of seven of the history plays in a series called *The Wars of the Roses*. The plays were produced in modern or "eclectic" dress. Sound quality is a problem. The videos are available online from Facets Video at *www.facets.org*.

About 450 films or videos of Shakespeare's plays are currently available, dating back to Herbert Beerbohm Tree's direction of an 1899 silent film version of *King John*, in which Beerbohm Tree also starred. With interest high in feature films of

Shakespeare's plays, and with many stage companies now videotaping productions, this number, which was reached after one hundred years, will double in the next ten. For current information on films and videos, refer to the Shakespeare Filmography online at *http://us.imdb.com/name?Shakespeare,+william.*

For fast ordering or tracking of a Shakespearean video or CD, a small store in Stratford, Ontario, Canada, is unusually well-stocked and willing to help you find a video or CD if they don't have it. Contact the Poor Yorick Shakespeare Catalogue, Tanya Gough, Chief Bard-tender, by e-mail at *yorick@bardcentral.com,* or see their complete catalogue and prices online at *www.bardcentral.com,* or call (519) 272-1999.

2. BOOKS FOR FURTHER STUDY

This list includes all works consulted for this book, some of which are mentioned in the text, and some other books useful to the actor.

Ackroyd, Peter. *Shakespeare: A Biography.* New York: Doubleday, 2004

Bartlett, John, ed. *A Complete Concordance to Shakespeare.* 18th ed. New York: St. Martin's, 1984.

Barton, John. *Playing Shakespeare.* London: Methuen, 1984.

Berry, Cicely. *The Actor and the Text.* New York: Scribner's, 1988.

Berry, Ralph. *The Shakespearean Metaphor: Studies in Language and Form.* Totowa, N.J.: Rawmon and Littlefield, 1978.

Bevington, David, ed. *The Complete Works of Shakespeare.* 4th ed. New York: HarperCollins, 1992.

Bloom, Harold. *Shakespeare: The Invention of the Human.* New York: Riverhead Books, 1998.

Boorstin, Daniel J. *The Americans: The National Experience.* New York: Random House, 1965.

Booth, Stephen. *Shakespeare's Sonnets.* New Haven: Yale University Press, 1977.

Bosco, Philip. *Philip Bosco speaks out. In Theatre.* 7 August 1998, 23–25.

Brook, Peter. *The Empty Space.* New York: Atheneum, 1968.

———. *Evoking Shakespeare.* New York: Theatre Communications Group, 1998.

Brown, John Russell. *Discovering Shakespeare.* New York: Columbia University Press, 1981.

———. *Free Shakespeare.* London: Heinemann, 1974.

———. *Shakespeare's Dramatic Style.* London: Heinemann, 1970.

———. *Shakespeare's Plays in Performance.* Revised Edition. New York: Applause, 1993.

———. *William Shakespeare: Writing for Performance.* New York: St. Martin's Press, 1996.

Bulman, James C. *Shakespeare, Theory, and Performance.* London and New York: Routledge, 1966.

Burson, Linda. *Play with Shakespeare.* Charlottesville, Va.: New Plays Books, 1992.

Cercignani, Fausto. *Shakespeare's Words and Elizabethan Pronunciation.* Oxford: Oxford University Press, 1981.

Davis, James E. and Ronald Salomone, eds. *Teaching Shakespeare Today.* Urbana, Il.: National Council of Teachers of English, 1993.

———. *Teaching Shakespeare into the Twenty-First Century.* Urbana, Il.: National Council of Teachers of English, 1997.

Doyle, John and Roy Lischner. *Shakespeare for Dummies*. Foster City, CA: IDG Books, 1999.

Epstein, Morrie. *The Friendly Shakespeare*. New York: Viking Penguin, 1993.

Freeman, Neil, ed. *Applause First Folio Editions*. New York: Applause, 1998 and on. (Shakespeare's thirty-six plays in modern print, available individually).

———. *The Applause First Folio of Shakespeare: in Modern Type*. New York: Applause, 2000.

———. *Folio Scripts: Shakespeare's First Texts*. 2nd ed. Vancouver: Self-published, distributed by Applause Books, 1999.

Garber, Marjorie. *Shakespeare After All*. New York: Pantheon, 2004.

Gielgud, John. *Backward Glances*. London: Hodder & Stoughton, 1989.

——— and John Miller. *Acting Shakespeare*. New York: Scribner's, 1991.

Granville-Barker, Harley. *Prefaces to Shakespeare*. 4 vols. Princeton: Princeton University Press, 1946.

——— and G. B. Harrison. *A Companion to Shakespeare Studies*. New York: Doubleday, 1960.

Greenblatt, Stephen. *Will in the World: How Shakespeare Became Shakespeare*. New York: W.W. Norton, 2004.

Guthrie, Tyrone. *A Life in the Theatre*. New York: McGraw-Hill, 1959.

———. *In Various Directions: A View of the Theatre*. New York: Macmillan, 1965.

Halio, Jay L. *Understanding Shakespeare's Plays in Performance*. Manchester: Manchester University Press, 1988.

Hall, Peter. *Peter Hall's Diaries*. Ed. John Goodwin. London: Hamish Hamilton, 1983.

Harbage, Alfred, ed. *William Shakespeare: The Complete Works*. Revised Edition. *The Complete Pelican Shakespeare*. New York: Viking Penguin, 1977.

Hinman, Charlton, ed. *The First Folio of Shakespeare: The Norton Facsimile*. New York: W.W. Norton, 1968.

Joseph, Miriam. *Shakespeare's Use of the Arts of Language*. New York: Hafner, 1947.

Kerrigan, John, ed. *William Shakespeare: The Sonnets and A Lover's Complaint*. New York: Viking Penguin, 1986.

Mahood, M. M. *Playing Bit Parts in Shakespeare*. New York: Routledge, 1998.

Mamet, David. *True and False: Heresy and Common Sense for the Actor*. New York: Pantheon, 1997.

Martin, Jacqueline. *Voice in Modern Theatre*. New York: Routledge, 1991.

McCrum, Robert, William Cran, and Robert MacNeil. *The Story of English*. New York: Viking, 1986.

Michaels, Wendy. *Playbuilding Shakespeare*. Cambridge: Cambridge University Press, 1996

Miller, Arthur. *A View From the Bridge*. In *Drama: An Introductory Anthology*, Otto Reinert ed. Boston: Little, Brown, 1961.

Moore, Sonia. *The Stanislavsky System*. Revised Edition. New York: Viking, 1965.

O'Brian, Peggy, ed. *Shakespeare Set Free*. Series of three books. New York: Washington Square Press, 1993.

Olivier, Laurence. *On Acting*. New York: Simon and Schuster, 1986.

Onions, C. T. A. *Shakespeare Glossary*. 3rd ed. Revised. Robert D. Eagleson. Oxford: Clarendon Press, 1986.

Parsons, Keith and Pamela Mason, eds. *Shakespeare in Performance*. London: Salamander Books, 1995.

Proudfit, Scott. Genius in exile. *Back Stage West*, 10 June 1999, 6.

Rees, Mandy, ed. *Shakespeare Around the Globe: and other contemporary issues in profes-sional voice and speech training presented by the Voice and Speech Review*. Cincinnati, OH: Voice and Speech Trainers Assn, 2005.

Reynolds, Peter. *Teaching Shakespeare*. Oxford: Oxford University Press, 1997.

Robinson, Randal. *Unlocking Shakespeare's Language*. Urbana, Il.: National Council of Teachers of English, 1988.

Rowse, A. L. *The England of Elizabeth*. New York: Macmillan, 1950.

Rozett, Martha Tuck. *Talking Back to Shakespeare*. Urbana, Il.: National Council of Teachers of English, 1994.

Rygiel, Mary Ann. *Shakespeare Among School Children*. Urbana, Il.: National Council of Teachers of English, 1992.

Schmidt, Alexander. *The Shakespeare Lexicon: A Complete Dictionary of the English Words, Phrases and Construction in the Works of the Poet*. 3rd ed. Revised by Gregor Sarrazin. 2 vols. Berlin: G. Reimer, 1902.

Shakespeare, William. "Writer Filmography." Online. Available from Internet Movie Database, 1999, at *http://us.imdb.com/name?Shakespeare,+william*.

Shapiro, James. *A Year in the Life of William Shakespeare: 1599*. New York: Harper Collins, 2005.

Shaw, George Bernard. *Man and Superman*. In *Seven Plays by Bernard Shaw*. New York: Dodd, Mead & Company, 1951.

Smith, Bob. *Hamlet's Dresser*. New York: Schribner, 2002.

Spain, Delbert. *Shakespeare Sounded Soundly: The Verse Structure and the Language*. Santa Barbara, CA: Capra, 1988.

Spurgeon, Caroline F. E. *Shakespeare's Imagery and What It Tells Us*. Cambridge: Cambridge University Press, 1935.

Tillyard, E. M. W. *The Elizabethan World Picture*. New York: Vintage, 1941.

Toropov, Brandon. *Shakespeare for Beginners*. New York: Writers and Readers, 1997.

Vendler, Helen Hennessy. *The Art of Shakespeare's Sonnets*. Cambridge: Harvard University Press, 1997.

Whitney, Craig R. *Hoffman as Shylock: London critics cool. New York Times,* 3 June 1989, A13.

3. BOOKS ON ACTING SHAKESPEARE

The bibliography of books about the skills required to act Shakespeare is slim. Many of the useful books are actually voice studies. But each book listed here is helpful to the actor in one way or another.

Barton, John. *Playing Shakespeare*. London: Methuen, 1984.

Berry, Cicely. *The Actor and the Text*. New York: Scribner's, 1988.

———. *Voice and the Actor*. New York: Macmillan, 1973.

Berry, Ralph. *On Directing Shakespeare: Interviews with Contemporary Directors*. London: Hamish Hamilton, 1989.

Bevington, David. *Acting is Eloquence: Shakespeare's Language of Gesture*. Cambridge: Harvard University Press, 1984.

Brine, Adrian and Michael York. *A Shakespearean Actor Prepares*. North Stratford, NH: Smith and Kraus, 1999.

Brockbank, Philip, ed. *Players of Shakespeare: Essays in Shakespearean Performance by Twelve Players with the Royal Shakespeare Company*. Cambridge: Cambridge University Press, 1985.

Brown, John Russell, ed. *Shakescenes: Shakespeare for Two*. New York: Applause Books, 1992.

Brubaker, Edward S. *Shakespeare Aloud: A Guide to His Verse on Stage*. Lancaster, Pa.: Author, 1976.

Cohen, Robert. *Acting in Shakespeare*. Mountain View, Ca.: Mayfield, 1991.

Daw, Kurt. *Acting Shakespeare & His Contemporaries*. Portsmouth, N.H.: Heinemann, 1998.

Guthrie, Tyrone. *Tyrone Guthrie on Acting*. New York: Viking, 1971.

Jackson, Russell and Robert Smallwood, eds. *Players of Shakespeare 2: Further Essays in Shakespearean Performance by Players with the Royal Shakespeare Company*. Cambridge: Cambridge University Press, 1988.

Joseph, Bertram. *Acting Shakespeare*. Revised Edition. New York: Theatre Arts Books, 1969.

———. *A Shakespeare Workbook*. 2 vols. New York: Theatre Arts Books, 1980.

Kaiser, Scott. *Mastering Shakespeare*. New York: Allworth, 2003.

Kermode, Frank. *Shakespeare's Language*. New York: Farrar, Straus, Giroux, 2000.

Linklater, Kristin. *Freeing Shakespeare's Voice*. New York: Theatre Communications Group, 1992.

Rodenburg, Patsy. *The Actor Speaks: Voice and the Performer*. London: Methuen, 1998.

———. *The Need for Words*. New York: Routledge, 1993.

———. *The Right to Speak*. New York: Routledge, 1992.

Scheeder, Louis and Shane Ann Younts. *All the Words on Stage*. Hanover, N.H.: Smith and Krause, 2002.

Sher, Antony. *Year of the King*. New York: Limelight Editions, 1986.

Silverbush, Rhona and Sami Plotkin. *Speak the Speech! Shakespeare's Monologues Illuminated*. New York: Faber and Faber, 2002.

Spain, Delbert. *Shakespeare Sounded Soundly: The Verse Structure and the Language*. Santa Barbara, Ca.: Capra Press, 1988.

Suzman, Janet. *Acting with Shakespeare: Three Comedies*. New York: Applause Books, 1996.

Tucker, Patrick. *Secrets of Acting Shakespeare: The Original Approach*. New York: Routledge, 2002.

Woods, Leigh. *On Playing Shakespeare: Advice and Commentary from Actors and Actresses of the Past*. New York: Greenwood, 1991.

4. BOOKS ON ACTING REALISM

Most of the classic books on acting, and the better new ones, are not concerned with playing verse. Shakespeare is rarely mentioned. Yet, these are excellent books that deal with acting primarily as it relates to modern text for stage or film.

Adler, Stella. *The Technique of Acting*. New York: Bantam, 1988.

Boleslavsky, Richard. *Acting: The First Six Lessons*. New York: Theatre Arts Books, 1933.

Chekhov, Michael. *On the Technique of Acting*. New York: HarperCollins, 1991; reprint and revised, *To the Actor*. New York: Barnes and Noble, 1985.

Bruder, Melissa, et al. *A Practical Handbook for the Actor*. New York: Vintage, 1986.

Hagen, Uta. *A Challenge for the Actor*. New York: Charles Scribner's Sons, 1991.

———— and Haskel Frankel. *Respect for Acting*. New York: Macmillan, 1973.

Mamet, David. *True or False: Heresy and Common Sense for the Actor*. New York: Pantheon, 1997.

Meisner, Sanford and Dennis Longwell. *Sanford Meisner on Acting*. New York: Random House, 1987.

Moore, Sonya. *The Stanislavski System*. Revised Edition. New York: Viking, 1965.

————. *Training an Actor*. New York: Viking, 1968.

Shapiro, Mel. *An Actor Performs*. Fort Worth, TX: Harcourt Brace, 1997.

Silverberg, Larry. *The Sanford Meisner Approach*. 2 vols. Lynn, NH: Smith and Kraus, 1994 (Vol 1), 1997 (Vol 2). Two more volumes are in preparation.

Stanislavski, Constantine. *An Actor Prepares*. Trans. Elizabeth Reynolds Hapgood. New York: Routledge, 1936.

————. *My Life in Art*. Trans. J. J. Robbins. New York: Theatre Arts Books, 1924, reprint, New York: Little, Brown, 1948.

————. *Building a Character*. Trans. Elizabeth Reynolds Hapgood. New York: Theatre Arts Books, 1949.

CHAPTER 39

Glossary of Terms

These terms are defined as they apply to acting Shakespeare.

Alexandrine—a six-foot verse line, usually with twelve syllables, e.g., "A thousand times more fair, ten thousand times more rich;" (*MV,* III, ii). Also called iambic hexameter.

alliteration—sequential words beginning with the same letter, e.g., Antony's "For I have neither writ, nor words, nor worth," (*JC,* III, ii).

ambiguity—uncertainty of meaning or intention; double meaning in a word or phrase; opposite of being clear or certain. The actor must play both the surface meaning and the second meaning, e.g., after being fatally wounded by Tybalt, Mercutio remarks, "Ask for me to-morrow, and you shall find me a grave man." (*Rom,* III, i), or Lady Macbeth's comment about smearing Duncan's servants with blood: "If he do bleed, I'll gild the faces of the grooms withal" (*Mac,* II, ii).

anapest—a foot containing three syllables, the first two unstressed, the third stressed. An anapestic foot. "To be THUS / is NOTH /ing; BUT / to be SAFE / ly THUS" (*Mac,* III, i). Common for words like "amputee" or "put it up." See Delbert Spain's *Shakespeare Sounded Soundly* for study.

anomaly—irregularity; a deviation from the common form; lines which depart from the regular blank verse line, such as those with four or six feet per line, rather than five, or a trochaic measure.

antithesis—opposing words or ideas set against each other, for example, "To be, or not to be—" (*Ham,* III, i), or "Give me liberty or give me death."

blank verse—unrhymed verse, especially unrhymed iambic pentameter.

caesura—a sense break in a blank verse line. Nearly every line will take a caesura after the second or third foot. Also used to set up a single word.

dactyl—a foot containing three syllables, the first stressed followed by two unstressed. A dactylic foot. Common with words like "memory" or "frequently."

elision—omitting a vowel, which results in a shortened word or words, for example, int'rest for interest, degen'rate for degenerate, virt'ous for virtuous, rev'rend for reverend. Also: "I had rather be a dog and bay the moon" (*JC*, iv, iii) (elide "I had" to "I'd"), or "Stir up the Athenian youth to merriments" (*MND*, i, i) (elide "Athenian" to "Athen'an"), or "An honest tale speeds best being plainly told" (*R3*, iv, iv) (elide "being" to "be'ng").

feminine ending—the unstressed eleventh syllable in a blank verse line, e.g., "To be, / or not / to be— / that is / the ques / tion:" (*Ham*, iii, i).

iamb—a foot of two syllables, the first unstressed and the second stressed.

iambic pentameter—a verse line of five iambs, or ten syllables.

imagery—word pictures; mental images, e.g., "Gallop apace, you fiery-footed steeds," (*Rom*, iii, ii).

irony—the use of words to convey a meaning that is the opposite of its literal meaning (Webster), e.g., Mark Antony says to the crowd, "And Brutus is an honorable man." (*JC*, iii, ii) Because of its double meaning, irony is always ambiguous.

metaphor—a figure of speech in which a term or phrase is applied to something to which it is not literally applicable in order to suggest a resemblance (Webster), e.g., "It is the East, and Juliet is the sun!" (*Rom*, ii, i), or "Life's but a walking shadow, a poor player," (*Mac*, v, v).

meter—the measured arrangement of words into a specific pattern, e.g., lines of five feet (each foot is a meter), where each foot has two syllables.

onomatopoeia—a word made by imitation of a sound, e.g., "bang," "mock."

oxymoron—a figure of speech that is an impossible statement, usually an adjective modifying a contradictory noun, e.g., Romeo's "cold fire." (*Rom*, i, i)

pyrrhic—a foot consisting of two unstressed syllables back to back. A pyrrhic foot.

rhythm—the recurring pattern of strong and weak accents within the meter, e.g., dee dum, dee dum, dee dum, dee dum, dee dum.

scansion—analyzing and marking the metrical stresses and caesuras in a verse line.

simile—a figure of speech in which dissimilar things are compared using "like" or "as," e.g., "She would be as swift in motion as a ball;" (*Rom*, ii, v), or "O sland'rous world! Kate like a hazel-twig/Is straight and slender, and as brown in hue/As hazel nuts and sweeter than the kernels." (The previous two lines include two similes and a metaphor.) (*Shr*, ii, i), or "The quality of mercy is not strained;/It droppeth as the gentle rain from heaven" (*MV*, iv, i).

soliloquy—a solo speech, often delivered to the audience or camera.

spondee—a foot consisting of two equally stressed syllables. A spondaic foot. Example: "green light."

trochaic foot or *trochee*—a two-syllable foot, like the iamb, but with the first syllable stressed and the second unstressed. Often the first foot in a line, e.g., "Let me not think on't; frailty, thy name is woman—" (*Ham*, i, ii), or midline, e.g., "From ancient grudge, break to new mutiny" (*Rom*, Pro).

Index

ABOUT THE AUTHOR

Wesley Van Tassel lived and studied in Minnesota, North Carolina, San Fransisco, Denver, and New York City before beginning a fifteen-year stint as a director in the professional theatre. During this period, he served as artistic director of the Westport Playhouse, the Mule Barn Theatre, and the touring Continental Theatre Company. With a Ph.D. in dramatic literature, he then became a professor and has taught at four colleges/universities.

Wes has coached "acting Shakespeare" to several hundred professional and student actors, staged twenty-four AEA productions, produced fifty-five others, and directed more than one hundred summer or university productions.

Wes and his wife, actress Dude Hatten, live with their dogs near Seattle. His son, Craig, lives in New York City, where he designs and engineers sound for Broadway shows. His son, Eric, who lives in Wyoming, is an artist whose primary emphasis is sculpture.

Wesley Van Tassel is available for voice and language coaching for stage and film, for short appointments in colleges or universities, or for workshops in colleges, secondary schools, or community theatres. He may be reached by e-mail at the publisher *PUB@allworth.com*, who will forward the message, or his personal address at vantass@kvalley.com. His web site is www.actingshakespeare.com.

Books from Allworth Press

Allworth Press is an imprint of Allworth Communications, Inc. Selected titles are listed below.

Mastering Shakespeare: An Acting Class in Seven Scenes
by Scott Kaiser (paperback, 6 × 9, 288 pages, $19.95)

Making It on Broadway: Actors' Tales of Climbing to the Top
by David Wienir and Jodie Langel (paperback, 6 × 9, 288 pages, $19.95)

Acting—Advanced Techniques for the Actor, Director, and Teacher
by Terry Schreiber (paperback, 6 × 9, 256 pages, $19.95)

Movement for Actors
edited by Nicole Potter (paperback, 6 × 9, 288 pages, $19.95)

Letters from Backstage: The Adventures of a Touring Stage Actor
by Michael Kostroff (paperback, 6 × 9, 224 pages, $16.95)

Improv for Actors
by Dan Diggles (paperback, 6 × 9, 246 pages, $19.95)

The Actor's Way
by Benjamin Lloyd (paperback, 6 × 9, 224 pages, $16.95)

Acting That Matters
by Barry Pineo (paperback, 5 ½ × 8 ½, 240 pages, $16.95)

Acting is a Job
by Jason Pugatch (paperback, 6 × 9, 240 pages, $19.95)

An Actor's Guide—Making It in New York City
by Glenn Alterman (paperback, 6 × 9, 288 pages, $19.95)

The Actor Rehearses
by David Hlavsa (paperback, 6 × 9, 224 pages, $18.95)

Please write to request our free catalog. To order by credit card, call 1-800-491-2808 or send a check or money order to Allworth Press, 10 East 23rd Street, Suite 510, New York, NY 10010. Include $5 for shipping and handling for the first book ordered and $1 for each additional book. Ten dollars plus $1 for each additional book if ordering from Canada. New York State residents must add sales tax.

To see our complete catalog on the World Wide Web, or to order online, you can find us at **www.allworth.com.**